Praise for
Memories of My Revolutionary Brother, Chokwe Lumumba

"Through the powerful pen of Chokwe Lumumba's sister, the esteemed poetess Shushanna Shakur, we are gifted an intimate perspective that only she could do justice to, as not only his blood sister but also his staunch confidante. Incorporating moving family and close associate remembrances, *Memories of My Revolutionary Brother, Chokwe Lumumba* captures the courage, compassion, and conviction of a giant of a man and resurrects his legacy for generations to rise."

—**Nkechi Taifa, Esq.**, author of
Black Power, Black Lawyer: My Audacious Quest for Justice

"Chokwe Lumumba was a great leader in our quest for independence and sovereignty. His influence is broad and lasting. *Memories of My Revolutionary Brother, Chokwe Lumumba* by his sister, Shushanna Shakur, provides first-hand accounts of his life by his siblings and law partners. They affirm that great leaders do not magically drop from the sky. Relationships in family and community nurture and shape them. Shushanna is an important leader in her own right, and we learn more about her journey as a student leader, teacher, community activist, and primary assistant to Chokwe in many of his most challenging moments."

—**Malik Yakini**, Black food sovereignty activist, urban farmer, and Mollywop bandleader

"Shushanna Shakur's *Memories of My Revolutionary Brother, Chokwe Lumumba* is an important addition to the literature of Black Power and New Afrikan Independence. Shakur's memoir focuses on her older brother's revolutionary leadership, activism, and legal advocacy of Black Liberation freedom fighters and victims of human rights abuses. As his sibling, comrade, and administrative assistant, Shakur provides unique insights that only she can offer to the world about her "revolutionary brother," the former mayor of Jackson, Mississippi, one of the most important political figures of the 21st century."

—**Akinyele Omowale Umoja**, author of
We Will Shoot Back: Armed Resistance in the Mississippi Freedom Movement

MEMORIES OF MY REVOLUTIONARY BROTHER, CHOKWE LUMUMBA

Shushanna Shakur
Edited by Edward Onaci

Copyright © 2026 by Shushanna Shakur

All rights reserved. No part of this book may be reproduced in any form or by any means without the prior written consent of the publisher, excepting brief quotes used in reviews.

Published by
House of Warriors Publishing Company LLC

ISBN: 979-8-9943498-0-9
Library of Congress Control Number: 2026901441

Book Cover and Interior Design by
Jessica Tilles of TWASolutions.com

Unless specified, all images are from the family collection.

Printed in the United States of America

Distributed by
Ingram Book Content
www.ingramcontent.com

Dedication

I dedicate this book to our beloved parents, Lucien and Frances Taliaferro (spiritual realm), who taught us the importance of the dash between our birth and death years and to leave the world in a better place than we found it.

Acknowledgements

This book is a labor of love detailing memories of my remarkable revolutionary brother who transitioned from this planet as an unsung hero. In my lifetime, I was able to observe my brother's evolution into a revolutionary with an unconditional love for our people. The admiration, respect, and love that I have for my big brother is enveloped in this book. Among the many lessons my brother and my parents before him taught me is that one does not achieve their goals without help. It takes the collective work of many to accomplish goals set forth in life. This philosophical belief, I believe, applies strongly to this book as well as to my brother's life. Therefore, I express my profound appreciation for the many individuals who contributed to bringing this book to fruition and say Asante Sana (thank you) to the following people:

From the depths of my heart, I reach out to my revolutionary brother, Chokwe Lumumba in the spiritual realm and thank him for living the remarkable life that inspired this book.

- My loving husband, Sherman Cain (spiritual realm) who supported my dreams always, and was the first to say to me, "You can write the book on your brother."
- Chokwe's Detroit law partners and special friends: Earl B. Ashford, Harry A. Davis, Jeffrey L. Edison, Georgia Manzie-Porterfield, Adam A. Shakoor (spiritual realm), and Nkechi Taifa who encouraged me to tell the story that only a close sister could tell.
- Gloria Elmore, for your love and support.
- Dr. Errol Henderson, Asante Sana for your input along my writing journey.
- Dr. Gloria Aneb House, Chokwe's comrade, my mentor, and our friend who guided me by my hand, helped lay the

blueprint for this book and extended her writing expertise to counsel me on this book.

- My friend Fatou Sao, who encouraged me to write my stories about my brother and helped with initial editing.

- My childhood friend Valarie Preyer, who proofed, edited my thoughts, and walked this writing journey with me.

- Chokwe's Comrades: Ahmed Obafemi (spiritual realm), Bilal Sunni-Ali (spiritual realm), Kwame Osagyefo Kalimara, Watani Tyehimba and Akinyele Umoja who provided information and photos.

- My big brother Reggie Taliaferro and my cousin Priscilla Atoa for holding the family memories.

- Dr. Denise Taliaferro-Baszile for giving me the encouragement to move on with the book after taking time to review the manuscript.

- Our siblings: Lucien R. Taliaferro, Gregory Taliaferro, Denise Glaspie, Mildred (Itari) Bowden, Robert (Jasiri) Taliaferro, and Mario (Gomvi) Taliaferro who contributed to our brother Chokwe Lumumba's development into a revolutionary.

- My daughters: Charlitta Hill, Shushanna Hill-Becton, Maisha Hill-Young, and my son Jeaco Hill (spiritual realm) who are my greatest achievements inspiring all my other achievements.

- My youngest daughter, Attorney Maya D. Cain, who is my voice of reason and the engine who drove me through this book writing process.

- John Hill of Zelman Unlimited for your documentation of invaluable book reflections.

- Dr. Peter Hammer, you read my heart and helped to connect the missing pieces.

Acknowledgements

- Jay D. Johnson, Jackson, Mississippi photographer.
- My comrade Kwasi Akwamu whose artistic support to our organizational movement and this book is greatly appreciated.
- Jessica Tilles @twasolutions, an angel who walked into my life to bring this memoir from the abstract to the tangible.
- Latorial Faison and Jessica Faison for your editing expertise and time dedicated to the book.
- Attorney Gerald K. Evelyn, you sir were my brother's close friend in life and remain his friend in death. I thank you on behalf of his children, his siblings, and my children for caring for our family in his absence. Asante Sana for helping make my dream come true…This Book!

A special acknowledgment to Dr. Edward Onaci, whose patience, guidance, and expertise were instrumental in bringing this book to completion. I am deeply grateful for your support. Dr. Onaci is an Associate Professor of History and African American & Africana Studies at Ursinus College and the author of Free the Land: The Republic of New Afrika and the Pursuit of a Black Nation-State (University of North Carolina Press, 2020), the first comprehensive history of the New Afrikan Independence Movement.

CONTENTS

Foreword by Gloria House xiii

Preface xxi

Chapter 1: Evolution Begins 1

Chapter 2: Growing Up in Detroit...16

Chapter 3: College, Law School, and Beyond 65

Chapter 4: Chokwe and the Republic of New Afrika 114

Chapter 5: Heartbeats 183

Chapter 6: Devoted Defender of the People 201

Chapter 7: Injustices from Jackson to Detroit 239

Chapter 8: Chokwe Joins Politics 271

Chapter 9: Chokwe Lumumba's Legacy Continues 293

Epilogue 304

Appendix 1 314

Appendix 2 318

National Conference of Black Lawyers 338

About the Author...341

FOREWORD

Chokwe Lumumba matured as a revolutionary during a period of heightened racial consciousness in African American communities throughout the United States (1960s–1990s). He was part of the generation that said "no" to the attitude of quiet endurance of systemic racism, which had characterized many in the previous generation. The generation of Black Consciousness and Black Power reached back into our history, reclaimed those great liberators of our past—from Nat Turner to Ida B. Wells, W. E. B. Du Bois, and Garvey—and rejecting strategies of accommodation, carried the fight forward in bold new ways. We organized the Student Nonviolent Coordinating Committee (SNCC), the Black Panther Party, the Black Liberation Army, the Republic of New Afrika (RNA), the New Afrikan People's Organization (NAPO), the Pan-African Congress, and the All-African Peoples' Revolutionary Party, organizations that broke definitively with ideas of slow, moderate calls for change. We also affirmed and supported a network of underground warriors of awesome commitment and courage.

This generation would reaffirm our African roots and culture through avid study and writing and appreciation of African religion, music, dance, customs, and clothing. We went home to Africa emotionally and spiritually to clarify our identity and to release ourselves from the dehumanizing definitions imposed by the hegemony of U.S. culture, government policies, and practices. Identifying with colonized people of color around the world, this generation of Africans in the United States recognized our own colonized circumstances and vigorously asserted self-determination as the necessary resistance to oppression. Through statements, demonstrations, draft resistance, and raising of funds and resources to support various causes, we practiced solidarity with other oppressed peoples and in this manner lifted our strivings as a people onto the international stage. This is the political and cultural context in which Chokwe Lumumba made his extraordinary contribution to the African liberation struggle in the United States.

Chokwe's political organizing in Mississippi reflected the audacious ideological contributions of the Republic of New Afrika to the freedom struggle in the United States: that we are an African people with an enduring and evolving African culture—captured, enslaved, and colonized by Europeans, having the right to freedom and sovereignty as a people; that the people's centuries-old relation to the land they have inhabited and worked must be respected; that people have the right to determine how they will govern themselves (the call for a provisional government); and that independence from the white supremacist United States is a perfectly legitimate objective. Working to advance these claims demanded substantive courage on the part of RNA cadre, as these ideas subverted the long-standing U.S. political assumptions that dismissed altogether African Americans' human rights.

RNA's revolutionary assertions, often viewed as preposterous by Black and White movement leftists, guided Chokwe's work as a community organizer, a people's attorney, and an elected official. In all these roles, he made the RNA principles come to life in ways that people could understand and accept as their own. Embedding himself and his family in the Jackson, Mississippi, community, Chokwe inspired community folk toward greater political independence, self-determination, and self-development. He explained:

> We were trying to build a new society. The New Afrikan Independence Movement was in direct opposition to the old, decadent capitalistic, racist,

white supremacist world, which was trying to hold us down, defeat, marginalize us and make us appear irrelevant.

Each step taken by the community toward greater political independence laid the foundation for a more radical assertion of freedom. Throughout this process, Chokwe must have said to himself, "What am I doing, running for Jackson City Council? I'm a revolutionary! I disavowed U.S. electoral politics years ago." Unheard of that a revolutionary who espouses self-determination, Black power, and political independence should be elected to the Jackson City Council! Unbelievable that a revolutionary whose ultimate objective is nationhood and sovereignty for Africans in the United States would be elected mayor of Jackson, Mississippi. How did this happen?

Though Chokwe had not intended to engage in electoral politics, that is where he found the people. Consequently, he applied RNA's ideological framework of nationhood to the practice of electoral politics. Winning the people's trust with honesty and ceaseless work, he urged them to use their votes to consolidate power and economic development for the Black community. Moreover, he framed their work together as advancing their human rights as a nation of people, bypassing the narrower politics of civil rights. Much of the contemporary progressive organizing in the South, particularly in the Peoples' Movement Assemblies, adapts and builds upon Chokwe's revolutionary approach.

As an attorney, Chokwe would bring this same human rights and internationalist orientation into U.S. courts in defense of liberation warriors, who were hounded and persecuted, and in some cases, as with Tupac Shakur, murdered by U.S. government forces.

Chokwe had received a "good" education in Detroit Catholic and public schools and later at the prestigious, private Kalamazoo College, where he excelled academically and assumed a leadership role in African American students' demands to end racist practices on campus. He was first in his class at Wayne State University Law School for two consecutive years but fought with others to ensure that expelled African American students would be reinstated to complete their degrees.

Having mastered U.S. jurisprudence, Chokwe was keenly aware of the legal system's intrinsic bias against everyone except the wealthy. Hence, he would not be constrained by that system in his legal practice but imagined instead bold defense arguments grounded in international human rights law. Presenting before racist, bigoted judges, who censored, jailed, and suspended him, called him a terrorist, and reprimanded him for wearing African clothing, he refused to be intimidated by court conventions or judges' derision. Rather, he took joy in his superior talents as an attorney: "I rose from poverty, went to their schools, finished as one of their best, and actually demonstrated more skill than the lawyers who were trying to persecute me."* In the Pontiac 16 case (1981), Chokwe argued that the defendants were prisoners of war, and that the State itself must be put on trial for its attempt to commit genocide against an oppressed people. Likewise in the Brink's case in Nyack, New York (1983), he contended that the defendants were members of the Black Liberation Army and prisoners of war held by the hostile U.S. government.

In his decision to move to Mississippi in pursuit of the RNA vision, and his unprecedented audacity in U.S. courts in defense of revolutionaries, Chokwe was very much the solitary warrior. Few of his associates in the legal profession would make similar choices, given the sacrifices entailed. However, his legal partners in Detroit, with whom he had remained close since law school days, revered and supported him in many concrete ways.

Chokwe lived a very full life, integrating his commitments as an attorney, movement activist, and family man. He was clearly exhausted a good deal of the time by these demands but remained dedicated.

Foreword

In all these arenas of struggle, he attempted to model the values he espoused by showing the respect, compassion, and concern for others that he hoped would characterize all our human interactions. He raised his children within the culture and social network of families in the New Afrikan liberation movement, wanting them to know their history, understand the political work in which he and others were engaged, and experience the love and camaraderie that movement friends shared.

Chokwe's sudden death stunned his family and the expansive circles of his friends, professional associates, and comrades throughout the United States. Fortunately, everyone was able to take some relief in the knowledge that, years before his passing, he had expressed a sense of fulfillment in his life: "I am grateful to God that I have been fortunate enough to meet revolutionaries, represent them, and fulfill my aspirations and dream to use the legal profession to represent people who are important to the struggle."[1]

Gloria House, PhD
(Aneb Kgositsile)
Detroit, MI
March 3, 2021

---

[1] Titilayo Akanke, unpublished interviews with Chokwe Lumumba, transcriptions dated October 2014.

Chokwe,
When you started on your journey,
It was as though you were
A blind man in a maze.
It was up to you to touch and feel
But never get lost in a daze.
Luscious temptations were there
To stop you from going anywhere,
But you didn't indulge.

There were obstacles put in your way,
Which you sometimes stumbled only
To get up again.
But knowing next time
You'd beat the man.

It took time.
You felt pain.
Some days your emotions were drained.

But in trying to get out of the black man's maze
That the white man designed
To damage your body and corrupt your mind,
You survived.

Chokwe, we are so proud of you.

–Shushanna

PREFACE

On February 25, 2014, Kwame's words "He is gone" vibrated throughout my entire body. This was a moment in time no one had predicted or expected. Scrambled thoughts ran through my mind. My brother Chokwe Lumumba is gone. My niece and nephews' father is now deceased. Our revolutionary brother Chokwe Lumumba is now gone. Our children's uncle is no longer here. The recently elected mayor of Jackson, Mississippi, has transitioned. The revolutionary known as Chokwe Lumumba is dead. I didn't quite know what to do with this information.

Throughout the entire tragic ordeal, what resonated over and over again is that his story must be told. The story of this amazing man must be shared. I thought the story of an exceptional attorney, activist, and mayor for the people must be documented. How did Chokwe Lumumba become a remarkable son, brother, husband, father, and friend? How did he become a man who loved his people so much that he sacrificed his livelihood and went to jail along with his clients? How did he become an amazing orator and brilliant attorney? How did he develop the courage, loyalty, determination, and perseverance to fight for justice and the rights of people? Who will tell this remarkable story? As his sister, who had a front-row seat into Chokwe's life, I can tell his story. I grew up in the same household, worked for his law firm, worked for him in the movement, was his representative in Detroit when he relocated to Jackson, Mississippi, and shared the duties of facilitating family affairs. Who better than I can tell the story of this great unsung hero?

Memories of My Revolutionary Brother, Chokwe Lumumba

While Angela Davis told her own story and Malcolm X revealed his through Alex Haley, I am chronicling Chokwe's story through his family (including myself), friends, and comrades. Interwoven with these accounts are Chokwe's thoughts on life in his own words, in his own voice. In the late 1960s through the early 1970s, the United States was experiencing a revolution. Many young warriors like Chokwe Lumumba joined the struggle and armed themselves with the knowledge of their fallen leaders and the guidance of their mentors to prepare for battle. The country was in turmoil and chaos from Los Angeles to New York, and they were right in the middle. Huey Newton, Angela Davis, and H. Rap Brown—they were right there organizing and leading the troops. From the 1960s until the day he died, like these heroic leaders, Chokwe Lumumba selflessly fought for, defended, and represented his people. His story should be told.

CHAPTER 1

Evolution Begins

"I think the single most important thing in my political development is Dr. King's death. You see, to my mother he was the Black Moses. She followed him and she always talked to me about him."
– Chokwe Lumumba

On an ordinary weekend day, our dad and mother loaded all the children living at home in Dad's comfy station wagon. I did not know much about automobiles at the tender age of ten, but I knew that my dad's station wagon was the best car to accommodate our big family of ten. There were three rows of seats and of course, if necessary, one or two of the younger siblings could sit on the laps of the older siblings. Yes, Dad's reliable station wagon always worked for us.

This trip was special, and I was told it was going to be a long ride, a little over two hours, so I gathered my Pebbles doll and jingle toy to accompany me on the ride. Our trip was a long and interesting ride with my parents, four of my brothers, and two sisters. The children's ages ranged from five to eighteen. There was a lot of chatting, singing, and many requests to stop and use the bathroom along the way. We finally reached our destination, and then the Taliaferros met Kalamazoo College. My first glance of this enormous building commanded my full attention. I could not understand why a school was so huge. Years later, however, I learned that this school was relatively small compared with most colleges and universities.

Memories of My Revolutionary Brother, Chokwe Lumumba

Our family was escorted on a tour of what they called the campus. It was incredibly beautiful. There were multiple buildings. The green grass and colorful trees were inviting. I liked it, and I wanted to stay there with my family. At the end of the tour, I became sad when Dad announced we were leaving our big brother Edwin (Chokwe) at his dormitory. As happy as I was to leave my brother in that beautiful place, I did not want him to leave us. Our oldest brother, Reggie, had already left the family for the army, and he was far away in another country, Germany. Now I had to let go of my big brother Edwin's hand. After exchanging hugs, kisses and goodbyes with Edwin, Dad and Mother once again loaded the remaining six children in our "old trusty" station wagon and we began our long ride back home.

We returned to K College four years later. I was older and did not bring toys with me this time, for I had parted ways with them a few years earlier. This time when we arrived at Kalamazoo College, I was able to observe things from a more mature perspective. I was observant of my surroundings, the beautiful K College campus, and all the students, graduates, and professors. It was all so amazing, so dignified, and so impressive.

To give more understanding on how Chokwe evolved into a revolutionary, one would have to learn about the years he spent in college. When I decided to write this book on my brother, I was fortunate enough to come across research on my brother's years in college. Eduard B. Avis, now a Chicago independent journalist, was a Kalamazoo College Senior in 1989 when he wrote his Senior Individualized Project (SIP) on "The Story of the Black Student Organization at Kalamazoo College in the late 1960's." Mr. Avis chose this particular subject for his project because he believed that it told an important story about the school and its history.

Reading Mr. Avis's paper evoked so many feelings in me. To actually read, in real time, the struggles, challenges, obstacles, and victories that my brother experienced early on in his revolutionary journey was amazingly heartfelt and poignant. Mr. Avis interviewed numerous individuals and reviewed expansive research for his SIP. "By reading the original demands and various 'position papers' on the crisis, I learned that many of the BSO [or Black Student Organization] members espoused Black Power—the belief that Blacks had to identify and establish themselves within the context of their own heritage before they could properly integrate into white society." Avis explained further that "an old Index article revealed that they organized into the Black Student Organization in the spring of 1968. This group gave them support, an organized bargaining unit to fight for their brand of Black Power. This fight involved making demands to the administration for such things as more Black history and culture classes, more Black professors and students, and separate dorm space and budget."[2]

Although I knew our brother was a revolutionary early on, Mr. Avis's writings gave me an in-depth look at his work. Also, it clearly shows how Chokwe learned from his experiences and then shared his knowledge with others. While I was reading about the strategy planning, protests, letters of demand, and other actions BSO performed, I was reminded of the protests that our sister, Itari (Millie), and I were involved in during the early '70s at Mumford High School. Michael Simanga (formerly Michael Humphrey) and Itari, both organizers of the Mumford protests, invited Chokwe and Dr. Imari Obadele, president of the RNA, to guide us through our protests.

Also, during the later '70s, I was able to share organizing ideas I learned from Chokwe with fellow students at Mercy College. The idea of sharing protest strategies continued from Mumford High School all the way to University of Detroit Law School in 1982,

---

[2]Eduard B. Avis, "Black on White: The Story of the Black Student Organization at Kalamazoo College in the late 1960s," Eduard B. Avis, Senior Integrated Project, Kalamazoo College, Fall Quarter 1989, 5.

3

when the majority of Black students were expelled from UDL, including me. I was grateful that we had a model template to utilize for our protest. Approximately ten years earlier Chokwe and fellow students at Wayne State University Law School held protests when the majority of the Black students were expelled from the school due to academic grades. Even though Chokwe was not among the number expelled, he helped to organize and lead all the students to victory, as the majority of the students were reinstated.

At UDL, we were not as successful. I too, like my brother before me, helped organize and lead protests against the expulsions. Even though a handful of students were reinstated, all were not, including me. One of the differences between the WSU Law School and the UDL protests was that UDL students were not unified and were divided on protest strategy, unlike WSU students who were fully unified. Another difference was that UDL students sued the law school and the courts decided who would be reinstated. WSU Law School protests resulted in all of the Black students' readmission. Although I have followed my brother's lead in the Black Movement, I did not and do not possess the skills of my brother, nor have I had the influence or impact on others as my brother had. However, my brother's teachings and influence on me and many others led to our contributions and positive gains in the liberation movement.

Mr. Avis's following interview with Chokwe highlights his college years and the period in his life when he was evolving into a revolutionary[3]:

My primary interest was learning what inspired Lumumba to begin his civil rights activism. In previous interviews I had learned that he was considered a shy, quiet young man until the death of Martin

---

[3]Reproduced with permission from Mr. Eduard Avis.

Luther King. It seemed like that would have created a convenient turning point for his biography, from shy boy to revolutionary overnight.

But that is not the way it happened.

"The death of King probably had, if there's any one thing that you can point to that had a traumatic impact...on me, that was it, no question about that," he began. "And not only me, we're talking about millions of Black people throughout America who experienced that as a traumatic impact. However, it would be unfair and unsound to believe that people are transformed to any particular kind of activity because of one event. I think, rather, what we should see is that what occurs is that you have life experiences which predispose you for a certain way of thinking because of the way that you physically impact with your environment or socially impact with the environment around you. Sometimes it takes a traumatic event to put you on course with what would be the logical consequence of living in the situation that you're living in and, as most human beings should, try to make it better, okay? And so what I'm saying quite specifically is that my experience probably begins at the very onset of my life."

Lumumba then told me about the various events of his early life that shaped his social conscience. "I mean I remember going to an all-white church...I was raised as a Catholic, and me and my brothers being told why we don't go where the niggers belong; you know that kind of stuff. I can recall Emmett Till's death, which was a traumatic experience...Those things stay with me. I mean I can remember times me and my parents (were) sitting in restaurants, drive-ins, and wouldn't be served, things of that nature, and I wondered about it. And as a kid growing up playing ball in the school, some of the simple things that happened every day that every Black kid just accepts as a reality and doesn't put any political significance to. When we played a basketball game it was generally our view, and this is a kid's view, this is not a bunch of hard-line political scientists or anything like that, that we had to win by at least 10 or 15 points when we played the St. Paul's or Grosse Points...We were one of the few teams that was predominantly Black in the Catholic division at the time...It was clear if the score was close we were going to lose, you know, and we understood that."

"When King died a lot of these things began to come back to me, they began to fit into a system, I guess we'd say of political thought {another thing} which was shaping me was coming to Kalamazoo College. Kalamazoo College to me the first two years...it was a bit of a cultural shock...People use to think I was real withdrawn and introverted and that kind of stuff...People was nice, some of them were nice, I mean I think I can remember some freshmen (with) some racialist kind of attitudes. But that wasn't the style of Kalamazoo College."

While at "K," Lumumba's social education was continued by foreign study in Muenster in the spring of 1966. He told me that he had heard that racism did not exist in Europe. It was immediately obvious that this was not true, but he found that the Europeans were genuinely interested in learning about the civil rights situation in America. Lumumba recalls getting rides hitchhiking more quickly than his white classmates because the Europeans wanted to talk to a Black to learn more about the situation. Even Jews, Lumumba said, who had endured the Holocaust only twenty years earlier, were amazed at how the Blacks stood the centuries of abuse.

It became clear to me that Lumumba's civil rights activism was not born of one shocking event. He kept bringing up more events that contributed to his education, even later in the interview when we had long changed the topic.

Three jobs he held at various times while at "K" seemed to have had a particularly strong effect on his development. The first was a job in a warehouse in Kalamazoo, where he worked on a mostly Black crew with just one white person. Lumumba described this white as a post-hippie, long-hair type and it was this man, rather than the Blacks, that greatly contributed to his development. He had been discussing the issues of civil rights with the group, and the discussion turned to King. King was quite popular at the time, and Lumumba saw in him a prime mover in the struggle.

Then the long-hair pulled him aside "Malcolm X is your real leader," he said. Lumumba then had his first indoctrination into Black Pride and Black Power, something that Malcolm X espoused, but King hadn't yet embraced. But he remembers that Black Power didn't seem right. His Catholic upbringing had taught him that any separation of races, as Black Power calls for, was prejudice.

Working in a steel mill in Detroit later on furthered his indoctrination. The Blacks working there were the most militant he had come across. Yet his doubts continued—if these men got their way, he thought, society would be destroyed.

To accept Black Power as a solution to the racial problem was something that he would have to learn on his own. He knew that racism existed—it had plagued him all his life. But King was not preaching Black Power; he was preaching Black rights, integration, and coexistence. Separatism seemed the opposite of integration. How could Blacks exist in this society without learning to make it within the existing structure? Separating themselves would distance them from that goal, wouldn't it?

It took one more job to change his mind. This time he was back in Kalamazoo, working for the city. His position was to find jobs for the hard-core unemployed, many of whom were Black. He talked to employers throughout the city, extolling the virtues of particular people, looking for open doors for his clients. But as he struggled for these people, and found success more and more elusive, especially for his Black clients, something became clear to him: some employers simply refused to hire Blacks. Some even admitted it: they did not want Blacks in their companies. This was no longer merely a matter of integration. These employers held the key to success for many Blacks, and they were not going to relinquish that key. Blacks could not get ahead without jobs, and these stubborn whites were not going to give them jobs. Would education change these people? Would a King speech open their closed minds? Perhaps, but Lumumba believed they were beyond help. He realized that if Blacks were to get ahead, they needed to control their own destiny—their own jobs, their own society.

For Lumumba the revelation that Black Power was the answer came before the death of King. It was the stubbornness of white employers which convinced him the Blacks needed a parallel social structure if true integration were ever to come about. Blacks had to become successful beside, yet apart from their counterparts, and then they could integrate. The white system on its own, Lumumba was convinced, was too racist to really offer a chance of success for Blacks.

King's death was merely the catalyst that sparked his struggle to put an end to a heritage of abuse. "When King died, to be quite honest with you, before King died, I had come to the point of view that there was something I had to do for the Black community that I wasn't doing. There was something I had to learn, that I wasn't learning. I didn't know exactly what it was going to be. I had begun to feel a lot more at ease on the campus, because I was a junior at that time. There were a lot of younger Black students who were coming in who kind of looked up to me for guidance and gave me some comradeship. Plus, I had known people in town better and I knew people at Western better. I just knew there was something I had to do. King's death made it an urgency."

Black Action Movement (BAM) was Western Michigan University's equivalent of the BSO. Immediately after King's assassination in April, 1968, BAM held a rally on Western's campus to which Lumumba and other "K" Blacks were invited. Lumumba recalls that BAM presented demands for Black advancement to

WMU's administration, and even occupied a campus building for a time.

Lumumba and his friend, Jerry Gray, asked "K's administration to send them to Memphis to attend a demonstration in King's honor. "K" gladly acquiesced, knowing well that the increasingly angry disposition of Black America would eventually hit home. The march solidified Lumumba's emotions and upon return to "K" he knew action had to be taken.

"After we came back from the march we became engaged in looking at "K" and saying to ourselves as Black students at "K": 'Is the Black experience really represented here? Are we educated as Black Africans in America...not only taking into consideration our African heritage but our heritage since we've been here? Are we being correctly educated in their perspectives? What will be of service?' I think that was the emphasis at that point in history: service to our people when we leave here and in fact service to ourselves. 'Or are we just passing through this benevolent white institution and will make either no contribution to our people or attempt to be a force to influence our people to be whiter than they are, which is the impossible dream?'"

The BSO was born shortly thereafter, and applied for official organizational status in May. Lumumba recalled that virtually every Black on campus joined the BSO, as well as a number of other students from third world countries, including East India, Asia and Africa. A total of 50 students became members at the peak of the organization.

The infrastructure of the group was similar to that of most campus organizations, with Lumumba and Jerry Gray as co-chairmen. All decisions made during the weekly meetings were voted on by the entire membership, and the co-chairs ran the show in the interim.

The emphasis for the group was on discussing topics of general interest to Blacks. Black liberation and methods making "K" a place more suitable and relevant to Blacks—including recruiting more Black students and pressing for more Black faculty.

As the BSO was forming, Lumumba had the opportunity to thoroughly cement his Black Power beliefs. The event was a Black Power forum being sponsored by some white students at "K" they knew Lumumba well, and they knew he was a prime mover in the BSO, so they asked him to give a speech. This turned out to be a vital turning point in his development. As he discussed the things he learned while preparing his speech, I felt as if I was approaching a turning point in my own thoughts. I had come to the interview trying to play reporter. I wanted the facts and some interesting anecdotes, but what Lumumba said taught me a vital point of Black Power: Blacks do have a unique and pride-worthy heritage. As he began describing his research for the speech, I tried to imagine what it would be like to have slaves for ancestors, and I realized how different that would make me feel. So much of Western society uses heritage as a factor in judgment—perhaps not overtly as in feudal Europe, but nonetheless family heritage is something that is looked upon with pride and respect. How would I feel if all I could see in my heritage were slaves? The thought had never occurred to me in research for this project. I think I finally began to see the Black experience from a fundamental level.

From this perspective Lumumba showed me how Black Power sought to bring Blacks out of this heritage rut. By looking beyond the slaves, to the time before the whites took the Blacks out of Africa, he showed me that Black heritage is more than slavery. In Africa, Black heritage was kingdoms and families and scientific developments and complex societies. By seeing Blacks as African-Americans I saw first the devastation of a people forced into Diaspora, divided from family and a familiar society, subject to humiliation and torture. Then I saw how this brief history could not be considered the final word; I saw how by looking beyond these horrible centuries one could see true Black Pride.

Evolution Begins

Lumumba explained his transformation: "It was almost like a new world opening to me...I'm learning first of all the way that our people had struggled against slavery, and struggled after slavery. And then I learned how they had been betrayed so many times, you know. And it's such a revelation to me...I think part of every Black person who doesn't understand the story is probably somewhat ashamed because they wonder. 'Why us? Why is it that my relatives wound up being slaves and why didn't we do something about it?' And that's why they like to forget it. So they don't talk about it...So I'm reading about the past...and how Africans actually were responsible for creating the first sense of mathematical systems...How they were responsible for medicine. Old Hippocrates just steals that from us! But it was a guy named Himbeltek [Imhotep] who really started out the whole organized modern medicine. And if you read the Greek philosophers they always talk about talking to somebody else or reading somebody else: these are the people who come from Africa, northern Africa for the most part. And the only reason that's true is because it just so happens that men and women apparently first came up in Africa, you know. That's apparently where human life first occurred according to the anthropologists. So it's nothing innate about being Black that makes you great, but it's just the coincidence of history that happened and that Blacks have all kinds of stuff to be proud of. And I didn't know it."

And I didn't know it either. And I realized that if I, a supposedly "enlightened" educated person, had not seen the truth behind Black beauty, many, many people had not seen it, and it would take some drastic measure to open eyes. Possibly even a measure as drastic as opening a campus building.

From this position I asked Lumumba about the first set of demands that the newly-formed BSO had presented to the administration. They were presented on May 16, 1968, and asked for such things as more Black courses, students and faculty.

"The first time, they met a lot of the demands in the first response, I believe. But there were some places they left open or it was kind of very arbitrary…Ultimately we got all of the first demands met. At least in terms of their agreeing to be done…

"I believe that people generally operate in what they perceive to be their self-interest…I have to believe that that's what the university was doing then, too. The historical events that occurred certainly were shaping a lot of the atmosphere on campus. Certainly we were beginning to work in our self-interest, more so than we had done before. And in the interest of our people, the way we perceived that interest. I think that we took a very strong position. I think it was correct to take that position at that time. It was correct for us and our own development and it was probably the best thing that could've happened to the university at that time…I think it was better even for us, much better for us than for them. Because first of all, given the fact that the university ultimately always acts in its self-interest, when the atmosphere changes a little bit—there had been many, many student demonstrations around the country—(people get) a little 'fed up.' It's interesting to me, you have to excuse me, but we've been going through oppression as Black people for some…at least 200 years, you know what I'm saying? And to think that people (after) we have one year of demonstrations, are beginning to get fed up, I don't have a great deal of sympathy for that. I have some human understanding of that because I know how people are. But in any event, they were. And so what that means is the university began to become more (open) toward our demand—until the later demands—as the society as a whole did."

I asked Lumumba what the BSO did in the year between the first and second demands. Basically, he told me, the BSO worked to further the needs of their people. They attended conferences at several small colleges sponsored by various Black student organizations,

Evolution Begins

and held study groups to study Black heritage. These study groups eventually evolved into the Black History Seminar that was added to the curriculum at "K" in the fall of '69.

K College Chokwe gradulation photos

A community outreach effort by the BSO was a tutorial program for Northside children. Kalamazoo College already had a program of its own, but the BSO saw that the children needed all the help they could get.

One of the more revealing projects in that interim period was an investigation of area food stores. "We did an investigation of the differences between food quality and food prices in the major food chains in the Black community and outside the Black community... It was a great difference. In terms of prices, food in the Black community was generally [priced] higher, and the quality was worse."

The BSO became aware of more things they needed from the College as the year progressed. Lumumba told me that visiting other colleges and attending conferences showed them what other Blacks were doing and how that could help them at "K."

Most of these things eventually became assimilated into the second set of demands, but not until they were requested through more regular channels. "The second ones didn't start off as demands. That grew into demands when the university didn't meet them... We were approaching them in a way that we wouldn't demand what we didn't have to demand. If we could get stuff by agreement, that would be fine. We didn't walk right in there and demand all that stuff at first... All these things had been discussed."

By the time the second set of demands was delivered, the BSO was well established and its message was clear: Kalamazoo College had to undergo significant change in order to be visible to the Black student population.

The rest of our interview was spent discussing the details of that long month in the spring of 1969. When we finally came to a breaking point, I realized that we had spoken for nearly three hours. That fact in itself showed me how seriously Mr. Lumumba took the movement, and still feels about it. It was not a passing fad for him—it is a continuing struggle. "It helped those of us who were in it. First of all, it helped us form a sense of dedication to our people, it also helped us to issue a resolution, and it helped us understand political dynamics of situations."

As I spoke with this man who still struggles for Black liberation, I got a sense of the passion that he used to drive the BSO in its first year. If the energy he exuded in the hours we spent simply talking about the situation is any indication of his potential, then the energy he used when the crisis was going on must have been phenomenal. The interview taught me a great deal about the early BSO, and about the African-American situation in general."[4]

---

[4] Avis, 22–34.

Evolution Begins

When we arrived at Kalamazoo College in 1969, our father could not locate Chokwe among the many graduates in the caps and gowns. When he did locate Chokwe, he was not dressed in cap and gown attire. Dad questioned Chokwe about the whereabouts of his cap and gown. Chokwe said he would not be participating in the ceremony because he believed the institution to be racist. Chokwe said they gave him a scholarship to K College so he could be their "token Negro" and he would not accommodate them. Also, by this time, Chokwe had become involved with the Republic of New Afrika, a group of Black Nationalists, who organized to claim five states in the United States to build and develop a Black Nation. Therefore, there was a lot of influence on Chokwe to stand his ground and not participate in the graduation ceremony.

Although Chokwe was strong and passionate with his argument, Dad was stronger and more passionate. Dad insisted that "We did not come all this way not to see you walk across that stage and get that degree." He told him, "Son, if you don't walk across the stage, you will break your mother's heart." I don't know if the pressure of knowing that my mother would be heartbroken or the fact that my father ordered him to put that cap and gown on changed Chokwe's stance. But I do know his stance changed. And I know, at that time, Chokwe had never really defied my father before. Although I did not know a lot about racism at that time, I remember that it was one beautiful moment in time to see my big brother walk across the stage in that sea of white faces and receive his Bachelor of Arts degree—political science major, history minor—that he worked for and earned. I left Kalamazoo College that day saying that I wanted to graduate from college, just like my big brother. Here again was his laying a foundation for me. I wanted to be so much like my big brother.

Although Chokwe's experiences at K College contributed to his evolution into a revolutionary, there were many other contributing factors. Chokwe's family and childhood are certainly among the most significant ones.

CHAPTER 2
Growing Up in Detroit

"My grandmother was a remarkable woman. She was one of thirteen children who raised fifteen children and helped some of those children raise their children."
– Chokwe Lumumba

Family photo (left to right) Mildred (Itari), Denise, Chokwe (Edwin), Gregory, Lucien (father), Bernadette (Shushanna), Priscilla-Frances (mother), Mario, Robert (Eldest sibling Reggie not shown)

Family Origins

Chokwe Lumumba (born Edwin Finley Taliaferro) grew up on the west side of Detroit in a family of ten: both parents, four brothers, and three sisters. Our father, Lucien Taliaferro, worked two or three jobs until his retirement. Our mother, Priscilla, stayed home and cared for the children until Mario, the youngest, entered elementary school. Although our parents were not wealthy and had to struggle financially to make ends meet, Chokwe had a strong, healthy childhood. He once said, "Some of my fondest childhood memories are of my father and mother loading the family station wagon with me and my seven brothers and sisters and going on outings to the drive-in or picnics." As one of the older siblings, Chokwe always believed it was his responsibility to set a good example and look out for his younger siblings.

Chokwe and our father, Lucien R. Taliaferro, Jr.

Our father was a hardworking, good-looking, well-built man. He was a very talented and resourceful man who worked many jobs: loan officer, security guard, construction worker, mixologist, taxicab driver/owner, factory worker, and private investigator, but the job he was most proud of was employment specialist for the Archdiocese of Detroit. There, he was able to help so many Black people gain employment. A few years prior to his death, at a ceremony honoring him for his work and contributions, the award presenter said that more jobs had been found for Black people during our father's tenure than during the whole history of the Archdiocese's Employment Program.

Several people told stories of how our father helped them. One of the clerks at the Juvenile Court in Detroit recalled how our father found her the first decent and stable job she had ever had. It appeared our father helped people on several of his jobs. Maureen Taylor, a renowned Detroit activist for welfare, mortgage, and water rights, said that if it had not been for our father, she is sure she would not have advanced in her career: "I was attending Marygrove College, when your father was a security guard there. I was experiencing problems in my personal and academic life. I, for sure, was ready to give up and throw in the towel. It was from talks with your father that I gained the strength and motivation to move on." Maureen brought tears to my eyes and joy in my heart when she shared that story with me. Another job he was particularly proud of was a private investigator. When Chokwe became an attorney and started his law firm, our father became the firm's investigator. He would serve subpoenas and conduct investigations into criminal cases for the attorneys. He would also provide services for other attorneys outside the firm.

Abena Hogan, Shushanna Shakur and Maureen Taylor

During our father's final working years, he was employed by an electrical company where our brother Reggie was employed as an electrician. Our father drove the work truck and did some construction, including on the People Mover in Detroit.⁵ Our father also worked on Interstate 96 (the Jeffries Freeway), an east-west interstate highway that runs approximately 192 miles entirely within Michigan's Lower Peninsula. This must have been a difficult experience for both of our parents, as they had previously in the late 1960s organized a group of largely middle-class Black neighbors to go to court to protest the city's taking of their homes by eminent domain to build the freeway. The group argued that the freeway would lower property values and that it would primarily serve suburbanites (mainly whites who had fled the city) to come in and out of the city, not the residents whose homes would be expropriated. In addition, homeowners were to be compensated only for the assessed value of their homes, not the market value. Although their efforts ultimately were in vain, this was one of many situations our parents used to model to their children how to "fight injustices."⁶

Our mother, Priscilla, was a beautiful, intelligent, compassionate woman. Although she was not a college graduate, she was knowledgeable about many subjects, including local politics. She was also our teacher. She taught us about God and the importance of maintaining a close relationship with Him. She modeled this lesson in her daily prayers and by taking us to weekly Mass. Through her marriage with our father, she demonstrated for us how to love and respect our own spouses, and through the close, loving relationship she cultivated with my siblings and me, she taught us how to unconditionally love our children. Our mother taught us how to care for the less fortunate and to never hold ourselves above them, and

---

⁵The People Mover is Detroit's only rail transportation. It is a 2.94-mile automated light rail system operating on an elevated track. It is like a miniature rail transportation system, as it only has one track and it travels from downtown Detroit to midtown Detroit.

⁶Lucien Taliaferro and Priscilla Taliaferro, Plaintiffs-appellants v. Henrik E. Stafseth, Director of the Michigan Department of State Highways, et al., Defendants-appellees, 455 F.2d 207 (6th Cir. 1972).

she taught us how to fight injustice everywhere and how to stand up for what we believe. Our mother was the one who introduced Chokwe to the history of our people and who inspired his activism. He said she was the one who compelled our father to load up the kids in the station wagon to see Dr. Martin Luther King Jr. speak in Detroit. Chokwe, who would have been about sixteen at the time, remembered it well. He said that was a moment of awareness for him. He often said that Dr. King's assassination and Emmett Till's heinous killing motivated him to be an activist.

Our beautiful mother emulated to all of her children how to be civic-minded and a responsible member of society. She often stressed, "It is up to each individual in society to take some form of action to improve it and make it better." Chokwe and our siblings were all introduced to civics and politics early. Our parents were civil rights activists who contributed selflessly to the movement, thereby laying a foundation for their children. Our mother once said, "When you do something for someone, make sure it is from your heart and not contingent on recognition or compensation. You may not be recognized or compensated for your charitable work, but you will be recompensed along the way by someone you would least expect." Our parents worked on the vision for Focus Hope in Detroit, along with other members of the Catholic Family Movement (CFM). Focus Hope is a nonprofit civil and human rights organization that was founded in 1968 after the Detroit Rebellion in 1967. Its mission is to unite a multicultural community in intelligent

Our parents, Lucien and Priscilla-Frances Taliaferro

and practical action to overcome racism, poverty, and injustice. Although Father William T. Cunningham and Sister Eleanor Josaitis are credited as the founders of Focus Hope, my parents and members of the CFM were there right from the start. Chokwe publicly confronted Father Cunningham at a speaking event at Wayne State University, where they were both presenters, asking him, "Why are the Black people, including my Black parents who helped create the vision for Focus Hope, omitted from its origin story?" I don't recall Father Cunningham's response. One of Focus Hope's early programs was a community food bank that provided free food for low-income residents. Our father took me to their distribution center on Oakman Boulevard once a month on Saturday morning to pick up government cheese, powdered milk, canned juice, and other nonperishable food items for my family. Our father often told me how he and our mother helped create the program.

Another significant contribution our parents made to the civil rights movement was organizing relief efforts in Detroit through the CFM while Dr. Martin Luther King Jr., Fred Shuttlesworth of the Southern Christian Leadership Conference, Stokely Carmichael, Ella Baker of the Student Nonviolent Coordinating Committee, and others were organizing marches in Selma, Montgomery, and other southern cities. My parents hosted two sisters who were active participants in the marches, thirteen-year-old Juliette and sixteen-year-old Charlene. The summer Charlene and Juliette stayed with us, they shared terrifying stories about their experiences during the marches in the South. According to them, during one march, the police turned water hoses on them and let ferocious dogs loose. Juliette said they were arrested another time and put into a jail cell made to hold four people with about twelve girls. One of the girls was pregnant and the guard entered the cell while we were lying down and stepped on her stomach. Our parents also welcomed guests from Africa in our house. Our cousin Pierre who resided in Liberia arranged for a few college exchange students to visit Detroit, and my parents hosted them. Our parents laid the foundation for Chokwe to become a revolutionary.

Paternal Grandparents

Grandfather,
Lucien Taliaferro, Sr.

Grandmother (Step),
Mary Starks Taliaferro

Our father would often tell stories about our grandfather, Lucien Taliaferro Sr., whom our father was so very proud of. Lucien Sr. left his home in Coffeyville, Kansas, around 1926 to relocate to Detroit to make a better life for his two sons, our father and his younger brother Edward Ranson. His Native American wife, Eunice Rogers, became very ill and died from tuberculosis while their sons were still quite young. Even though Lucien's sister Lemmon helped raise the boys while Lucien worked, she had her own family to take care of. Lucien did what he thought was best for the boys and placed them in a Catholic orphanage temporarily and left for Detroit to make a living. While he was in Detroit, he met and married Mary Starks, a well-bred, church-going, educated widow who had a son, George, and a daughter, Cevelia. Lucien went back to Kansas and got the boys and brought them to Detroit to live with his new bride and her family.

According to our father, Lucien Sr., who was a brick mason by skill, helped build landmarks and roads around the city of Detroit. One of the construction projects he worked on was the Davison Freeway, which runs east-west between M-10 and Interstate 75, arguably the first urban freeway constructed in the United States.[7] He also worked on the Fisher Building, Harper Hospital, and many other buildings throughout Detroit. Our father recalled the times he would walk a few miles to take our grandfather his lunch or dinner when he worked overtime. Lucien Sr. was a talented bricklayer and cement mixer who worked tirelessly for long hours. However, he watched his white coworkers get higher pay and overtime and time and a half for their labor while he received the minimum pay. His employers justified this discrepancy by saying they were skilled craftsmen who had certain licenses that our grandfather did not have. At that time, Blacks could not gain admission into trade programs or receive additional training. Even though our grandfather did not have an official piece of paper indicating his qualifications, he and his brothers, John and Ted, all were able to build structures from the ground up. John and Ted even built their houses next door to each other on Scotten Street on the west side of Detroit. Lucien Sr. purchased a home on Marston Street in Detroit's North End, a relatively modest neighborhood at the time.

When we were growing up, our grandparents were significant figures in our lives. We went to holiday dinners at their home, and our paternal grandmother, Mary Taliaferro, would often give our mother her credit card to shop for her children. Our grandfather and our father shared a very special and close relationship. They enjoyed watching the Detroit Tigers on television together, even though Lucien Sr. believed that the organization was one of the most racist in Major League Baseball. Walter Owen Briggs Sr. was one of the owners of the Tigers. According to Michigan Chronicle writer Branden Hunter, "See Briggs thought Black people were good enough to work for long hours and little pay in his factories but not

---

[7]https://detroithistorical.org/learn/encyclopedia-of-detroit/davison-freeway.

good enough to play for his baseball team. He would not even allow Black people to sit in the boxes near the dugouts at Briggs Stadium on the corner of Michigan Avenue and Trumbull. No Black players ever played for the Tigers while Briggs was the owner. The saying around the clubhouse was, 'No jigs with Briggs.'"[8]

Our father and grandfather also enjoyed building things together. At our last house at 4762 Spokane Street (we lived in three different houses on the same block), they built a six-foot-high brick wall encasing the side of our house. Although our father said they built it because our house was adjacent to an alley, he likely did it to keep his daughters' future suitors off the property. Our grandmother Taliaferro tried to teach her granddaughters to be "fine and proper." She was also a faithful member of the African Methodist Episcopal Church. When Chokwe was coming into his Black consciousness, I thought our grandmother would be against it, because she was so proper and conservative, but I was wrong. Both she and our grandfather were proud of Chokwe and often read articles about his activism. Grandmother Taliaferro would enlighten the women at her tea parties about her soon-to-be attorney, militant grandson and his activism. Our grandfather was not much of a conversationalist, but when he spoke of his grandson Chokwe, he spoke with approval.

Our father said that he did not know much about his mother's side of the family and that he knew very little about his family beyond his father's generation. His father, Lucien B. Taliaferro, was born to John Taliaferro and Tular ("Lula") Davison-Taliaferro of Kentucky. They had five boys and two girls: Finis, Martha, John, Theodore, Lucien, Paul, and Lemmon. Our father's grandfather died in 1917, before our father was born in 1921, and his grandmother died in 1937, sixteen years after his birth. Our father often told stories about his father and uncles. He was so proud of them for their building and construction skills. He talked most about Finis, who was his father's eldest sibling. He owned

---

[8]Branden Hunter, "Racism, Baseball, and the Detroit Stars Negro League Team," *Michigan Chronicle*, March 30, 2018.

his own store as well as other businesses. He also shared fond memories of when he and his brother, Edward, stayed with his aunt Lemmon for a short time after his mother died when they were boys. But his fondest memories were about his time spent with Edward and his father. Some of our relatives said that Edward, who preceded our father in death, was the spitting image of their mother. He had a beautiful long ponytail, reddish skin, and high cheekbones. He was an outdoorsman who loved to fish and hunt. Although our surname, Taliaferro ("iron cutter"), is Italian, our limited knowledge of our ancestry on the Taliaferro side does not show any European blood. Our grandfather Taliaferro was a mahogany-complexioned man with black features. His brothers and sisters we knew or had seen pictures of were of a lighter hue than our grandfather. However, our grandfather's mother's portrait portrays a chocolate-dark woman with African features. Many people have described our father as having features of a Black Sicilian. He would sometimes tease and say he was a Black Sicilian, but our mother would quickly scold him and say, "Lu, stop telling those kids stories."[9]

Mother and Dad

Maternal Grandparents

Our maternal grandparents, Willie Tillman Finley and Rydonia (Donnie) Barrow Finley, were from a little town in Alabama called Lafayette.[10] Our father used to say our mother came from the

---

[9] One time when my husband Sherman and I visited my eldest brother, Reggie, in Atlanta, he showed me a map of Georgia and pointed to a county named "Taliaferro." Reggie told me then that he believed the county was named after a wealthy slave owner. This would come to make sense over my adult lifetime, as I met many Black people with the surname of Taliaferro and the majority of them had African features.

[10] Chokwe learned of information about our mother's maternal family that the Barrow family actually first appeared in this country in West Point, Mississippi. According to Chokwe, he and our mother attended a Barrow family reunion in New Jersey sometime in the late '70s or early '80s where someone produced a genealogy chart with this information.

Memories of My Revolutionary Brother, Chokwe Lumumba

Grandfather, Willie Tillman Finley & Grandmother, Rydonia Barrow Finley

Buckalew Mountains. I always thought he was joking until I read about our mother's birthplace and learned the Buckalew Mountain area is a historic African American community in Chambers County, located off of Veterans Memorial Parkway halfway between Lafayette and Valley, Alabama. I never knew our Grandpa Finley because he died in 1946, the year before Chokwe was born. The portrait we have of him depicts a red-haired, green-eyed, white man. However, our mother said he was not a white man. I believe Reggie, our oldest brother, remembered him best. His memories consist of going with our grandfather to work on the ice and coal wagons he owned. Priscilla, our oldest cousin, remembers family members talking about what a wonderful man he was, taking in seven children from our grandmother's first marriage. Our mother said her father was a man of few words; when our father asked for Grandpa Finley's approval to marry our mother, he gave it in very few words while intimidating our father a bit. Our mother said Grandpa Finley actually liked our father, but her relationship with her father was special, and he did not like the prospect of losing her. Chokwe was named, in part, after our grandfather, as Chokwe's birth name was Edwin Finley Taliaferro.

Grandma Finley was the matriarch of our family for a very long time. She was the type of woman you would read about in Black history books. She was born May 3, 1891, in Lafayette, Alabama. Grandmother was a bona fide healer as well as a midwife. But most important of all, she was a spiritual woman who had a powerful gift of prayer. People came from all over to ask her to pray for them.

Donnie Finley was married first to William Raye, a man as black as a skillet with African features. He was a widower and brought three children, Annabelle, James, and Jessie, into their marriage. Donnie and William then had four children together, William, Betty, Frank, and Alonzo. William Sr. dug wells and worked in the coal mines. In 1918 he died when he fell into a well, leaving our grandmother a widow with seven children. She met and married our Grandpa Finley. They then had eight children together: Booker, Ellen, Priscilla-Frances, Katherine, Robert, Zipporah, Ruth, and Deleon. Our grandfather and grandmother raised fifteen children together until our grandfather's death in 1946, leaving our grandmother to continue raising the younger children and several grandchildren until her death in 1977. Our grandmother's children were a rainbow of colors—from the darkest dark to the lightest light. There was never an issue of lighter ones receiving more love than the darker ones. We did not participate in colorism in our family. In fact, our uncle William was one of the darkest men I knew, and he was one of the most loved men in our family. He had a great sense of humor about many things. His nickname for our mother was "Blackie," even though he was the dark one and she the light one. Our mother always taught us to never compare ourselves with others and think we are better: "We are all the same and no one is better than you and you are not better than anyone else."

Our family ancestry included greatness on many levels. Chokwe and our entire family were very proud of our family lineage to one of the greatest men who ever walked the planet. Donnie Barrow Finley's brother was Munroe Barrow, Heavyweight Champion Joe Louis's father. Thus, our mother and Joe were first cousins.

Joe's mother, Lillie Barrow, paid for our grandmother Donnie to bring our mother and several of her siblings to Detroit from Lafayette, Alabama. Lillie Barrow called our grandmother sometime after she had relocated her own family to Detroit, while Joe was building his boxing career, and told her to pack up her family and come to Detroit. Grandmother complied, and lucky for us she did, because our beautiful mother met our handsome father here.

Joe Louis Barrow

Our father, who had been a boxer while serving in the armed forces, met Joe Louis while he was dating our mother. In the early 1940s, our father had taken our mother out to the Graystone Ballroom in Detroit, and in walked Joe Louis. At some point Joe, accompanied by his entourage, walked over to our parents and engaged in conversation. Before parting, Joe looked over to my father and balled up his huge fist and said, "You better take care of Pretty Frances or else."[11] Later, after our parents' whirlwind courtship, it was Lillie Barrow who paid for their beautiful wedding reception at St. Stephens AME Community Center.

---

[11] Our mother appeared in a book about Joe, in which the caption under her picture described her as Joe Louis's "beautiful Cherokee cousin." The author was trying to illustrate Joe's Indian heritage. Our mother had a beautiful olive complexion with dark, silky long hair and high cheekbones.

Early Education and Activities

"Even when I was a little Fat Man, I understood that I was going to make my mark on the world."
—Chokwe Lumumba

Our family always supported Chokwe's educational, professional, and political ventures. Our oldest brother Reggie and younger brother Greg contributed financially to his education, while our sisters and youngest brothers assisted in various ways from attending his sporting events to helping with his community organizing. Our father got up early with Chokwe and went to bed late driving him around to his numerous activities, and when Chokwe attended college and law school, it was our father who made sure his needs were met, even if this meant having to work three jobs simultaneously or asking other family members for a helping hand. Whatever it took to ensure Chokwe's progress and that of his other children, our father found a way.

Although he was happy at home, Chokwe seemed to experience a lot of difficulty in school in his earlier years. He fought a great deal with other children and received poor grades. He recalled fighting to protect others. Even though he attended a predominantly white school for all of elementary (Holy Ghost Elementary School) and some of high school (St. Theresa Catholic School), racism did not play a major role in his troubles. St. Theresa was mostly white when he began in the second grade, but it was predominantly black by the time he graduated in 1965. Chokwe believed the racism he encountered directly during these years was subtle. His peers tended to associate and mingle with members of their own group and generally did not harass others, although he did recall in one of his many fights a white boy telling him he had stayed in the oven too long.

However, Reggie's experiences with overt racism made an impact on Chokwe. Chokwe witnessed a nun admonishing Reggie for dancing with a white girl; another time a white man questioned Reggie about why they were going to a Catholic church: "Why don't you boys go to the nigger church?" Because of the overt prejudice and cruelty of St. Theresa's older students, Mother and Dad eventually transferred Reggie to another school. Despite our brother's tribulations, Chokwe excelled in high school. However, Chokwe felt he experienced "the changing of the guard" when he attended St. Theresa. Most of the older white students had moved on and now the Black students dominated.

Chokwe and eldest brother, Lucien R. Taliaferro, III (Reggie)

Chokwe said it was Reggie who pioneered the way and laid the foundation for him and others to build on, especially his siblings. Chokwe once said that Reggie was "among my heroes. I have always admired him for his intelligence and strength. It was Reggie who motivated me to play sports, he was such a good athlete, and it was Reggie whose academic achievements encouraged me to excel in my studies." Chokwe excelled in high school, both academically and athletically, earning numerous awards and accolades: honor roll for four years, member of the National Honor Society, president of the junior class, president of Student Council, and winner of forensic speech two years in a row. He was the captain of the football team; in 1964 he was awarded All Catholic Football Honorable Mention; in 1965 he was All Westside Catholic League for basketball; and in 1964 and 1965 he was All Catholic League in track.

Chokwe's early job experiences in his teens included delivering pizzas at Famous Pizza and driving an ice cream bike. Later, he worked during the summer at Frank's Nursery Warehouse, loading and unloading trucks; at Chrysler Corporation in the Hamtramck Assembly Flint Plant; at Vernors Company, delivering soft drinks; and at Great Lakes Steel Company in downriver Detroit. Chokwe also held jobs while attending college in Kalamazoo. There, he experienced working with youth as a day camp counselor, and he gained insight into local government when he worked for the Kalamazoo's Community Relations Department finding placement for Black job seekers.

Chokwe's Siblings' Reflections

Front Row (L to R) Itari, Greg, Shushanna
Back Row (L to R) Chokwe, Mario, Reggie, Robert

Chokwe had loving relationships with all of his siblings. Each of us has memories of our experiences with him. We shared some of these memories to give others insight into Chokwe.

Reggie's (Arki) Memories

Chokwe got his spirituality from our maternal grandmother, Donnie Barrow Finley. He received his revolutionary zeal from our father, Lucien R. Taliaferro Jr., who was a freedom fighter at heart. His love of people came from our mother, Priscilla Frances Taliaferro.

Our family first lived on Watko Street in Detroit. Watko was located in the projects, outside of Conant Gardens, between Ryan Road and Conant and Nevada and Seven Mile Road. After we lived in the projects for a while, Florence Ballard of the Supremes and her family moved in across from us, and then again, when we moved to Spokane, they moved across from us. The other members of the Supremes, Diana Ross and Mary Wilson, lived over in the Brewster Projects.

Growing up on Watko, Mom and Dad had five children: Chokwe, Greg, Denise, Millie, and me. I think Millie was probably just a baby when we moved from the projects. We definitely did not grow up with a silver spoon in our mouths on Watko. We were among the many poor families who lived in the projects. The nickname for the projects where we lived was "Cardboard Alley." The project units were made out of asbestos board, a tough cardboard material. If a tenant would get angry and punch the wall, their fist would go through to the neighbor's house.

All of the tenants in the projects were Black, with the exception of one white man. He lived in one of the only two houses on the street. He lived in a dug house that was made of tar pitch, where tar was used to close up spaces between the boards. The house was all black, and some of the kids used to make fun of him and called him Farmer John. He would just chase them away when that happened.

The two-bedroom unit we lived in was not very big at all. We had a potbelly stove in the living room and a galvanized tub, where Mother bathed the younger children. We only had a stand-up shower in the bathroom. This picture should give you some idea of our economic standing in the community. Despite our impoverished surroundings, I have fond memories of growing up there. There was a big baseball diamond on Ryan Road almost at our back door. There, we used to play baseball, kickball, and all those sports. In the wintertime, when the ice and snow were on the ground, we played hockey. Most of the guys wore shoes or boots, but I had some skates, and I would be skating around.

One story I can share with you is the story involving our babysitters, Gussie Mae and Nettie Ruth. They were our older cousins who used to babysit us. One evening, one of the two introduced us to the following story: Someone had been stealing from Mr. Charlie. Mr. Charlie sent his work boy, John, to find out who was stealing from him. John went away one day in the basement to look for the thief. John had been gone for some time when Mr. Charlie came to check on him. Mr. Charlie came up from the basement and said, "I couldn't find John, but I found some pork chops left." That night at midnight there was a noise coming from the basement. Gussie Mae or Nettie Ruth, depending on who was telling the story, would then say there was a noise from the basement, and a strange voice saying, "I died one time…I died two times…I died three times…and you going to die if you touch my pork chops." The first time Chokwe and I heard that story, we both had to use the bathroom immediately after she finished the story. We both were peeing into the toilet at the same time when a voice said, "I'm Bloody Bones, and I died one time…I died two times…I died three times and…" Chokwe and I ended up squirting urine all over the bathroom in every direction. It's memories like this one that remind me of the fun we had in spite of our circumstances.

One other memory I have of our childhood is not so funny, looking at it as an adult. Chokwe and I used to play cowboys and

Indians a lot. Often, when we played, I would tie him up, and he would always get loose in a matter of minutes. One day, I wanted to get rid of him, so I tied him up pretty good, and he could not get loose. He was screaming so badly. I felt bad about it and untied him. However, sometimes I felt like I was tied up, with my little brother hanging around me.

Eventually we moved from Watko to Spokane and Grand River, where our family grew even larger. Bernadette came along after we moved to Spokane, then Robert, and then Mario, who became the eighth child. We had a unique housing situation on Spokane. My dad was buying the first house we moved into from Watko, and along came a recession, and we lost that house. We then moved almost directly across the street and rented there for a while. Then later on, after I had gone into the service, Dad purchased a different home on the same block, down at the end of the street near Grand River. Perhaps we would have stayed in the last house on Spokane, but the Jeffries Highway (I-96) came through and the city took the house to make way for the freeway.

Spokane was different than Watko in many ways. The neighborhood was middle class as opposed to the poverty-stricken projects we came from. We knew all the neighbors and they knew us. We enjoyed that neighborhood very much. There was some racial diversity on Spokane. When we moved there, there were about four white families still living on the block, although they gradually moved away. However, there was one white family who lived in the largest house on the block. They stayed there for a very long time. I remember they were still there when I left to go to the service.

There were no real problems between Chokwe and me growing up. I was four years older than him, and I was his big brother. The only issue with my little brother was whenever Chokwe was given chores to do, he would find a way not to do them, and I would end up doing them. For example, when he was given the chore of doing the dishes, he would play with his toy soldiers and submarine in the dishwater, and then he would eventually fall asleep. The dishes were not done, so I had to do them, and that was something that happened on a regular basis. I have heard that Chokwe's grandson Qadir, Rukia's son, also likes to play with his little toy figurines. So, I guess it has been passed on in the family.

Chokwe was just as happy playing with his toy soldiers as he was with his imaginary friends, Dee Dee and Bubbles. One day, Chokwe just announced that Dee Dee and Bubbles were there. Mother and Dad included them in the family. They had to have chairs at the table and plates on the table. I don't remember if they had food on their plates.

During Chokwe's and my teen years, we were both involved in basketball at school and in the neighborhood. We played baseball at Pattengill School, which was located near us. I was also in the Boy Scouts. I don't think Chokwe was in the Boy Scouts, but I remember walking all the way up to St. Leo's on Grand River and 14th Street. That was quite a distance to walk to Boy Scouts.

We were friends with another family, the Fullers, who had sons our ages. Sonny was my good friend, and Jerry was Chokwe's good friend. Sonny and I were both the older brothers, and we were both mama's boys.

Chokwe and I both attended St. Theresa Catholic School. There was just a handful of Blacks when I first started school there, and there were not too many more when Chokwe started. There were racial undertones. There was not much overt racism, but you knew where you were welcome and where you were not, and we went by those guidelines. When Chokwe started the ninth grade in the high school at St. Theresa, I had already left and gone to Catholic Central, where I graduated from high school.

Of course, there were some racial undertones that impacted us in different ways at St. Theresa. When Chokwe was in high school, he became a very good basketball player. Years prior, when I played high school basketball at St. Theresa, I did play first string, but I did not feel the coach was giving me the benefit of his knowledge, as he did his other players. Anyway, I played ball as best I could. I remember one incident during my time at St. Theresa that occurred at a school dance. I was dancing with different girls, a few Black girls and a couple of white girls. I danced with the white girls because they asked me to. One of the nuns came up to me afterward and told me it would be better if I didn't dance with the white girls. At first, I did not feel too good at all about the situation, but then I took it in stride. Since I knew well what to expect from the environment that I was in, it did not upset me.

Chokwe and I maintained relationships with Sonny and Jerry Fuller as adults. We were involved with Sonny Fuller, whose African name was Chaka, in the Republic of New Afrika (RNA).[12] I first became involved in the RNA when Chokwe was in college. Later, Chokwe and two of my sisters and two of my brothers joined the RNA. What initially attracted me to the RNA was that I saw they were not afraid to protect themselves when accosted by the police. That was ideal for me, and their objective of land for Black people in the five southern states was appealing to me—at least at first. Then I thought about it, and I said I didn't know if I wanted to live there. I liked the idea that Black people would have control over their own government, not that I wanted to get away from white people.

I joined the RNA after the New Bethel Incident at Reverend C.L. Franklin's church (discussed further in chapter 4). Subsequent

---

[12] The founders of the movement originally spelled Africa with a *c*. They began using the *k* on November 30, 1975. It appears they did so in agreement with Zimbabwean writer Ruwa Chiri's claim that the choice was a way to honor pre-colonial practices. See Edward Onaci, *Free the Land: The Republic of New Afrika and the Pursuit of a Black Nation-State* (Chapel Hill: University of North Carolina Press, 2020), 106–107.

to living in New York after leaving the service, I returned to Detroit and joined the RNA. The trial involving my friend Sonny (Chaka) was going on at the time. My understanding of the incident was the RNA was having a meeting at the church and they had some rifles. Someone called the police and told them they saw someone with a rifle. The police showed up to take the rifles away from them. Some type of scrimmage evolved, and there was some shooting. The police shot into the church, and some of the RNA members outside the church with rifles returned fire. Allegedly, one of them who returned fire was Chaka, and another one was Rafael Vierra. Those were two of the brothers they put on trial, and they were found not guilty. It seemed about six months after the trial acquittal, Chaka was found stabbed to death. He was stabbed many times. I believe they found him in a car. We never did find out exactly what had happened. They thought it might have been revenge for Chaka's vindication in the New Bethel police shooting. Chaka's murder impacted me greatly because he was a dear friend.

Chokwe had a great deal of success in his career and professional life. My younger brother, who used to be unmotivated about his chores, had evolved into a hardworking man, juggling a law practice, family, and community activism. He became well known for his success in the courtroom fighting cases. I always admired him for that very much. When he rose to be the vice president of the RNA and then to interim president, I thought that was good for him because that is what he wanted to do. I had left the RNA by the time he took on those positions. He went on to build his own organization, New Afrikan People's Organization (NAPO), but I did not know too much about that because we didn't really discuss it. The only place I knew NAPO existed was in Atlanta. That is the only time I came into contact with it. I had been gone from the movement for many years by the time NAPO was organized.

When Chokwe became mayor of Jackson, Mississippi, I thought it was great. However, I had concerns about his running into some problems. After living in the South myself, I knew that southern Black people were very conservative. I didn't know if they wanted to be mixed up with his politics, but I was wrong because he won the election overwhelmingly. That was a good thing. He won because he had done his homework. He had been there for years and had done some things that he needed to do to become intimately acquainted with the community.

One of the last times I was with Chokwe was at a surprise party for me and our brother Greg. I was very surprised that day. There was Greg trailing me, and I was trying to get him to come on up because I thought the party was for him, which it was. The party was for both of us, but I didn't know that. I was there a good ten minutes before I realized what was going on. The party was held a week before my birthday. If it had been three days after my birthday, I would have been in the hospital dying. Actually, I was at Beaumont Hospital battling pneumonia for one month. After I won my battle with death, then to learn my brother had died hit me hard.

Jackie, my wife, and I went down to Jackson to see Chokwe when he got out of the hospital prior to my going into the hospital. That was in June or July. Shushanna called and told us that Chokwe was sick, and we decided to go down and see him. At some point, he and I had discussed that he might need a type O donor (I believe) for bone marrow. After that I never heard any more about it. Shushanna told the family that the results of the autopsy showed that the cancer problem was not connected to his death. The independent autopsy, which the National Conference of Black Lawyers (NCBL) and Minister Louis Farrakhan arranged, found that Chokwe died from a heart aneurysm.

The last time we were together with our brother Chokwe was in October. We attended the NCBL event that was held to honor Chokwe, mayor of Jackson, Mississippi, and Deborah Jackson, mayor of Lithonia, Georgia. Several of us attended that event with him at the DoubleTree Hotel in downtown Detroit. Prior to that event, we went over to Mrs. Fuller's house to celebrate her 100th birthday with her. Mrs. Fuller, Sonny (Chaka) and Jerry's mother, was turning 100 and it was important to us to go see her. Mrs. Fuller and my wife sang hymns together. We shared stories with Jerry and with each other. The whole evening we shared together was nice. That was the last time I was with my brother Chokwe. I want Chokwe to be remembered in the way everyone knew him.

*Cicero Love, Chokwe, Jerry (Chico) Fuller
(Photo courtesy of Jeff and Shaakira Edison)*

Gregory's Memories

My relationship with Chokwe did not involve the movements he participated in or his organizational work. Ours was more a familial one. I think about the times Chokwe and I spent together in our early years. We moved to Spokane Street when I was about three years old, and that was in 1954. We had a great neighborhood-block-community. Of course, Chokwe and I were a part of that. I remember all the different things we used to do and the fun we used to have. We played football in the streets. We built pushcarts. We made bows and arrows out of tree branches. The tips of the arrows were made of bottle caps smashed onto the thin tree branch. We had a great time, and I think we bonded with the neighborhood kids.

Our neighborhood was middle class, in my opinion. But, quite naturally, when you try to label a neighborhood poor or rich or whatever, there are still differences in individual families financially. We were so close-knit on our block. It was an integrated neighborhood in the process of change. I don't recall any problems existing between the Black and white neighbors.

The neighbors in general were the type of people who would involve themselves when they observed something wrong, even if it was with other people's children. The image that has been passed on about the old days of the neighbors whipping other neighbors' children for wrongdoing—I don't remember anything like that occurring on our block. But I definitely remember parents whipping their own children. I was included in that. We did have a lot of fun coming up, but that's not the same as there weren't issues on the block. It is important to remember children, as well as adults, had a community spirit.

One of the most memorable incidents I recall on Spokane was one that involved fun but turned into something else. It happened one night when we had a lot of family (relatives) over to the house. If it was for a specific occasion, I don't remember. Our family often came together to socialize. I know our maternal grandmother was there, and our paternal grandfather was there. I know our maternal cousin, Tyrone, who was my age, was there, and I later found out our paternal cousin, Rosemary, was there. So anyway, I remember Mama telling me not to go back outside because it was dark. Although she had told me that and made it very clear, I could not hold back from showing Tyrone this little clubhouse that my friends and I had half built. It was dark outside and there was no light in the clubhouse. I had a candle to light the way as I showed him the clubhouse. As I was guiding the tour of the clubhouse, the breeze from outside caused the candle to ignite my shirt. I remember vividly that I ran out of the clubhouse because I was on fire. The next thing I remember was Chokwe. The clubhouse was next door to where we lived. When we went to the clubhouse, Chokwe was not in the yard. I don't know where he came from or how he got there. I don't know if he saw me from our house and jumped the fence into the next-door neighbor's yard, but I remember this: Chokwe pushed me on the ground and rolled me over and put the fire out.

During that period of time, fire safety was not being taught in school, so I don't know where he learned that lesson that enabled him to save my life. This situation motivated some regrets that I have later in life. Chokwe and I did speak of that frightening incident, but we did not go in depth about it. I never did find out where he came from to rescue me and what was going through his mind. I was amazed with him being only four years older than me that he knew what to do. Chokwe definitely saved my life that day, and after he saved my life, our grandmother saved my life. Grandmother Finley was such an important part of all of our lives. They got me in the house, and our Grandfather Taliaferro wanted to rush me straight to the hospital. I found out later that Grandmother Finley said, "You all can take him to the hospital, or you can let me work on him first." They decided to let Grandmother do her down-home doctoring. Cousin Rosemary and our older brother Reggie had been there watching. Rosemary later shared with me that our grandmother put something on my chest. I remember being in the bathtub and she put something on my chest that calmed me down. Mama told me later that the doctors in the hospital said to her, "If you had rushed him straight to the hospital, he would have died from shock." So Grandmother made the difference.

Chokwe, St. Theresa Pirates, Detroit, Michigan
(Photo courtesy of Denise Lawton)

Johnny Woodle, St. Theresa Pirates, Detroit, Michigan
(Photo courtesy of Denise Lawton)

Chokwe loved sports, and he played every sport St. Theresa had to offer. He was on the basketball team, football team, and track team. At St. Theresa that was pretty much it; they did not have any other sports. He was an outstanding athlete. This is a story I recall that speaks to his athletics. I was at the Detroit Jazz Festival a few years ago, and I was with a group of people. A member of another group was Judge Gershwin Drain. At one point, Judge Drain asked me if we knew each other.

I said, "You might know my brother," the logic being that as a judge, he might know my brother, an attorney. When I told him who my brother was, he was amazed to find out that not only did he know Chokwe, but their connection was not from the law but from high school sports.

When I told him my brother was Chokwe Lumumba, he said, "Oh yes, your brother and John Woodle were not too kind to us at St. Gregory's."

When I told Chokwe about the incident later, he laughed and said what was ironic about that was that Gershwin Drain was St. Gregory's best player. Edwin Taliaferro (Chokwe) and John Woodle were the best players in the Catholic Basketball League, probably more so John than Chokwe. Everyone who knew about the Catholic Basketball League knew John Woodle and Edwin Taliaferro.

John Woodle was drafted into the Vietnam War, and that is probably what ended his potential career in basketball. He was good enough for professional ball. After Vietnam, John got into some trouble with the law, but Chokwe remained true to their friendship. There were some other athletes that Chokwe grew up with who gained success in sports. I was not into sports as much as Chokwe, but I remember he was not just respected by the Catholic League's opponents and teammates but also by the neighborhood guys. Two of the neighborhood guys who stuck out more than the rest were Joe Neely, who played basketball, and John Mayberry, who also played basketball but ended up making his living playing professional baseball. Neely and Mayberry both attended Northwestern High School, while Chokwe was at St. Theresa, so they did not play in the same organized basketball league. Chokwe competed against them in street basketball.

Chokwe's love for basketball extended past the neighborhood, high school, and college. His love of sports and his awareness of what

Memories of My Revolutionary Brother, Chokwe Lumumba

sports could do for young people existed throughout his life. When he moved to Jackson, Mississippi, he organized and sponsored a youth basketball league while maintaining his law practice. Piston player Lindsey Hunter's son or younger brother played on Chokwe's team. A couple of his players went on to play professional basketball. Maurice "Mo" Williams played for the Cleveland Cavaliers, and Isaiah Canaan played for the Houston Rockets. Also, a couple of his players played overseas.

In addressing Chokwe's character, I want to share an incident I recall, but all the details are hazy. There were a couple of white guys at St. Theresa who were very popular, and they were somewhere between my class and Chokwe's class. Chokwe and I were four grades apart. I remember them doing something negative while taking advantage of their popularity. I remember Chokwe saying publicly, "I'm not impressed," about what they did. However, I was so impressed with what Chokwe did. My thinking on this incident is that there are a lot of kids who will just go along with whatever the popular kid does, even if what the popular person says or does is demeaning to someone else. But Chokwe was saying, in so many words, that's not cool. Even though I don't remember all the details of the incident, I clearly recall the integrity my brother showed. That said a lot about his character, even back then.

Another incident that the older siblings recall about Chokwe's character and what type of courage he possessed even as a teenager happened on Spokane Street. Charles Hootsell (a neighborhood friend) had done something, and two members of the Grand River Gang were looking for him. It started with Reggie and Chokwe playing catch in the street. I had been sent to the store, and when I returned, I saw the aftermath of what had happened. Two of the members of the Grand River Gang, Jackie Bridges and Peppy Ballard, were walking down the street. Jackie said something to Chokwe about "Where is that damn Hootsell? Tell him I am looking for him." It just so happened that when he said that, our father pulled up in the driveway and was getting out of the car. I don't know what was said, but there was a heated exchange of words between Dad and Jackie. Then, Reggie ran up on Jackie and swung on him. I remember Reggie explaining that if he hadn't done what he did, Dad could have easily gone to jail because Dad would have done something to Jackie. As I was coming back from the store, I ran into Jackie and Peppy. We were coming towards each other, and I saw Peppy helping to support Jackie. Jackie was holding his jaw because Reggie had "messed him up."

Later that night, Peppy, who came from the Ballard family (our families were friends since way back in the days of living in the projects), had the nerve to bring Jackie's older brother and sister to our house. They came in getting loud with Chokwe, whom they had mistaken for Reggie. Chokwe never told them any different, but Reggie came down from upstairs and immediately got it straight.

When we were young, of course, I never thought about Chokwe becoming a revolutionary, lawyer, and mayor and accomplishing all of the great things he did. There was a time when Chokwe and I were very close, even closer than he was with Reggie. We were probably closer because Reggie had found girls at that time, and Chokwe and I weren't there yet. Even though Chokwe was almost four years older than me, we basically had the same friends and played with the same people and did some of the same things. As Chokwe arrived into his middle teens, things started changing between us. I didn't realize at the time, but Chokwe had probably started thinking about his life. I, on the other hand, found that it was important to me what our peers thought about me at a time when it did not seem important to him. That to me is a very telling thing in the life of Chokwe Lumumba. What he valued was so much more important than my peers' thinking I was one of them.

The last time several of us saw our brother Chokwe was at the surprise party for Reggie's birthday and my retirement. When I think about that time, I know if it was left up to me that wouldn't have happened. I would not have wanted a big celebration for my retirement. But I'm grateful because that was a happy occasion. Most people could probably identify with the premise that when you get to the point in your life as we had, and when family members are separated by miles, often it's more funerals that bring everyone together than happy times. The event was well put together and Reggie was surprised, and I was surprised. A lot of people made some nice remarks, but when Chokwe got up and spoke his words were exceptionally heartfelt. When he spoke, you would not have realized he was a politician because he recognized the night was only for the celebration of his brothers, and that meant a lot.

Chokwe's humility was so impressive. Chokwe said that night, "our older brother Reggie is my hero, and my younger brother Greg is my confidant who I can talk to about anything." That was saying a lot because it was easy to see that there may have been times, although Reggie was the oldest, that he would have been in Chokwe's shadow because of all that Chokwe had accomplished in life. But Chokwe did not look at it like that.

With regard to Chokwe's death, I think his dedication for the movement could have contributed to his departure. There were so many people like Malcolm X, Martin Luther King Jr., and Marcus Garvey, who had found the thing that defined their lives. It wasn't only what they lived for but what they died for. I think most people have trouble comprehending that. It has been said in so many different ways. For someone whose passion is that great, their service for the community is what causes them to leave here.

If Chokwe could hear me today, I would tell my brother I love him. I talked to Chokwe in Mississippi on his election day, and I remember telling him how I wish Mama and Daddy had been there. There is just so much I would like to say to him, but I would like to convey to him that so many of the things he started with our family, we will not forget. They will continue!

Itari's (Millie) Memories

When we were growing up, some of us in the family called Chokwe "Poindexter" because he had glasses that were thick. I remember seeing him sit at a desk in the house doing his homework and reading. Another fond memory I have of Chokwe is when he was in a play at St. Theresa, and I was shocked to see him acting because he was so quiet and reserved, and he had the starring role. Later in life, I realized how important Chokwe's role was in that play. He portrayed Moses, and that is who he ultimately became, a leader of his people to guide them through the wilderness of racism and oppression. In the play, Chokwe said in a loud voice, "Let my people go."

Chokwe was very protective of me and my sisters. He was always interested in teaching us things after he started going to college. What he was learning he wanted to share, and he wanted us to be a part of it. I remember working in a summer youth program with him as the director. I must have been seventeen years old, and I recall him being a very strict disciplinarian and very regimented, and behind his back we called him "FL," which meant Fearless Leader.

I remember Chokwe was a spiritual man and believed in prayer. He would ask our grandmother to pray for him and his team before games, and when he and his friends were taking the bar exam, he called my grandmother and asked for her prayers. He would also call Grandmother to pray during his closing arguments on a trial.

Nubia adored Chokwe and their children, but she seemed to dote on Chokwe Antar. I remember her telling me, "My son is a genius." She said it emphatically and meant it. I would laugh and tell her, "Well if he is, he gets it from our side of the family."

I want people to remember that Chokwe sacrificed his entire life for the service of others and that he died fighting for the liberation of our people to his very last breath. He was a beautiful soul, and he was a man among men. He was an extraordinary man who was fearless like the lion he was. He was a Leo, Leo the lion. If I am interpreting the Bible correctly, the lion Judah was fearless. A lion is supposed to be created without fear. This is how I want my brother Chokwe to be remembered.

Jasiri's (Robert) Memories

Chokwe was eleven years older than me. He was my big brother who taught me a lot. I remember him bringing me into the movement, where many life skills were developed. In the Republic of New Afrika, we would sell BAMN (By Any Means Necessary) papers and collect donations for the Malcolm X Community Center located on Dexter and Tyler. Many activities and learning went on at the Malcolm X Community Center. It was there where I became a member of the African Drill Team, which was a big part of my life.

The Simba Wa Chungas (Young Lions) was a drill team for the young men in the RNA. There were several of us that went through training together. We—Sundiata Keita, Ade Thurman, Jaribu Shahid (Henderson), and I—were mostly around the same age, ten to fifteen. However, my younger brother Gomvi (Mario) and Entandaji (Eliot Holmes) were also a part of our drill team. Although Chokwe instructed us on various aspects of the RNA, our drill instructor was Ché, who was a dedicated disciplinarian instructor. The drill team was extremely important in our growth and development, because it taught us discipline. Later in life, as adults, we all went on to become productive members of society: Sundiata, a master drummer known worldwide; Jaribu, a respected musician on the West Coast; Ade, a health care aide; Entandaji, a real estate agent. I became a chess instructor, and my brother Gomvi was the one whose profession was most related to the drill skills we developed in the Simba Wa Chungas. He became a security guard for several large companies and then ventured out and opened his own security business.

Although the skills we learned from the RNA guided us into different areas, most involved training or teaching youth certain skills. We were well-rounded, disciplined young men. Chokwe and the RNA are responsible for a lot of that. Chokwe made it clear that you must first teach discipline before drill, gun security, or anything else. That lesson remained with me when I became an adult and began teaching chess.

Prior to teaching, I played chess with Cooley High School, never lost a game against another school, and when we went to Lansing for the state championship, during my final year at Cooley, we won second in the state, and I placed first in the state championship.

I taught Dexter Thompson, who later became a chess master, the year after I left and Detroit Public Schools (DPS) did not have a league for at least another four years. Dr. Paul Graham started the organized chess league in DPS in the early 1990s, about fifteen years after my graduation from Cooley High School. I have taught for twenty-five years in the DPS Chess League, and in several suburban schools and youth programs. Another one of my chess students, James Canty of Mumford High School, became a chess master. Also, I have shared my skills with my own three children, Robert, Natalya, and Nigel, who also have carried the title of Chess Champion in city and state tournaments.

The RNA days also enabled Chokwe and me to spend time together. I would often ride with him to RNA events, and we would have discussions on many issues and just life in general. Chokwe, being my big brother, would often give me advice and direction. He would correct me when necessary and encourage me to reach higher heights. I recall one incident where I believe he was attempting to encourage me to grow. We were at a conference at the Shrine of the Black Madonna about STRESS (Stop the Robberies Enjoy Safe Streets), a group of police officers who were terrorizing the Black community. Chokwe put me on the spot by calling my name to speak. I was not comfortable speaking, and I thought my presentation was very poor. Unlike my brother, who was a good speaker and able to deliver an impromptu speech, that was not who I was. Chokwe had a keen sense of delegating work to others in the RNA. I believe he learned from that incident that speaking was not my forte, because he never asked me to speak again. Chokwe trained a lot of good people right who will carry on his legacy. Chokwe had many admirable traits and characteristics. However, I think his ability to lead was the primary one. He could show people things and motivate them to want to do what he was doing. He possessed the knowledge as well as the leadership. Some speakers will speak on things they do not know a lot about, but not Chokwe. He spoke on what he knew, what he researched, and what he had learned.

Finally, I admire my brother for his ability to delegate what needs to be done. Delegation of assignments is crucial to any organized group. As much as Chokwe helped others, including those in our family, I believe we helped him too. The fact that he had a family that was supportive of him definitely helped. Often, what Chokwe believed in and was advocating was not popular. However, we, individually and as a family unit, supported Chokwe's dreams and aspirations, as he did ours.

Mario's (Vincent) Memories

Growing up with my brother Chokwe was inspiring. My father and Chokwe were early inspirations for me to play athletics. Chokwe played basketball and football and ran track. When I saw what he was doing, like playing basketball at Kalamazoo College, I wanted to do it too. I saw Chokwe as a very motivated person with a positive attitude. I also admired Chokwe because he was very driven and he knew the direction he wanted to go in life.

Chokwe definitely had talent, and he was a very hard worker. When he was studying to go through law school, he worked twice as hard as most other students. I recall him telling us we had to work twice as hard as the next person, referencing our white counterparts.

There have been times when I have met and/or worked with former athletic rivals of Chokwe.

I met Stanley Clifford, one of Chokwe's athletic rivals back in the day. I worked with him at MGM Casino. He said although Chokwe was his rival, everyone liked and respected him. When I was the president of the Local 1111, SPFPA (Security Police and Fire Professionals of America), one of the former local presidents, Tom Smith, mentioned to me he knew Chokwe from Wayne State University. Tom's face would light up when we talked about Chokwe.

Chokwe was a superior athlete and prided himself on staying in shape. He loved playing a variety of sports, even after he graduated from college. After he became a lawyer and was working at the Public Defender's Office, he played with the Black Stars. This baseball and basketball team was made up of members of the legal community like attorneys Paul Curtis, Gerald Evelyn, and Chokwe Lumumba. The team continued to play after Chokwe's and Jeffrey Edison's law firm started. It was at their firm that he brought me and two of my brothers-in-law (Ronnie and Charles) on the team along with another one of his partners, Ernest Jarrett.

Chokwe's playing college sports influenced me athletically. He played a center/forward while he was at K College, and I played similar positions when I was at the University of Colorado at Boulder. Chokwe would hustle and dive. It was not an ego thing with him either. He was always striving to make the team better. He would commend me on the court, and he would give me constructive criticism.

My older brother brought me and our brother Jasiri (three years older) into the Republic of New Afrika. Chokwe put us into the Simba Wa Chungas, the drill training team for young brothers. There were several of us young brothers that were trained in the Simba Wa Chungas by Brother Ché, our proficient and skillful trainer. He was often assisted by his brother Bokeba. Ade, Jasiri, Sundiata, Jaribu, Entandaji, and I were in our drill team group. Amazingly, all

Memories of My Revolutionary Brother, Chokwe Lumumba

of us grew up and found positions in life that represented helping and/or teaching others: Ade became a medical assistant and worked with senior citizens in the health field; Jasiri, chess instructor and youth organizer;[13] Sundiata, community activist, culturalist, master drummer, and teacher; Entandaji, realtor; Jaribu, musician and entertainer; and I went into security, providing security for some of the large companies in Detroit. I opened my own security firm as well, and a DJ business. Entandaji and I also joined the Phi Beta Sigma Fraternity, Incorporated, when we were in college. We both were able to utilize our drill steps from the Simba Wa Chungas drill team. Entandaji, in fact, taught our Sigma Brothers stepping. Needless to say, we were all well trained and disciplined from our beginnings in the Republic of New Afrika's Simba Wa Chungas.

Although Chokwe did not train us in the drills and military program, he talked, advised, and guided us young brothers in life matters. He would talk to us and tell us what he knew, and he had a wealth of information he imparted to us. Chokwe was fourteen years older, so he definitely served as a mentor to me. He was a serious disciplinarian, and there were a lot of situations where he had to set me on the right path. He would tell all of us, "We don't want to drag our people down. We want to lift them up."

I spent a lot of time around Chokwe, and when I was doing security for him, I would stand firmly and erect while he made his speeches. This required a lot of discipline. Once, the RNA was having a program at Wayne State University, and I was providing security for Chokwe and Brother Imari. Many people could not stand still around them while they were making speeches. When he said he was going to make it short and sweet, it would still be lengthy. He had so much to teach. I recall another time, when I was by Chokwe's side in Jackson, Mississippi, during his mayoral campaign, I was standing

---

[13] Chess Coach Robert Taliaferro (Jasiri) was awarded the Harold Steen Hall of Fame Chess Award by the Detroit City Chess Club for his 40-plus years of contributions to chess in 2021.

by him to make sure people did not overwhelm him. Even though he was my big brother, I felt proud to be his 6'5½", 325-pound little brother protecting him. When Chokwe would speak, he made me proud to be security for the RNA.

Chokwe was a great communicator who knew how to talk to people from all walks of life. When he did the segment on "Can I Kick It" (YouTube), he was able to reach out to young people in a special way.[14] He has always made me proud of his oratorical skills. There have been times in my life when people have commented on how I had picked up some of Chokwe's oratory style. Many would say, "I could tell you are Chokwe Lumumba's brother because you sound like him."

What I probably admire most about my brother is he followed his dreams and aspirations. There are some people who talk about what they are going to do, but Chokwe did it. He became a lawyer because he aspired to defend our people. He became the minister of defense and vice president of the RNA because he aspired to do the people's work. Chokwe had a love for our people everywhere, but he had a passion for Jackson, Mississippi. This was not something that happened overnight. I think he moved to Jackson to purposely help them rise, and it was not by accident that he served the people on the city council and became the mayor; it was in divine order.

I would like to see my brother remembered as a man who meant what he said and said what he meant. That covers his commitment and work he put in for the betterment of our people and the movement as a whole.

Shushanna/Bernadette Memories

There are things I remember about my brother Chokwe from my first years because that is how much he meant to me. When I

---

[14]Can I Kick It featuring Chokwe Lumumba | MPB "Can I Kick It featuring Chokwe Lumumba," Mississippi Public Broadcasting, YouTube, September 24, 2012.

was in the second grade, Chokwe's high school class participated in the St. Theresa Christmas pageant; Chokwe volunteered me to place the star on the Christmas tree. Our sister Itari's fond memory of that particular Christmas pageant is that Chokwe also selected her to participate in the play. Although her part was minor, she realized that Chokwe's part was major. He played Moses. Imagine that—the nuns allowing a Negro boy to play their beloved Biblical figure. Even though the truth is Moses was of colored descent, most Europeans, Catholics, and other religious sects have taught and represented Moses, Jesus, and all biblical figures as white. The paintings in our history and religious books depicted them as white. The irony of Chokwe playing the role of Moses is incredible to me. First of all, a traditionally racist Catholic school allowed a colored Chokwe to portray one of the greatest biblical characters next to Jesus Christ in the Bible. Second, Moses led his people out of bondage, and that is exactly what Chokwe was working on during his entire adult life.

Among many things that my brother taught me when I was a child were how to tie my shoes, how to write my letters, and how to ride my bike. He also taught me about the value of money when my prankster brother Greg told me that a nickel was more valuable than a dime, because it was bigger in size. It made sense to me, but Chokwe could not stand by and allow this injustice to exist, so there was my first lesson in arithmetic from him. However, there was a bittersweet twist to the writing lessons he gave me. Although he introduced me to writing the letters in the alphabet, he taught me how to hold my pen incorrectly, as he held his. That lesson that I excelled in resulted in poor penmanship for life and a crack on my knuckles by the nuns when I refused to hold the pen correctly.

Now the bike lesson didn't go off very well at all. Even though Chokwe was teaching me through instruction and demonstration how to ride the bike, I had a fear of riding the bike of which he was not aware. One day at the park on a family outing, after numerous unsuccessful attempts to teach me how to ride a bike, he relented and told me to get on the back of his bike. Unfortunately, I did not have a lesson in riding on the back of a bike either. I didn't hold my feet out, my foot got caught in the spokes of the bike, and I had to be rushed to the hospital. I don't remember much about the trauma, but I do remember Chokwe visiting me at the hospital, and I overheard my mother trying to reassure him that it was not his fault. He felt really bad about my injury. Although it was my fault, as a little kid I guess I didn't know how to convey that to him.

Chokwe attended a private Michigan college where there were very few Black people. Although our parents were excited about him going to Kalamazoo College, I missed my brother. He and our older brother Reggie were both gone. Reggie was in Germany serving in the army at the time Chokwe was in college. I remember writing both of my brothers regularly (sometimes weekly). My letters consisted of the latest updates of the family, my school, and extracurricular activities. I even told them about my favorite TV shows and movies. I let them know who did what at home. One might say I was the family reporter. I often wonder whether they read all those childish letters and what it meant to them. I want to think it meant an awful lot to them, whether they had time to read them or not. Even in our adulthood, I continued to serve as the family reporter for Chokwe, and I think he relied on me for that purpose.

Our father was involved heavily in Chokwe's sports activities (track, basketball, football). He encouraged him and made sure the entire family would attend as many of his games as possible. There were many things that our family shared together: church on Sunday, Sunday dinner at the table (all ten of us), drive-in night, Belle Isle, and later, Palmer Park picnics and Chokwe's football and basketball games.

Chokwe and I shared an exceptional sibling relationship. Chokwe was second born in our sibship of eight, and I was the sixth child born. Although we were eight years apart, we connected on many levels.

Memories of My Revolutionary Brother, Chokwe Lumumba

He played many roles in my life: brother, teacher, mentor, protector, collaborator, advisor, boss, and friend. He was my big brother who rode the Good Humor Ice Cream bike and made me the celebrity among my little friends on the block. Later, he became a big deal in high school as a top athlete and honor student. It seemed like, there again, a certain notoriety and popularity was attached to being Edwin Taliaferro's little sister. So later in life, when he became a revolutionary-attorney-mayor, it was not surprising to me. He had always been a star in my book.

Over the years, it just seemed Chokwe and I intersected more than the others. Although several of our siblings were in the Provisional Government of the Republic of New Afrika (PG-RNA) with Chokwe, it was I who went the long haul with him. Itari, initially, was more involved with Chokwe's RNA work than I was. She worked with Chokwe and traveled with him to conferences. I was missing in action many times due to baby births and school. Not only was I Chokwe's legal secretary/filing clerk/receptionist at his law offices, but I typed for him as well for RNA business, and sometimes I typed for Imari. Therefore, I had keen insight into Chokwe's activism activities. Itari also took over some of those roles at both the Malcolm X Center and the law office when I was in school. Eventually, Itari's activism decreased due to job commitments, and I returned to assist Chokwe with his work in Detroit and remained his Detroit assistant until the day he transitioned from this planet.

In hindsight, I see several pivotal points that demonstrated our special, exceptional relationship. When Chokwe's oldest son, Kam, was shot in Jackson, Mississippi, and placed on life support, he called me first. Many years later when my son, Jeaco, was shot and killed, Chokwe was the first call I made to my siblings. When Kam was shot, it was an extremely scary situation for all of us but especially for Chokwe. I recall at one point the doctors were trying to remove Kam from life support. Our mother had, by that time, arrived in Jackson to help Chokwe. It was our mother who said, "There is no way they will remove my grandson from the machines." Our mother saved Kam's life, and he has always been so grateful to his Grammy for looking out and caring for him during the most critical time in his life.

When Chokwe's marriage was in trouble, I was there. Chokwe and Nubia experienced a marital separation over Chokwe's infidelity, and the separation completely crushed him. I have seen my brother prepare to fight at the Supreme Court with no trepidation or fear. I have seen him go up against law enforcement agents, and not once was he intimidated or deterred. I have even seen video footage of him going up against the Ku Klux Klan, and he did not stutter or flinch once. However, it was a different story when Nubia asked him to leave their marital home due to his infidelity. He acquiesced and moved away from Nubia as well as the children. When that happened, he was a man I did not recognize. He was staying with Brother Kwame Kalimara, a comrade and a friend. I recall both of us tried to minister to him on his unfortunate situation. When I saw my brother depressed, fatigued, and spiritless, I had to reach within to counsel him. He reminded me of myself when I separated from my first love and husband. I was devastated and apparently walked around looking depleted and depressed. Our Aunt Mitt, who was in her late seventies at the time, told me, "Bernie, you cannot walk around feeling bad for yourself. No man wants a woman who is down and out. Pick yourself up and concentrate on you and your children, and the rest will come in time." I shared this wise advice with Chokwe. "Chokwe, you've got to pick yourself up and let Nubia know you are truly sorry, and you are going to take care of business while making the changes you need to make for your marriage." Kwame told me later that he thought my talk with Chokwe helped him. I don't know how much it helped, but thank God, he did get Nubia and his family back together. They grew stronger every day, until Nubia's earthly transition. Chokwe became more family oriented and took over more of the caregiving of the children when Nubia was away on her work trips as a flight attendant.

Memories of My Revolutionary Brother, Chokwe Lumumba

Certainly, the scariest moment in Chokwe's life was in June of 2003 when Nubia had an aneurysm in Detroit while on a flight layover while he was in Mississippi. Our cousin Michelle, who lived in Oak Park, invited Nubia to dinner and to spend the night at her house, as opposed to staying in the Westin Hotel by herself. Sometime after dinner, Nubia complained of her head hurting and she went to lie down. Shortly after, Michelle and her fiancé heard some strange sounds coming from the guest room. They found Nubia in an incoherent condition and they immediately called EMS.

Chokwe was called and notified of the dire situation. I immediately picked up our sisters, Denise and Itari, and headed to the hospital. We saw Nubia in the emergency room. It was apparent that something was awfully wrong. We each took turns trying to talk to her while rubbing her hands and forehead. However, there was no response from our beautiful, talkative sister-in-law, who could talk just as much as any Taliaferro woman. At some point, the doctors came in and let us know just how grave Nubia's situation was. He said she had suffered a brain aneurysm, but they were going to give her the best medical attention.

Later, someone explained to us that when a patient suffers an aneurysm in the brain stem, it is impossible to recover. A patient who suffers an aneurysm in one of the brain lobes, for example, the frontal lobe, has a better chance for recovery. I don't know about our sisters, but I could not believe what these people were saying. It was difficult speaking to Chokwe about Nubia, but I assured him that we were going to take good care of her until he got there.

Doctors and nurses explained to us that Nubia had suffered severe brain damage, and her brain was not functioning. They said she was fully unresponsive and the ventilator was breathing for her. However, once when I was at Nubia's bedside rubbing her arms and legs, I swear she moved her head from side to side. I thought for a second, I'm not crazy. I know what I saw. I cannot recall who was in the room with me at the time, but they said they saw the same thing. Then how, I wondered, could she be moving? Medical personnel had an answer for that question too. They said brain-damaged patients sometimes had spontaneous movement in their limbs. I could not comprehend what they were saying. Although I did not have any background in medicine, I did study physiology and psychology in college. They taught us that neurons (sensors) from the brain are transmitted to the body with direction; for example, a neuron is transmitted from my brain when I raise my hand in class, directing my hand movement. I could not understand how, if Nubia's brain was not functioning, she could move her head from side to side.

Chokwe arrived from Jackson within hours. His son Chokwe Antar arrived shortly after, and we awaited the arrival of Rukia, his daughter. I believe she was out of the country at the time. By the time Chokwe arrived, a family and friends vigil had already begun, and it continued around the clock. Chokwe confirmed the doctor's diagnosis with me of an aneurysm in the brain stem. They told him there was no chance of recovery, because she was brain-dead. Chokwe, in his pain, was very concerned about Nubia's family and their position on her treatment. The treating physician had recommended taking her off of life support.

I said to my brother, "You must get another opinion."

He said to me, "They already have two concurring opinions from experts at this hospital."

I then said to him, actually digging deep into his persona, "Chokwe, then you have to get an independent opinion, outside of this hospital." Also, I did have extensive personal experience with the medical profession that he did not have. At that time, I had undergone five major surgeries, and I had helped with the medical care of both of our parents. I said, "Of course they are going to agree with each other."

Many people (including me) thought of Chokwe as one of the most brilliant lawyers in the country, and he had definitely procured outside expert medical opinions on his clients involving autopsies.

Although he was not a malpractice attorney, he was smart enough to know not to rely solely on the hospital doctors. However, this situation was not about a client; it was more personal, it was about his wife, the mother of his children, his soul mate. So I said what Chokwe already knew but could not think at that time, or maybe he did think about it and just wanted my perception. He often did that with me and some others: looked for our perspectives on something that was weighing heavily on him.

"Chokwe, you will have to get an outside doctor to give a third opinion." With his many connections, this was immediately done. Unfortunately, the independent doctor confirmed the hospital doctors' opinions. Rukia had arrived at the hospital by this time. Chokwe and the children spent time alone with Nubia while family and friends continued to hold vigil. The mood in the waiting room was very somber but loving. People were engaging in floating conversations, while grasping for words to fill and fit the conversations.

Next, I recall a very painful but beautiful moment. Chokwe had requested a separate room where he could meet privately with his immediate family. It was both surprising and heart-stirring when he asked me, out of our other siblings who were there, to join him and the children in this meeting room. Chokwe opened the meeting with a pained but clear voice and said, "We have to make a decision about whether or not to remove your mother from life support." Chokwe explained what had transpired with the doctors, their treatment, their diagnoses, and their recommendations. The bravery of my brother and his children was amazing. With pain pulsating through their eyes, they all stoically held the necessary but undesirable discussion to determine their mother's fate. It was something that will never leave me. At one point, Chokwe had the doctor explain to his children what had been explained to him previously. It appeared that they understood that their mother was no longer mentally or physically with us on this planet. Thus, the decision was made to terminate the life support.

Nubia was already admired and loved by so many, but in her death, she became even more so. Nubia, like her mother before her, donated her organs. Her mother donated her eyes, and I thought at the time, "how honorable." The children said Nubia wanted her organs donated, too, and it was even documented on her driver's license. The hospital determined that her kidneys could be donated. There was a woman from some organization, like the "Gift of Life," who remained vigilant with the family day by day. She explained to us that she was there waiting to see if her services would be needed. I did not like that at all. I thought her presence was very peculiar, and I didn't want her there. She was nice and polite to the family, even waiting on us from time to time, getting coffee and other things. Chokwe and the kids never said anything about her presence, but I'm really not sure they knew who she was or why she was there. In addition to our family, there were so many friends who came daily that they did not know. I thought of her as the grim reaper or something, waiting for the word to take Nubia's body away. When I expressed my feelings to a couple of my siblings, one of them said, "She is just doing her job." Whether she was or not, I didn't want her there. And if her job was to have Nubia's organs matched with a recipient on an organ donor waiting list, she was deprived of that duty.

Nubia was spending the night at the house of my cousin Priscilla's daughter, Michelle, when she had the aneurysm. Priscilla made a special request when learning Nubia's kidneys would be donated. Spiritually, ironically, coincidentally, Priscilla had a very close friend who needed a kidney at that crucial time. Nubia's kidney was given to Priscilla's friend, and the transplant was successful. The recipient contacted Chokwe and the children to express her appreciation and gratitude.

There were a couple of other heartbreaking and tragic events Chokwe and I shared. When my son, Jeaco, was murdered in Detroit, Chokwe was in Mississippi, but I reached out to him daily for guidance with this horrific situation. When the police and prosecutors failed to do their duty, Chokwe sent his investigators, Hondo and Mikhail, from Jackson, to investigate Jeaco's case. Chokwe even came to Detroit to attempt to persuade Kym Worthy, Wayne County prosecutor, to do her elected duty and prosecute the people who were alleged to have killed my son.

There were many more intercessions with Chokwe and me evolving around his political work, legal work, my work, and family. As his personal representative in Detroit, I handled his law referrals, political organizing, speaking engagements, fundraisers, petition drives, and other related activities. But, most important of all, when our parents began to age and were no longer able to govern their business, it was Chokwe and I who handled those affairs. Early on I took on the job of taking our parents to doctors and business appointments and assisting with their care. However, it was our sister Denise who stopped working to care for their physical well-being at home. Chokwe and I still continued to discuss, develop, and make plans surrounding our parents and family as a whole.

Prior to our father making his earthly transition, I kept day-to-day and then hour-to-hour contact with Chokwe in Mississippi. The doctors had given us little hope for his survival during his last days, and that's another story in itself. Chokwe came once to see our father before his health deteriorated, and Dad was so happy to see him, along with all the others who came to see him. Chokwe asked that I call him and let him know when the time came. I called him and he made it before our father departed this life. I heard the pain in Chokwe's voice and saw the sorrow in his eyes. Our father was Chokwe's biggest supporter and fan in life since he was a young boy. Sometimes I think our father, who himself was a brilliant, talented man, whose aspirations and dreams were cut short because of his responsibility to care for his wife and eight children, may have lived vicariously through Chokwe.

Unfortunately, when our mother's time came to make her transition, things did not go as smoothly as they had with our father. Chokwe called and spoke to our mother briefly when she was coherent, but by the time he arrived from Mississippi she was unable to speak. It was painful for me this time to see Chokwe trying to reach our mother, but she was unreachable. Watching him bend his tall frame down to our mother's bed to speak quietly into her ear was heart-wrenching. Mysteriously, several hours before he arrived, she was talking. After that period, I do not recall her talking again. I don't know what he quietly said to our mother, except calling her name repeatedly. But no one could have told me convincingly that my brother Chokwe would follow our mother into eternity fourteen months later.

Choose Your Battles

Male testosterone was shooting everywhere. After working a late night at the law office, Chokwe had to go out to talk to a client. We had worked late and would be going home together since I did not have my car, and I lived upstairs from him. When we arrived on a very narrow street where the client lived, I noticed there was no passageway for two cars to pass. A man driving in the opposite direction attempted to pass through. He appeared to be a very angry man who was shouting objections at Chokwe concerning the problematic situation of passing on this very narrow street. At one point, the men (Chokwe and the angry man) were shouting at each other with no apparent resolution in sight.

All of a sudden, a big robust, thick Black man exited his vehicle, cursing at Chokwe over the passing situation. "You dumb m— f—, get the f— out the way." Chokwe, also angry, responded, "Man you move, I've got the right away." Boy, I did not think this was going to end well. However, as quickly as it started, it ended when Chokwe reentered his car and went out of his way to get to our destination.

Chokwe backed up, not the angry man. I felt very bad for Chokwe because I don't think he wanted to back down.

In my opinion, the other man was not only wrong, but he was the aggressor; but I did feel proud of my big brother for being the one who backed up and gave in. Chokwe must have assessed the situation and concluded he was dealing with an unpredictable, aggressive hothead, and he had his younger sister in the automobile. Though he kept eyeing his briefcase, which I knew contained more than his legal files, he made the best decision to back down and give in. This reminded me of our Aunt Rachel's husband's situation, who was stabbed to death during an altercation with a neighbor over a parking space.

One of the most valuable lessons Chokwe taught me in life is to "choose your battles." He would often say that to me when I would bring issues and situations to him that were upsetting me. "Shushanna, you have to choose your battles. You can't fight everything, and you have to decide what is more important. You have to let some things go and concentrate on what needs your attention most." That night on the narrow street with the angry man in the other car, Chokwe demonstrated that lesson to me. I recall Chokwe also advising my ex-husband once that "Sometimes, you just have to walk away. It takes a real man to walk away." That is what Chokwe did that night. I shudder to think how things could have turned out if Chokwe did not back down and walk away. Someone could have been arrested and incarcerated or hurt, or even killed.

CHAPTER 3
College, Law School, and Beyond

"When I left law school to go and work with the Republic of New Afrika, my father encouraged me to return to school. I reread Malcolm X and I decided I would come back and be the type of lawyer that Malcolm would have been."
– Chokwe Lumumba

Edwin Taliaferro, later known as Chokwe Lumumba, graduated from St. Theresa Catholic school in 1965 as a top athlete with honors. He then transitioned to Kalamazoo College where he went on to experience life events (in and out of K College) that developed his political constitution. Chokwe never, no matter what the cost, wavered from these principles for the rest of his life. This was one of my brother's attributes I aspired to possess among many.

Chokwe's hard work in high school on and off the field paid off. He was awarded both academic and athletic scholarships to attend Kalamazoo College. Chokwe was on the freshman and varsity basketball teams and also on the varsity football team. He played college sports until a serious injury ended his ability to play. Academically at Kalamazoo College, he pursued a Bachelor of Arts degree with a political science major and a history minor, which he earned in 1969. It appeared the more education Chokwe pursued, the greater his achievements and the more awards he earned.

After graduating from Kalamazoo College in 1969, Chokwe attended the summer Pre-Law School Institute at Wayne State University Law School through the Council on Legal Education Opportunity (CLEO). He finished the institute with honors and was second in his class. He then attended Wayne's Law School from 1969 to 1975, graduating cum laude. Again, he earned awards for his outstanding achievements: He finished first in his freshman class, he received the Law School Bronze Key Award, and he finished first in his contracts class. He was granted the Contract and Hornbook Awards and received an invitation to join Law Review.

While in law school, Chokwe gained experience through his commitment to the legal profession but also because of the challenges he faced. He was a law intern for the Wayne County Neighborhood Legal Services for the Domestic Affairs Division and the Home Purchase and Economic Development Division in Detroit. He also worked at the Free Legal Aid Clinic as a law intern defense counsel for indigent clients in misdemeanor cases. As a law intern at Legal Aid and Defender Association at Landlord Tenant, he represented tenants in landlord-tenant actions. In addition to being a law intern, he worked as a legal researcher for the American Civil Liberties Union in Detroit.

However, his stint in law school was also a battle. Once, while speaking at the Wolverine Student Bar Association Conference, Chokwe shared his experience protesting against WSU Law School. He had helped spearhead a protest at the law school in 1971 when 64 percent of the Black students at the school were dismissed. Chokwe and others formed a human chain in front of the law school and ultimately locked it down. The brave student warriors said, "If we can't come in, no one is going in." Subsequently, all of the students were reinstated and all but two became lawyers and/or judges.

Another significant incident of racism occurred after Chokwe successfully completed his first year of law school. He took a leave of absence to initially go to Mississippi to work with the RNA. His leave, however, lasted three years due to the RNA 11 Incident because he committed to help with their legal defense. With that experience, he learned firsthand how unfair and biased the American judicial system was. Chokwe, I believe, became frustrated and disillusioned with the desire to practice law from that experience. New Afrikan Brothers and Sisters were being tried for defending themselves against a police and FBI attack, with an arsenal of weapons on them, while they were lying asleep in their beds before dawn (like Fred Hampton in the Black Panthers in Chicago). Years later, Chokwe shared with a group of law students, lawyers, and judges about his conflict over returning to law school. "When I returned to Detroit after working on the RNA 11 case, my father talked to me about returning to law school. I always wanted to be a lawyer. I reread Malcolm X, the appendix and how Malcolm told the story about how he expressed the desire to be a lawyer to his teacher; a teacher who liked him a lot said, 'Malcolm that is an unrealistic dream for a nigger.' So what I decided was I would come back and be the kind of lawyer Malcolm would have been." However, when he returned, he was required to repeat his entire first year. This was not a traditional practice.[15]

In addition, while attending Wayne State University Law School, as a student-teacher, he taught contracts review. After law school, he served as a part-time instructor at Wayne County Community College teaching American Government and the Black Struggle, Regionalism and the Black Community, Black Sociology, Black Psychology, Criminal Law and Process, Corrections, Constitutional Law, Business Law, Black History, and Political Science 101. He also served as an instructor at the Criminal Defense Association of Michigan in Detroit. His teaching

---

[15] Author's note: The exact quote is "A lawyer–that's no realistic goal for a nigger." See, Malcolm X and Alex Haley, *The Autobiography of Malcolm X* (New York: Ballantine Books, 1964), 38.

spanned from high school students to college students to law students. Chokwe taught Street Law at Independent High School YWCA in Chicago. Then, through Malcolm X Community Center for Black Survival in Detroit and as the Program Director, Chokwe taught the community Street Law, Political Education, and Awareness.

Edwin F. Taliaferro entered Wayne State University Law School as a compassionate, very intelligent young man aspiring to be an attorney. Through his law school journey and acclimation into the Republic of New Afrika, he graduated law school as Chokwe Lumumba, an evolving revolutionary. Chokwe passed the Michigan Bar on May 6, 1976, and received a license to practice law in all Michigan courts. His quest for justice and his drive for liberation led him to successfully complete additional law programs beyond law school and to earn law licenses beyond Michigan.[16] He practiced primarily criminal law for most of his legal career in Michigan.

Chokwe began his legal career under the supervision of Attorney Myzell Sowell, former director of the Legal Defender's Office on Gratiot in Detroit. Chokwe treated his indigent pro bono clients with dignity and respect. When Chokwe was assigned a case the Recorder's Court judges knew they were in for a long haul. Chokwe tried each case like it was the most important case. Chokwe's law practice and experience in the courts contributed to his evolution into a revolutionary. He was able to see up close the workings of an unjust justice system in America. These experiences also provided him with an opportunity to defend Black people. He began practicing law at the Defender's Office in Detroit in May 1975. In his position as deputy defender, he provided criminal defense of indigent clients until September 1977.

---

[16] He participated in Michigan Bar Review from December 1975 through February 1976. In 1977, he successfully completed the National Institute of Trial Advocacy, Ithaca, New York; BARBRI–Bar Review, Jackson, Mississippi; Member Magnolia Bar Association from April 1991; Member of National Conference of Black Lawyers 1975.

College, Law School, and Beyond

*(Left to Right) Chokwe, James Cannon, Earl B. Ashford
(Front) Shushanna*

In 1977, Chokwe joined two other attorneys and opened the law firm of Ashford, Cannon, & Lumumba. This law firm evolved as they acquired new partners and associates over the years. While practicing at his law firm, in Detroit, Chokwe eventually gained the respect of most of the judges. Even the ones who disliked him had to admit they respected him. Also, even the judges who held Chokwe in contempt appreciated his dedication and integrity. However, judges all over the country understood that Attorney Chokwe Lumumba was determined and relentless.

On several occasions, Chokwe told a judge politely but directly, "Your honor I motion for you to remove yourself from this case."

"On what basis?," the judge would ask.

"On the basis that you are a racist, Sir, and you are unable to preside over this trial fairly or impartially."

The Wayne County Prosecutor's Office would gear up for a "Chokwe Lumumba case," so much so his cases would generally be the talk of the office. Some of the prosecutors feared him, some disliked him, but all of them knew and understood that Chokwe Lumumba was a good advocate and, more often than not, a winning advocate.

Chokwe won over 80 percent of his legal cases, including winning the overwhelming majority of his murder cases during the early part of his career as a lawyer in Detroit. He came to the public's attention in particular for his successful representation of Hayward Brown in the early 1980s. Brown was one of the most sought-after individuals in U.S. history for his alleged involvement with attacks on Stop the Robberies Enjoy Safe Streets (STRESS) undercover police officers. Mayor Coleman Young was credited with dispersing STRESS subsequent to reports of their terrorizing and killing members of the Black community (see chapter 5).

On April 24, 1991, Chokwe passed the Mississippi Bar and received a license to practice law in all Mississippi courts. He practiced law as a general practitioner in Mississippi from 1991 to 2013. When he moved to Jackson, Mississippi, in 1991, he initially provided legal services as an attorney through Southwest Mississippi Legal Services. He started a law practice in Jackson shortly after. Chokwe remained a member of the law firm until 2013 when he became mayor of Jackson, Mississippi.

Friends and Partners for Life

(Left to Right) Soffiyah Elijah, Earl B. Ashford, Chokwe, Georgia Manzie-Porterfield, (seated) Adam Shakoor

The law firm that Chokwe opened in 1977 with Earl Ashford and James Cannon expanded several times to include partners Jeffrey L. Edison, Adam Shakoor, Ernest Jarrett, Naomi Ottison, and Harry Davis and to include as associates Juanita Christian and Judge Norma Dotson. Judge Diane Cynthia Stephens and attorneys Paul Curtis, Samuel Perkins, and James McGinnis were also affiliated with the law firm. Chokwe served as "of counsel" to the Law Offices of Curtis and Edison and the Law Offices of Jeffrey Lee Edison. In addition, Chokwe was an active member of the National Conference of Black Lawyers. When Chokwe moved to Jackson, Mississippi, in 1991, he opened a general practice specializing in criminal matters with his partner Harvey Freelon. Attorneys Imhotep Alkebulan and Chokwe Antar Lumumba also worked with the firm Lumumba, Freelon and Associates.

Several of Chokwe's law partners began their relationship with him during law school and maintained those friendships during Chokwe's life. Here are their reflections on Chokwe.

(Left to Right) Chokwe, Jeff, and Earl (Photo courtesy of Earl B. Ashford)

(Left to Right) Jeff Edison, Chokwe, Gerald Evelyn, (Front) Walter Pookrum, (Photo courtesy of Jeff and Shaakira Edison)

Judge Earl B. Ashford

I first met Chokwe Lumumba at Wayne State's law library. He was about a year ahead of me. We met just as two Black law students. Since there weren't too many brothers over there, when you saw one,

Memories of My Revolutionary Brother, Chokwe Lumumba

Law Firm Partners and Associates

Attorney Harry A. Davis
(Partner)

Attorney Naomi
Ottison-Truman (Partner)

Attorney Samuel L. Perkins
(Associate)

Attorney James W. Mcginnis (Associate),
Itari, and Chokwe Antari

Judge Norma Y. Dotson
(Associate)

Judge Cynthia Diane Stephen
(Associate)

Attorney Ernest L. Jarrett
(Partner)

you had to greet him. So, at first, I was just pleased to meet another brother who had a little bit more experience in dealing with that particular institution than I had. I thought he might have something to say to me that I didn't know. At that time, WSU [Wayne State University] had a relatively small percentage of Black students in the university overall but especially in the law school. There were tensions because it was the time of...student activism, the problem with how Blacks had been dealt with in America. Those real-life issues showed up at the law school and college in general. Just the very fact that the numbers were quite limited made you have to seek refuge in a similar Black person you met and hopefully in a kindred soul. That was a survival issue. You had to join with somebody. At first, I didn't know what we might have in common, except we were both planning on fighting the system from within by virtue of the occupation we had chosen. We all got involved in the Black Legal Alliance (BLA). Jeff Edison was the president. Daphne Means, I don't remember what her office was, but she was an officer. Chokwe was the community liaison. I was the bookkeeper, I believe, some type of financial responsibility. The BLA encompassed all Black students, and we were officers. [...] The Association of Black Legal Alliance was part of the student activism movement. Some of our primary purposes were to assist one another with the experience of surviving law school and dealing with the system we were involved in, and also as an organization, there was a substantial amount of effort to get additional students into the law school. Students who had trouble getting into law school in the ordinary and usual fashion would also come to the BLA for assistance, and we were able to often go to the dean and other school officials and sometimes get some other students into the law school. There was a protest at the law school prior to my term there (Derrick Humphries, Virgil Smith, Longworth Quinn, and others). What happened with those guys impacted me; it helped me understand the atmosphere I was walking into. It happened during one of Chokwe's first years in law school. You know he was in his first year in law school twice.

Chokwe told me that he had been in law school before at Wayne State. As I recall, what he explained to me is that he had previously been in law school at WSU under his original name, Edwin Taliaferro, and when he came back the second time, he applied under the name Chokwe Lumumba. He had an excellent academic record anyway, so his academic records were impeccable. It wasn't until he got back in the second time that they found out he had been a previous student there.

Our BLA group felt a need to organize for several reasons. First off, a lawyer has to have an obligation to understand the history. So we studied the history of the United States number one, number two the history of Detroit, the history of Wayne State University number three, and having learned what the history of the law school was made it clear that we needed to be prepared for a rigorous encounter with the system.

Remembering our protest, I recall that our group was so tight. We were studying together so closely. We were monitoring each other; we were nurturing each other. We went against the approach that the law school expected students to take. They had a higher interest in the more individualistic approach, a more combative approach with each other, and a more competitive approach. Our whole approach was contrary to the way they expected us to behave as law students, and because we were working so closely with each other and honing each other's skills, getting ready with our practice court and all that kind of stuff, they actually started objecting to the students observing the presentations of the behavior of other students because we were going back and helping each other improve their participation. The law school did not like that, so they actually banned the students who had been through that process from participating and watching because we were going back and helping those still to come get even better. It was not a part of the system. It really seemed that the system was designed for us each to carry knives and to be ready and willing to stick those knives in the backs of each other. I am sure other students who came after us were able to benefit because of our protest.[17]

The administration of the Black Legal Alliance changed. I was still aware of some of the changes that were taking place, some of the officers and their activities. It was always interfacing with the law school and challenging the way they were approaching it, but specifically about tutors, I don't remember that because we were each other's tutors.

Our vision for a law firm started in law school. While we were students, we were talking about it. A number of us had just decided that we were going to work together in a firm. It started off with a number of breakfasts that were put on by Adam Shakoor and his wife. Those were some of the informal settings where we talked about opening a firm before we got out of law school. The plan at all times was that we would not have a traditional law firm but that it would be community based. At the same time, we had plans that we were going to cover all areas of the law. Some were going to be criminal lawyers, some were going to be civil lawyers, and I was going to be a business lawyer. We had in mind, and subsequently we put into practice, to cover the full range of the legal profession. Actually, Adam was a little more anxious to get to it than the rest of us. Adam opened the first law office that was really affiliated with ours. Then later, Chokwe, James Cannon, and I found the building at 11000 West McNichols, which was in the heart of the Black community. It was a nice enough building that it showed that we were taking care of business, but at

---

[17]Shushanna interjects, "As a law student at U of D [University of Detroit], we did not have any resources, like tutoring, mentoring, or library assistance. However, law students at WSU during this same period were able to benefit from these resources due to the protest that you all waged." When Georgia Manzie and Leroy Soles came to WSU Law School, they were able to benefit from those resources that came about after your protest.

the same time, it was located close to the clients we had and would expect to have. Then, Adam came and got with us. We were all talking about it. Jeff came later; he was always in the conversation, but he had decided he was going to spend a little more time in training. Jeff had decided to specialize in criminal law, and one of the best venues for that training was at the Legal Aid Public Defender's Office. Chokwe had been there at least for a while; Jeff wanted to hone his training skills a little longer at the Public Defender's Office.

We had dreams when we opened the law office, but the first thing we had to talk about was Chokwe's political activities. We perceived that the phone was tapped in the office. Everybody at all times recognized that. There was going to be high scrutiny; there was no question about it. His involvement with the Republic of New Afrika made it very clear that any activities we engaged in would be under extreme microscopic observations. We were not planning on doing anything illegal. We were only going to be exercising our rights and the rights of our clients. After you get the understanding that the phones are going to be tapped and the government was going to be watching everything else you do, then you start your dreams of what you want to do and how you are going to do it. One of the main things that we had in mind was that we decided we were not going to represent any drug dealers. That was an essential aspect.

Chokwe was an officer with the Republic of New Afrika, which was an organization that had existed for a while with the goal of having the United States concede to Blacks' demand for five states in the South for us to run on our own as an independent nation. Because this was such a revolutionary idea, we knew that if we affiliated ourselves with Chokwe, we were going to be associated with that. Although Chokwe was the primary activist with the Republic of New Afrika, his involvement with the community and his interest in the well-being of Blacks, and the future prospects of us as a people doing well, are what made us want to be affiliated with him. We were all as deeply steeped in the more radical aspects as he was.

Chokwe made it his mission to excel in law school, and he did. He was at the top of his class for at least two of the years he was in law school, and he was invited to participate in the highest levels of student activity because of his record. He rejected some of the invitations because of his outlook on the people who were making the invitation and the message that was to be delivered if he accepted or participated in that activity, but he made it his business to be a top student and he was very diligent in his studies. As a matter of fact, it seemed he was studying someplace else besides the rest of us because I don't remember him being there all the time when we were studying. He was there sometime, but I don't know where else he was studying; but I do know that he was roaming around the county because he never did give up his political activism. He would be here and there, but he managed to stay a good student. As a matter of fact, Chokwe told me he had a photographic memory. He could see the page of a book after he looked at it.

The legal profession as practiced by the dominant culture is very competitive—not just competitive but with an eye toward defeating and undercutting your competition, so the cooperation that we were participating in was the exact opposite of what they expected us to do and what they expected to train us to do as incoming law students. They wanted us to come in and fit the mold and fit their expectations, and we were subverting that by not participating in that particular approach. A lesson that could be learned from our law school group is that there is no question that the only way a group of people can do really well is if many or most and perhaps all the group do really well, and any effort to separate out or treat as different or divide and conquer is against our interest. You should always keep in mind the importance of work and cooperation among like-minded people for the benefit of the entire group.

My best memory of Chokwe. [...] Well, I was his lawyer. I am not going into the circumstances as to when or why I represented him, but another memory I have is one of my best memories. As knowledgeable as Chokwe was about history, culture, and political system, he was a little off about one situation. I remember he represented Tupac Shakur. One day someone gave Chokwe some tickets to a "pop concert," and we didn't know what a pop concert was, but I think four of the partners and their wives and/or girlfriends went with Chokwe to this concert. Let's say it was a little different from our expectations of what pop was. It was a type of music that was very far from the Motown experience, Black blues type of music we were used to, and it was at the Light Guard Armory. It was packed full, and when the people started singing, we started running. That was all because Chokwe had decided to be a social director, a position he was not quite qualified to perform.

The first time I heard that Chokwe was going into electoral politics, when he ran for city politics, this was a bit of a departure from a position of a man who had advocated secession from the United States to end up in a position to take up a political office. As a matter of fact, in some of our private conversations when we were still in law school, I used to challenge Chokwe on what his position would be if we were to have a nation like the Republic of New Afrika. One of the things I asked him was, "Ok, Brother, now that we are going to be in charge, you are the champion of the people when it comes to the criminal courts and dealing with the oppressed brothers. When we are in charge, what I want to know is, will you be the prosecutor?" He kind of thought we would not need a prosecutor, and I disagreed with him quite strongly. I told him, "we will be in charge, but there will be a need for some police officers, and I just want to know, are you ready to take on that job?"

When I found out Chokwe had passed, it was a shock beyond any kind of understanding because he had just reached that lofty position of being the mayor. He was just getting started with his plans and programs for what he wanted to do in that southern state.

So to hear that he was gone was quite devastating. It was not just a personal loss, but I thought it a loss to the entire group of Black people he had served so many years and so valiantly, especially the group that had adopted him in Jackson, Mississippi. I think if we keep in mind that he always tried to make sure that justice was done with individual people and to us as a whole and that his goal was to see Black people progress and have autonomy with regard to decisions affecting them—if we keep those things in mind, I think we will all do better. I would tell young people about Chokwe that as you grow up, you will find that there are certain people that have spent some time on earth who have demonstrated by the things they have done while they were here the things that are important in life and how you should go about trying to serve not yourself but others. I would say discussing and looking into his life and history would be an example they could consider following.

Attorney Jeffrey L. Edison

When Chokwe made his earthly transition, my wife, Shaakira, and I were in Ghana, West Africa, specifically in Accra. There is a W. E. B. Du Bois Centre where W. E. B. Du Bois is entombed, and there is a center there where people from the African Diaspora congregate. In addition to the center, there is also an African Diaspora forum that was established by Dr. Erieka Bennett, who is the Diaspora Ambassador to the African Union. There is a wall of heritage, an ancestral wall where there are plaques that people can purchase in the names of their own ancestors to be placed on the wall forever. Shaakira's father and mine had both passed, and we had gotten name plates for our fathers on the wall.

After Chokwe passed, we felt that it would only be fitting that we get a nameplate not only for Chokwe but also for his wife Nubia. When we were there in March, right after Chokwe's passing, we got nameplates in both of their names. Coincidentally, Chokwe's name

Memories of My Revolutionary Brother, Chokwe Lumumba

Attorneys Myzell Sowell and Milton Henry

Attorneys William Waterman and Elbert Hatchett

Attorney Cornelius Pitts and Shushanna Shakur

Judge Daphne Means Curtis and Chokwe Lumumba

(Left to Right, Back Row)
Attorney Kenneth V. Cockrel,
Attorney Ted Spearman
(Left to Right, Front Row)
Defendant Hayward Brown,
Legal Investigator Gregory Hicks

Injustices from Jackson to Detroit

Lumumba Family on NCBL Nassau Trip, 1991
(Photos courtesy of Jeffrey L. Edison)

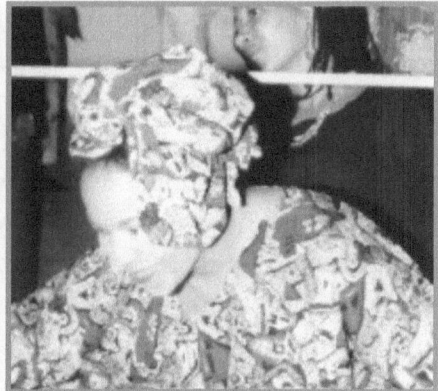

is right next to Brother Nelson Mandela's, together with Nubia. We had that enshrined, and it is also very personal to me, too, because Chokwe's passing on February 25th was four years to the day that my father had passed on February 25, 2010.

Jeff and Shaakara Edison placing Chokwe and Nubia Lamumba's name plate next to Nelson Mandella's name in Ghana. (Photo courtesy of Jeffrey L. Edison)

I first met Chokwe in August 1973, right when the academic year was beginning. I was in the law library, and he had come into the library, walking down the aisle. As Earl Ashford stated earlier, when you see someone, a kindred spirit, you are automatically attracted to them. We met one day at Wayne State's law school. I believe it was one of Chokwe's first days returning to the law school. I just happened to be in the library, and he had come in, and of course being two brothers, we were attracted to each other, and we struck up a conversation about the law school. I was saying I was there in the summer program, and I was using some choice words to describe how I felt about the law school and what the law school represented. Chokwe shared his experiences from a few years before. We just hit it off and became great friends and, later, great partners.

Chokwe was in law school twice. I am not sure if it was because of the change of names or because of the school's policy. He was out for three years (because he left in 1970) and now was coming back three years later. They just felt we are going to give you an added hoop to jump through. His objective was to get back into school and to succeed. Whatever they put on his plate, he was going to be able to deal with [it] in one way or another.

I believe he left the first time because of his involvement and position with the Republic of New Afrika. I believe the raid [on the RNA properties] occurred in 1971 in Jackson, Mississippi, but there were other activities that required more attention than his desire to be at law school at the time. He had to refocus and deal with his political activities. Then, after organizing around the legal team for the RNA 11 in 1971 and together with all of his other political and social activities, he knew that he needed to be back in law school to do what he needed to do to become a lawyer. So he then returned to law school and had to repeat his first year to achieve this goal.

The law school at the time was a microcosm of what we all experience[d]. Generally, in terms of the legal profession at the time, if I recall, African/Black American lawyers only comprised less than 1 percent of the legal profession. It certainly was not because of Africans being unqualified but rather the institution of racism that excluded Africans from being a part of the profession. As a result, there was tension between the institution and Black applicants. They would let us in, but they would kick us out of the school, and they would not graduate us. That was the tension that Chokwe and others dealt with in his first year in 1970.

Things had not changed by the time he came back in 1973. Carl Edwards, Ivy Riley, Bob Twitty, and a few others were in Wayne before 1973. I think they began in 1972, so by the time I came, Earl Ashford came, and others came[,] the groundwork had been laid to have an organized effort to resist those institutional policies that kept us out. There had been discussions previously about the whole dynamic that we would enter into because law school really perpetuates elitism and individualism, contrary to our collective frame of reference, which would get as many of us out as possible. We ran up against the wall often as teachers and professors would take advantage of us one-on-one. They would try to belittle us and demean us to discourage us from moving forward. However, we would not let that happen, and those who were doing well in a certain subject certainly shared their knowledge and expertise with those who needed their assistance. It was a good time [for] organizing among the students to have a collective learning experience, collective resistance to policies, and collective agitation to change those policies so that more of us could get through that process.

I don't think Chokwe had problems dealing with anybody. There may have been certain obstacles put in front of him, as we all had, but Chokwe had such an overwhelming personality, drive, and commitment. I never experienced any kind of weakness or concern about his own personal ability to survive and prevail through anything. He was always helping others who may have questioned their own personal abilities to succeed, because the institution itself was structured so that you questioned yourself as opposed to questioning the institution. So we had to struggle, oftentimes, to understand that it was not our inability because we were all admitted to law school.

We all had excellent backgrounds coming from undergraduate school, and now we were in this place that was telling us that we were not qualified. Some people had a tendency to believe that as opposed to the racism and institutionalism—the racism of individual professors and the institutional racism of the law school that would exclude us—but I never saw Chokwe question his ability to succeed.

In law school, we had the Black Legal Alliance (BLA), which was created the year before I got there. Carl Edwards, Ivy Riley, and others created the BLA. I did accept leadership of the BLA; however, we really had more of a collective leadership approach. I may have been a bit out front, but there wasn't any one particular individual that was held up, so we were able to really tap into the talents and wisdom of a collective. We had a great group of students who were prepared to struggle to get through.

The contributions the BLA made at WSU Law School had a lasting impact. One of the biggest challenges was not only the admissions policies of the school but also readmission policies. These policies impacted students who may have had some challenges their first year and their ability to continue on. We challenged the school to change the policies to allow more of us in and to keep us in school in terms of creating support mechanisms, not only in terms of studies but also in financial aid. Those struggles brought us in contact not only with the law school administration but also with the Board of Governors at Wayne State University as a whole.

Challenges against racism existed not only at the law school but across the campus in other departments too. We were able to present our grievances before the Board of Governors at WSU to make changes across the campus. It was at the Board of Governors that we came into contact with Myzell Sowell, who later became one of our mentors and allowed us the opportunity to become the lawyers that we have become. Myzell Sowell was the chief defender of the Defender's Office. Chokwe, Daphne Means, and I went to the Defender's Office to practice after law school. We went there because Myzell saw something in us that prompted him to invite us to come to the Defender's Office. Certainly, for me, it was one of the best things to happen to me in terms of my career.

What made our group successful was each person's commitment to struggle and our own commitment to the liberation of our people, based on each person's own history and experiences. It was just a matter of timing and opportunity that happened to bring us together at the same time, and because of that, with each person's talents and skills and motivations, we were very fortunate that the timing was right. I don't think it was anything special other than the timing and our own personal commitments that brought us together.

Chokwe was inspired to go to law school by Milton Henry, who was one of the founders of the Republic of New Afrika, and Kenneth Cockrel, who was an outstanding legal advocate during the time. Coming along the way as we developed in our law careers, Milton Henry was an inspiration. Cornelius Pitts was a trial lawyer we looked up to, particularly when we were starting the practice of law as young lawyers. Ray Willis, in the Defender's Office; Tony Axon, an outstanding trial lawyer; and Albert Hatchet[,] another outstanding trial lawyer, all inspired us. As a matter of fact, Chokwe and I went to observe Albert when he was representing Cicero Love in the retrial of a murder case that Albert successfully defended. Cicero was a local community activist who was wrongfully accused and later vindicated—in fact, vindicated by Judge George Crockett Jr. in the first trial where Cicero was convicted. Judge Crockett made an extraordinary move in setting the jury's guilty verdict aside. It was just about unheard of in most parts, and that was appealed and the charges were reinstated. Cicero was retried and acquitted.

Detroit has many outstanding criminal defense lawyers that we all benefited from, such as George Lee and Robert Mann, with whom Adam Shakoor worked for a while. Mann was an outstanding trial lawyer. There were sister lawyers that Chokwe admired like Deborah Gaskin and Brenda Maxwell, to name a couple.

Chokwe appreciated numerous judges as fellow attorneys. I mentioned Judge Crockett, and he has the history but bar none to date. One of the best trial lawyers is Judge George Crockett III, and he never got the recognition that trial lawyers deserve. Dalton Roberson was an incredible jurist. In fact, when Chokwe represented Bilal Sunni Ali and members of the Black Liberation Army in the Brink's robbery trial, Judge Dalton Roberson came to New York and testified on Chokwe's behalf. When they tried to keep Chokwe from practicing in New York, Paul Borman, who at the time was the chief defender of the Federal Defender's Office, happened to be in New York, and when he heard what was happening with Chokwe, he came and testified on Chokwe's behalf to allow him to practice in New York. Paul Borman became a United States district judge locally in Detroit.

When Chokwe sought admission to the Mississippi bar, they challenged his admission. Judge Henry Heading, who was a native of Canton, Mississippi, right outside of Jackson, came down to Jackson to testify before the Character and Fitness Committee of the bar. There were judges who stepped out and directly supported Chokwe. The Recorder's Court had a lot of great judges.[18] Really, the reason why there was an attack to abolish Recorder's Court was because of the quality of justice that was being meted out in the city of Detroit, together with a predominantly African pool that served on the juries. Jurists in Recorder's Court, at the time for the most part, were outstanding. Recorder's Court also received national recognition for administration of courts' systems and was used in some law schools as a model court, and that was under Black leadership.

Recorder's Court was unique because it was a reflection of the Detroit population that was majority African, so you had a majority African bench. The Recorder's Court was the criminal court for the city of Detroit. Not only the jurists but the staffing, the clerks, and probation officers were majority African, and juries were majority African. You had a quality of justice that was not experienced in other areas of the state, at least for African offenders and African lawyers who had to practice, so that in and of itself was unique regardless of what the decisions were. Whatever was decided by a judge or jury, you at least had a feeling that it was not racially motivated; that was the critical aspect of Recorder's Court.

The Recorder's Court was also the type of court that a lawyer like Chokwe Lumumba could walk into the courtroom with a dashiki on and practice law. There was no basis for challenging him on his

---

[18]The text here uses both "The Recorder's Court" and "Recorder's Court" interchangeably to reflect the ways that people refer to that entity.

attire. He wore a tie and was dressed appropriately. Even courts that challenged him on his dress had no basis. To challenge his wearing of a dashiki would be artificial. There really was no dress code saying you had to wear an Italian suit to practice.

Chokwe represented defendants and political prisoners throughout the country. In New York he represented Bilal Sunni-Ali, who was one of (in terms of this particular trial) four or five brothers and one European who were charged with being involved with the Black Liberation Army and their expropriation of monies from an armored Brink's truck. One or two guards or police were killed, and so it was a very politically charged case. One of the brothers, Sekou Odinga, took a position of not being a political prisoner but rather a prisoner of war that was based on the history of the U.S. government's war on African people here in America.

It was in that context that the criminal charges were being defended against. During the course of the trial, there were tensions and antagonism between Chokwe and the judge. The judge tried to limit what Chokwe could advocate, to limit his style, and that occurred in terms of questioning what types of evidence could be presented in court, and it was just tension throughout. During the course of the trial, Chokwe was held in contempt on two occasions. However, he was not adjudicated for the contempt until after the trial, and Chokwe's client was in fact acquitted when Chokwe was held in contempt. At the time, it was not just myself who went to New York (because I was here in Detroit maintaining the practice), but it was Harry Davis, Anthony Adams, Paul Curtis, James McGinnis, and Robert Dawkins. There was a group of us out of the 11000 West McNichols office that understood our brother had been attacked, and we had to go and represent him.

Hayward Brown was one of Chokwe's Detroit cases that received a lot of news attention. Initially, Hayward Brown was represented by Kenneth Cockrel as a result of a shootout in Detroit with the police when they were chasing him across the country. Kenny successfully defended Hayward when chief of police John Nichols made some comment about Hayward and the other brothers who were with him, Mark Bethune and John Percy Boyd. Nichols referred to them as "rabid dogs." Kenny's whole piece [response to Nichols's comments] was "What do you do with rabid dogs, and that is to kill them." That created the atmosphere for Hayward and the others' conduct to be perceived as defending themselves. The police force had already demonized them as rabid dogs. Then later, after that acquittal, the police were after Hayward. All he was trying to do was live his life. Hayward was arrested repeatedly and charged repeatedly for various offenses. Chokwe represented Hayward in a number of those cases, at least two, maybe three or four.

One case that stands out in my memory was when Hayward was a passenger of a car that was stopped in Dearborn. There were about three or four guys in the car when the Dearborn police stopped them. They ended up getting a gun out of the car, and it was a challenge to the stop and search of the car. The cop was asked, "What is your basis for stopping this car?" He said, "Because there were three or four Black guys riding through Dearborn." He said it that blatantly. Fortunately, the court understood that was certainly illegal. Ultimately, this was the basis to suppress the case. Out of all the cases, I don't believe that Hayward was convicted of anything, at least of the cases Chokwe represented. It was unfortunate that he ended up making his transition later.

Chokwe, in his vigorous advocacy, challenged the whole institution of the criminal process in representing a client. It has been said previously that not only did Chokwe represent political activists, but most of his clients were just everyday folks charged with various types of crimes in a very racist criminal system. He was in Mississippi on a case, challenging the process where a brother was convicted and facing an extraordinary amount of time. I believe it was at least fifty years, certainly the rest of this brother's life. Chokwe was trying to bring out the defects in the process, and I think this is when one of the jurors had done something improper, and he was trying to have a hearing to make a record of what had influenced this particular juror. There was a back-and-forth exchange with Chokwe and the judge. It really got down to the judge telling Chokwe to "look it up in the books," and Chokwe told the judge, "I probably finished higher in my law class than you did."

The judge told Chokwe, "Shut up and sit down."

It was just a back-and-forth exchange as a result of Chokwe protecting the interest of his client and the judge not wanting to hear it. He felt threatened by the advocacy of this African lawyer challenging his authority. The judge held him in contempt, and after the hearing, a newspaper reporter asked Chokwe to comment, and Chokwe said, "The judge has the judicial temperament of a barbarian." As a result, the incident was referred to the state bar. The National Conference of Black Lawyers stepped up to represent him. Adjoa Aiyetoro was the national director at the time. She and I and Imhotep Alkebulan, who was Chokwe's law partner at the time in his practice in Jackson, Mississippi, were also on the team representing him. He ended up being suspended for about six months, but he didn't miss a beat. During the suspension, he was able to commute to Michigan and represent clients here. Chokwe retained his law license in Michigan, and he was counsel in my law firm in Detroit. The Michigan bar did not choose to take any action against Chokwe based on the Mississippi discipline, so he was able to continue practicing law in Michigan at this time.

When we were in law school and the Defender's Office, we often talked about sports, and he supported sports. He thought he was a dynamic athlete along the way, so when we were in law school, we had the basketball intramural team, the BLA Stars. We had a pretty good team: Gad Holland, Dennis Burnett, Paul Curtis, Chokwe, and Dave Mason. Gerald Evelyn got a Wayne State ID to play with us. Papa Wells would always come and hang out with us. We also had a softball team at the Defender's Office, and we played flag football. Chokwe thought he was a wide receiver. Folks don't really know that side of him, but he enjoyed sports and the competition. He had that competitive drive.

Each of us had our own experiences with Chokwe. He was just so special. I really don't know how to define it. He just had a way of affecting you in his relationship. He got you to do things that you would not ordinarily do. He got you to think about issues. He really was a critical, dynamic thinker. To talk about his being creative, when he was held in contempt in New York, one of the issues he raised was one Imari Obadele had brought up in the RNA 11 case. Imari had raised the issue of immunity. He took the position that he was the president of a sovereign nation, the Republic of New Afrika, and therefore immune from prosecution. When Imari raised it, the Appellate Court rejected it in short script. However, he taught Chokwe that, consistent with the "social engineering" practices of Charles Hamilton Houston, you lay the groundwork. Chokwe applied that idea to his various cases to create constitutional challenges at the time discrimination and segregation.

However, Chokwe raised the issue of diplomatic immunity because at the time, he was not only the Vice President of the Republic of New Afrika, but he was also the Minister of Justice for

Adjoa Aiyeterio and Jeff Edison

the RNA when he represented Bilal Sunni-Ali. So Chokwe asserted diplomatic immunity because he was an official of the RNA during his representation of Bilal. This time, the Second Circuit, although they rejected it, gave a little more attention to his argument. The court referenced the Vienna Convention on Diplomatic Relations and the corresponding statute of the United States Code. There were no expectations that the court was going to recognize the provisional government, but Chokwe was laying the groundwork, like Charles Hamilton Houston, former Dean of Howard University Law School, admonished his law students to become social engineers in the struggle against racism and oppression. We don't know what precedent this might set for future generations of lawyers, or when a legal advocate or a person of leadership may argue diplomatic immunity. They can reference this case. You never know, but Chokwe claimed it.

Chokwe was such a phenomenal individual. He was courageous, he was fearless, and he was just dedicated and committed to African people and all oppressed people. He would advocate the elimination of all oppression and exploitation across the board. One of the things that was mentioned was Chokwe getting involved in electoral politics. It was a surprise, but when you stop and think of it, I think I recall him talking about it. It wasn't like Chokwe was looking to be involved in electoral politics. He would always say, and I know Chokwe Antar referenced it in his comments, "You have to have love for the people, because if you don't, you will eventually betray the people." I think his getting involved in electoral politics was a manifestation of the will of the people in the Jackson community that propelled him into electoral politics. I think it was the people in their organizing looking around for leadership. It was out of the grassroots that identified Chokwe as their representative and their leader. Chokwe's love for the people would not allow him to not assume their request for his leadership in electoral politics. Even though we were surprised by his involvement in electoral politics, when we look at it from this perspective, we certainly understood his decision to do it. Then, for him to be successful as a councilman and mayor, without compromising any of his principles and beliefs, and for him to say in his campaign motto "One City, One Aim, One Destiny," taking on Marcus Garvey's mantle, is outstanding, and that was embraced by white Jacksonians.

Chokwe was just one of those spirits that comes along every now and then and stands out among us. Let me say to his sister, Shushanna, you have always been his big sister as his younger sister. No matter what challenges Chokwe was going through, no matter personally, politically, or family-wise, you have been his biggest supporter and protector. I think as we go forward, you will always continue to protect his legacy and protect his spirit and his vision, despite what others may say, challenge, or raise. I think you are one of the keepers of that, and I know that's how your father and mother would want it to be. You are just the one out of all the siblings, you are the one for that. Everybody is supportive in their own special way, but you are the one to personally protect Chokwe. You know he was always calling Shushanna.

If we all can in our special way be committed to struggle against injustice, exploitation, and oppression, I think we all will have served his legacy well. Whenever that opportunity comes along for us to personally be involved in resisting injustice, do it. I think Chokwe will be proud of us. We certainly are all proud of him and respect him for his leadership, for his love for us personally, and his love for our people.

Attorney Gerald K. Evelyn

I met Chokwe through points of intersection. I went to Mumford High School with Jeff Edison, and [at] that time during significant protest, Mumford had a student protest. There was a young man there named Michael Humphrey (now Michael Pili Simanga), and I knew him from school. The RNA was coming into fruition, and he actually brought Imari Obadele (president of RNA) to Mumford. That was my first exposure to Chokwe, and later, Chokwe came to speak. Chokwe served in an advisory capacity, or he was there to direct the activism at Mumford. I do know that Kenneth Cockrel was also providing leadership at Mumford through Gregory Hicks and his organization. However, I did not meet Kenny until later in life after the Hayward Brown and the John Percy Boyd incidents and through his sister Melba Boyd. We went to Michigan State together. The students were just mad, and other than Michael, there was not a lot of internal leadership to the school. After I went to law school in D.C., Jeff and I maintained a relationship because of Jeff and Chokwe's relationship and because of the fact that there were law students around the country [who were] very active and organizing. Some of the things that were going on at Antioch overlapped with some things that were going on at other law schools. Antioch was a little different school, but there were some of the same struggles, so my relationship with Jeff kind of segued into a different relationship with Chokwe. When he came to Mumford, he was like a developing icon. I was a high school student. Later on, we developed more of a peer relationship and that was because of my relationship with Jeff.

After law school, we worked on cases together. You could not know Chokwe and not be involved at some level. You might be co-counsel. You might be providing support. The Defender's Office was kind of a point of intersection, especially when Myzell Sowell was running it. It was really like a community law office. You found lawyers there who were active and women activists. That is where I met Erma Henderson [in 1972, the first Black woman elected to the Detroit City Council] and where I first met Papa Wells, one of the original founders of the RNA. He would be there with Chokwe and

Jeff. The Defender's Office was like a community law office, and that is what the law office at 11000 West McNichols became. I went to the Defender's Office as a clerk, and Chokwe was already working there as a law student. Then, I got to know him on a different level. My first exposure to him in a case was the Pontiac case. They were doing something at the Defender's Office to support that case. The Pontiac case [1978] concerned a rebellion of inmates at a prison in Illinois, and a number of guys were arrested and were charged with death penalty crimes. Chokwe successfully defended several of those people.

I did go to jail with Chokwe while defending a client. There was an organization in Battle Creek (most of the members were women) called the Coalition to End Police Brutality and Racism, and there were a number of National Conference of Black Lawyers who got involved in various aspects of legal issues that came out of that activity, some of which produced criminal cases. Jeff was involved, Carl Edwards was involved, I was involved, and Chokwe was kind of the centerpiece as usual. There was a case where a guy named Larry Guy was the lead defendant, and they were charged with planting pipe bombs and some other activity that arose out of their political activity. Chokwe, another lawyer named Fred Moore, and I were involved in one particular preliminary examination, and we had a judge by the name of Alfonso A. Magnotta, Jr. It was a district judge in Battle Creek who was very racist. He actually filed a grievance against Chokwe and me because during the course of the examination, we accused him of being racist, or we accused him of having racist motivation in some of his decisions. He filed a grievance against both of us that was ultimately dismissed, but in any event during the course of that representation, Chokwe was held in contempt and I was held in contempt. Fred managed to avoid it on that particular occasion. I was given eighteen days in jail. Chokwe was given twelve days in jail. I remember at the time he sentenced us to contempt, we had a rather long hearing in front of another judge, who was a friend of Judge Magnotta Jr., and that judge actually convicted us of contempt.

Every defendant has a right to speak before they are sentenced. In this case, the judge left the bench without allowing us to speak, and if you don't get that right to speak, it is pretty clear that the sentencing will be invalidated. We would then have a perfectly appealable issue. But telling Chokwe not to speak wasn't going to happen. So Chokwe made a very eloquent speech. At that time, Nelson Mandela was in prison, and he was saying, "If Nelson Mandela can do twenty-five years for standing up for Black people, I can do twelve days standing on my head, so go ahead and give it to me." The judge did give it to him, and he gave me eighteen days. We appealed that conviction, and I remember one day I was taking my oldest son to the barbershop, and we were driving up I-75, and I heard on the radio that our conviction was reversed and the case was overturned.

After the case was overturned, we never had to go back and retry it, and the judge who actually sentenced us and held us in contempt died of a heart attack right after it happened. I used to always accuse Chokwe of killing that judge. Despite all of what happened with [the] Larry Guy case, I still wanted to work with Chokwe on other cases. Actually, you never had a choice if you were committed to the same types of activities as Chokwe. His energy and personality had a certain kind of momentum. Being held in contempt was not my idea, but you are in the same case with him, and his leadership had a contagious quality because some people who may not have had courage would be inspired to do courageous things and would look back and say, "I can't believe I did that." But he had a way of inspiring people that would cause people to do things they did not believe they could do or think were even possible.

To address the type of lawyer Chokwe was, we could look at the qualities people want in a lawyer. It is often said that you want a lawyer who is smart, prepared, and committed. Those qualities exist in different lawyers from one degree to another. He is probably one of the only lawyers I have ever seen whom you would consider a five-star lawyer on every level. He was creative, intelligent as he was committed, and people always kind of marveled at his militancy. He was charismatic and articulate, he expressed himself well, and he was fearless—those are the things that were in his public persona. What you didn't see was how hard he worked to prepare a case, how much time he put in to prepare a case, and how creative he was because he would never limit himself; he would always come up with a creative way to get himself out of a difficult situation. So I would tell a client that you are going to get a very special talent if you manage to get Chokwe Lumumba to take your case. After you have been in court with him, you know that.

Chokwe will impact future lawyers. From a legal perspective one of the things that made Chokwe unique is that we have this civil rights tradition that arose to break down the barriers of segregation, and Charles Hamilton Houston and other well-known Black lawyers are given credit for having articulated an alternative view of the Constitution. Chokwe was unique in so far as his letting you understand [that] as a lawyer you could not let yourself be limited by traditional interpretations of the Constitution. You have to come with an alternative view of how to view the U.S. Constitution and American law because if you limit yourself to those traditional definitions of how the law should be applied, then you can't possibly defend oppressed people. People who are oppressed by that same legal system require that you take a more creative approach and not just accept the stare decisis of how the law works.[19] He was the person

---

[19]Stare decisis is the doctrine that the court "abide by or adhere to, decided cases. Policy of courts to stand by precedent and not to disturb settled point. Black's Law Dictionary," Henry Campbell Black. M.A., St. Paul Minnesota West Publishing Co., 1968, Revised fourth edition, 1577.

who took the law and said there is a way to turn it inside out to benefit Black people and oppressed people. Being involved with the National Conference of Black Lawyers, an organization that sees itself as the legal arm of the revolution, that by its definition means you have to understand a revolutionary change was necessary for Black people to not be oppressed, and that is opposite of what you are taught in law school. Law school says the law is supposed to change very slowly and not very much. Well, if you are being oppressed by the legal system, then slow change is not going to get the job done, and he was a person, as a lawyer, who taught people to think out of the box in a way that will cause you to be much more creative.

You could not know Chokwe and not be inspired by what he was doing in representing political prisoners. What was interesting, though, was that Chokwe had a lot of "ordinary" clients too, for lack of a better term, and he gave the same quality of attention to them as he did to someone in the Republic of New Afrika or in the Black Liberation Army. If you were just a person who came to him and said, "my son is charged with armed robbery" or "my husband is charged with this crime," he would be the same lawyer.

Chokwe and I shared more than the law in our friendship over the years. We both loved sports. People who know Chokwe well know there are a lot of things he liked to do and enjoy. I worked with him on a lot of cases, but we would always have, especially in more recent years, shorter conversations on those because he would say, "Gerald, I need you to do X" or "Jeff is going to do X, and I need you to do Y." So I would call Jeff and we would discuss it, and I would end up doing X and Jeff would do Y. Then we would turn to something that was more entertainment. We would talk about the Pistons, the Lions, the Tigers, especially basketball. He really enjoyed basketball, so we might spend hours on the phone. I have been on conversations with him, and Nubia would pick up the phone and say, "Alright, that is enough, you boys are done!" and hang the phone up. So that is one thing I miss a lot about him, that aspect of our friendship that

College, Law School, and Beyond

Jackson Panther AAU Team

we could share as friends. Frequently, when we were talking about some aspect of a game, he would reach back and talk about his years when he was an athlete at Kalamazoo College or St. Theresa when something was done to him that may have not been done to other athletes. He never forgot or let you forget his history as an athlete.

When he started the Jackson's Panthers AAU Basketball Team, that organization really helped a lot of young people get scholarships to college. Moe Williams of the Cavaliers was one of his players. There were several players that came through that same program, so that was a very successful program. He was very quick to tell me about somebody he was developing who was going to be an NBA player, and twenty years later he said, "See, I told you Moe Williams is a great player, and he came out of our program," and I would say, "Alright Chokwe, I got it."

When Chokwe became mayor, as Earl Ashford said earlier, you had to enjoy the contrast because he was always the person opposing the government and the state. I actually told Chokwe, "When you become the mayor, you are going to be the defendant of police brutality. How are you going to defend that?" But it was hard not to appreciate and have some elation over the election on the other hand, as one of his friends and people who were close to him. We experienced his persistent victimization by the system—being held in contempt, being threatened, and having his license taken away from him—and so with his having been a victim of the state for so long, it was really kind of refreshing to know that that could happen in Jackson, Mississippi.

After Chokwe passed away, his son Chokwe Antar ran for his father's mayoral seat. I supported him, not just because he was Chokwe's son but because Chokwe Antar was a partner to his father. He grew in his father's footsteps, and he shared in the vision his father had for making Jackson a better place for all people who lived there, and I thought that was the only way and the best way to ensure the legacy Chokwe had established even in that short amount of time. You have to remember Chokwe had done a lot of groundwork that led to his becoming mayor; being elected mayor was just the next step in the process of the movement. Chokwe Antar, I felt, was the truest way to ensure that that legacy continued. We know with politics all too often the people promise things, but when they get into office, things are different. I am convinced that Chokwe Antar shares his father's vision. He is his own man, but he shares his vision for progress for the people in Jackson, and that is the best way to make sure that legacy is continued. That is why I supported him then, and that is why I will support him the next time he runs. I hope he does.

Honorable Adam Shakoor

I have known Chokwe longer than any of the law partners. My first meeting with Chokwe occurred during the hospital delivery process, I assume. Chokwe's mother and my mother were in Henry Ford Hospital maternity ward together, and he was born August 2nd and I was born August 6, 1947. So we used to joke and say we have known each other since birth. In law, we call that constructive knowledge.

Adam A. Shakoor and Chokwe, (Background) Robert Taliaferro, Jr.

We renewed our acquaintanceship and friendship in the 1960s. Of course, that was with the historical development and honorable activities surrounding the Republic of New Afrika's foundation. I was not a part of the Republic of New Afrika, but I was around during that time period, active with an organization called the Dodge Revolutionary Union Movement (DRUM), and we were close to Imari and other members of the RNA. We engaged in revolutionary activities combating the UAW's [United Automobile Workers] racism in their selection of union officers in locals that were becoming predominantly African American, Local 3 and Local 604.

So we had a lot of crossover in terms of RNA members who also were members of DRUM, as they worked in the plant. DRUM was General Gordon Baker's organization that developed into the League of Revolutionary Black Workers, as we organized in other plants outside of Dodge Main. There were other plants in Michigan and Indiana where workers were suffering some of the same issues as DRUM and wanted to join in with our efforts. So we expanded to go into various other plants. That is when we changed the name of the organization to the League of Revolutionary Black Workers as opposed to identifying it as DRUM. We also had FRUM (Ford Revolutionary Union Movement). We organized in high schools. We had young people at Mumford High, Northwestern High School, and other people, also in relation to those activities. We had an affiliation where we brought Kathleen Cleaver in when they opened a Black Panther chapter here, and [a] couple of our members went out to Oakland, California, and met with Bobby Seales and others. Basically, they wanted to unite with us, and we thought that their focus and our focus were similar but not enough that we would become a part of the Panther organization.

When I returned to Wayne, after the 1967 riot, we began to actively engage in the organizing efforts with DRUM, and in 1969 I was assigned to work with organizing a Black construction local, Local

124, with a gentleman named Calvin Stubbs who was their president. So I went into organizing there, and we were pretty successful. We got accreditation through the Department of Labor to have our own apprenticeship program. I felt I needed to finish my undergraduate degree in order to go to law school and obtain additional skills. I returned to Wayne in 1969 and renewed my friendship with Chokwe. He was going to law school at the time, and I was finishing up my undergraduate work. When I got out of undergraduate school I went into a master's program in urban planning at the Center for Urban Studies. We worked sporadically with some of the folks over at the law school because our co-director, Otto Hessler, was also a professor in the law school. He and Richard Simmons were the co-directors. Of course, after that I had a desire to go onto law school, and that is what I did.

When the Detroit riots broke out in 1967, I was living on campus. I lived where the [Michigan] Science Center and the Charles H. Wright Museum of African American History are now located. I lived in an apartment at 252 Farnsworth Street, the Burdell Apartments. A lot of the events of the riot were happening over on Warren Avenue, Trumbull, 12th Street, and so forth, so we were engaged in some of the activities that were going on during the riots in protecting the Black folks' property, and I had friends that were right there in the thick of the Clairmount/12th area, and we were over there assisting and helping.

The experience of the race riots, which I like to call the rebellions more so than race riots, was like this. When the activities of the rioting or rebellion were going on, it was Black and white helping together. Someone white who may have seen a TV first and a Black who wanted the TV at first, and he said, "Man I saw it first," they let him pass. So there was no racial animus to what was going on. It was a class struggle. It was an effort to stop the oppressive actions of the Detroit Police Department in our community: the history of

Detroit. Maybe ten or fifteen years in my life of that time period, I was aware of police officers shooting and killing Black women, calling them prostitutes, planting knives on them and saying they were, when they were actually giving favors to the police who were pimping them and doing other kinds of things as well. So it was a corrupt police department. It was the "Big 4," as we called them. The plainclothes white police officers were not much different in that era than some of the issues that are going on now, but it was just more blatant. Four white officers, with plainclothes, would ride into the Black neighborhood and have the youth—fifteen, sixteen, seventeen years old—called to the car and they would harass them and sometimes beat them. So it was something that was akin to any oppression that you would see in Third World countries in terms of police and community.

These types of experiences helped shape and guide my generation as it relates to Black people especially. We were very aware of the system and that it could not remain the same. It built up in us, those who experienced it or saw it. And when we got the skills, we had the firm belief that we should make change happen. That was our experience of that generation, and it was shared by many. Unfortunately, some of those who rebelled did not have the necessary approach so that they could stay alive and not land in prison. So many of the people of that era landed in prison and, of course, that was during the war in Vietnam, and many of them were drafted and put on the front lines in Vietnam, and that was also something that impacted people in terms of drugs.

After the rebellions, we noticed that hard drugs began to impact our community. There had been no major heroin operations in the African American community. Marijuana was there, but even then, a young person could not buy marijuana. Musicians and others may have had some. Society was such that young people could not buy from older people. You would get a real lecture: "Boy you don't need this, get the hell out of here," something to that effect. But as the riots and rebellion of 1967 occurred, there was what we called in street language a "panic" on marijuana. There was no marijuana around, but there was ample heroin. They brought it in, and more and more came. Then, of course, some of our young men got caught up in it, and some of them got caught up in the criminal justice system as an aspect of the drug scene. It was a situation that impacted organizations, whether they were social, radical, or militant. We had people who would snort what we call "scag," mixed heroin, and they were out there marching, and they were out there demonstrating. It was just a proliferation of drugs, and of course, as they had consciousness, they often got clean. We didn't tolerate it, but it did happen, and of course, we were able to ensure that people got the kind of help they needed.

When we were finishing law school, our vision forward was discussed many times. Often, we met at my house where my wife then, Nikki, would prepare us a meal. Jeff, Earl, and Chokwe were a year ahead of me, and of course, I had known Chokwe previously. I was introduced to Jeff, Earl, and James Cannon, and others like Gad Holland. We all talked about post–law school and if you had hesitancy about whether you were going to make it. There was no question you were going to make it because of the things the Black Legal Alliance put into place, by way of the tutorials and outlines, information on the approaches of different professors, going over the exams; but we were all studious folks, and because we knew the kind of codes, the language, the inclinations of different professors and being on top of the game, so to speak, we knew we would do well.

We knew that we would one day come out of law school being activists, militants, radicals—however you wished to name it. All of us had a conscientious mindset that we wanted to be "social engineers," a term coined by Professor Houston, the famed professor at Howard Law School who trained Thurgood Marshall. We knew we wanted to make changes in society. We had talked as we struggled in law school together about having a firm that would be a catalyst for change in our community, and that was our plan. I did not go to the Defender's

Office with Chokwe and Jeff; I went to work with Cornelius Pitts, Bob Mann, and Larry Patrick. So I got some good training in terms of the practice. I went to the Defender's Office after that and got some additional training.

Jeff and Chokwe would school me too because they were going around the country getting seminars and having the practical experiences of what they called the "baptism by fire." They had to do cases, some of which were very dynamic cases, that most lawyers would never have an opportunity to do in their first year. I felt that they had the experience and I had some experience, so I said now is the time, but as Brother Earl said, some were not as ready. I left Pitts, Mann, and Patrick and went over on the northwest side of Greenfield and waited for everybody else. We had the breakfast meetings. The time was right. They were ready, and I had to finish up my lease. I think I had a month left on Greenfield and I joined the firm. I paid my fourth—Earl made sure of that—and we all came together. The firm was then Ashford, Cannon, Lumumba, and Shakoor.

I think the firm was able to achieve some of the goals we set forward. One example was the reciprocal arrangement we made with David Rambeau who had a Black awareness TV program called *Project Bait*. Rambeau wanted us to represent *Project Bait*. The state bar had just approved advertisements by law firms. David and the firm had a sharing of "We help you, and you help us." We became the first legal firm, not Black but the first firm white or Black, to have TV advertising. We also did name changes, as African name changes were taking place throughout the community. It was a process of going through probate, which was a costly process, and it was one where sometimes people did not want to pay to assert their cultural right and heritage. We developed an affidavit after researching the law that allowed under Michigan law the right to change your name as long as it was not for fraud. Since we were a paper-oriented society, we developed an affidavit, notarized it, and so forth. Many of the members of various organizations, members of the Republic of New

Afrika, members of the Muslim community, and other organizations and people wanted their name changes done. We only required a $10.00 fee for the process for paying the typist and the notary fee, and that was that. They got passports and licenses and everything else. That was thirty-five years ago. Many who changed their names applaud the fact that they were able to do so. In this process, we were representing various segments of the community.

David Rambeau and Ed Mwalimu Vaughn

The firm grew and developed over the years: Ashford, Cannon & Lumumba; Ashford, Cannon, Lumumba & Shakoor (later, Ashford, Edison, Lumumba & Shakoor; Ashford, Davis, Edison, Lumumba & Shakoor; Davis, Edison, Jarrett, Lumumba, Ottison & Shakoor; we wanted to do it all alphabetically, the continuity of our idea). People knew they could come to our law firm at 11000 West McNichols and get assistance, no matter their issue. Even when other lawyers had messed up their case, they would come over and we would try to straighten them out. There were times when Brother Chokwe would straighten them out with no fee, if he knew them and they were of a strong consciousness in the community and, of course, we would work it out and there was no problem. That was just Chokwe: he was an activist dedicated to the community, he had a lot of friends, and of course, a lot of friends need help, especially when they are out in the community doing things. We knew that from the outset, so we all contributed. Sometimes the publicity Chokwe got, while it was not necessarily compensational, it was still beneficial to the growth of the firm. So we enjoyed that time. When you look at it, in terms of life's journey, you look back and see that those were some of the most productive and high points of our professional lives.

We were able to excel because of the way we thought our roles would be as lawyers. We knew we had to be good because we were working on behalf of our people. We knew we had to be better than others because it was talent, although devious talent, that kept us oppressed. We had to be certainly as smart as and smarter than those enemies of the people, so we came with a desire and motivation to make change. We weren't there to just be functionaries and keep something of a profession that is a good profession in terms of monetary substance.

In law school, we helped organize the National Conference of Black Lawyers. We weren't yet lawyers. We had some members who had graduated but joined to allow the National Conference of Lawyers to come into existence. Jeff and Chokwe were in their third year, and I was in my second year, but we knew that was the direction we were going in. We talked about the need to be at the top of our game, so to speak. As you take that to the level of what we did as lawyers, then I believe that the commitment we had, the skill set we developed, and the people who had serious issues of oppression influenced our direction.

Chokwe was certainly at the forefront of identifying and assisting in those fights, and we all had to develop those skills. I think that those efforts were attributes that allowed us to succeed on levels that none of us thought we would but just came as a result of the challenges we faced, the training we had, our mindset, and our purpose. It still is a part of us, even though law school was in the 1970s; we are still doing the tasks that need to be done and trying to train others. If you look at Chokwe with his family, his son Antar was his partner. When I last visited with Chokwe in September 2013, prior to his death, we had an opportunity to travel some three hours by car to Memphis to the classic football game. He wanted to go, so we went. While traveling back, we had a chance to talk a lot about his plans for Jackson, and what he wanted to do. I asked Chokwe if Antar was going to handle the law firm, since he was mayor, and if Antar was going to get involved in politics. He said, "I would like him to perhaps look at it one day." I also asked him, "Do you think he should be mayor someday?" and he said, "Absolutely." Antar is the vision of his father as mayor of Jackson, Mississippi.

Antar was his son and his partner, whom he very much loved and mentored. Of course, that was Antar's choice, but we all know—Gerald and Jeff and all the others know—that Chokwe had a vision, and he shared it with his son and his son was certainly a part of helping make his vision a possibility. Now Antar is carrying the torch as mayor of Jackson.

In reflecting on Chokwe's home going services in Jackson, I must say that I had the good fortune of being Mrs. Rosa Parks's attorney during her life. I also served as her trustee and handled some of her probate matters, along with her personal representative, Elaine Steele. So when Elaine, Judge Damon Keith, and I planned her home going services in Montgomery, Alabama, Washington, D.C., and Detroit, there was some criticism because of the many celebrations in different places, and Detroit's then mayor wanted it all here in Detroit. I said no, "She was a world-renowned civil rights leader." There was much love for her, so we had to go to her hometown. We had to go to Washington and come back here to her adopted home. Throughout the process, everywhere we went there were many people and just so many great words said in various places where she either laid in state or at the ceremony at her home church in Montgomery.

Memories of My Revolutionary Brother, Chokwe Lumumba

(Left to Right): Rukia Lumumba, Chokwe Antar Lumumba, Rosa Parks, Cynthia Steele, Chockwe Lumumba

Throngs of people were in the procession from Chokwe's home going ceremony to the cemetery. Hundreds of people along the way were screaming "Chokwe," "Mayor Lumumba," and so forth. It was phenomenal. The only funeral that I can think of, and I have been to many, that was comparable or close to Mrs. Parks's homegoing was Chokwe's. That was the legacy of love that Chokwe left, and the legacy was expressed by the people in so many different ways. They had embraced Chokwe. While Detroit can claim that Chokwe was born in the city, Jackson claims him as their leader and their mayor.

CHOKWE
(August 2, 1947 – February 25, 2014)

Chokwe,
hunters who trapped slave catchers
in the nets of trees
live in the law books of the gifted
not in what is said

but what is left unsaid
between the lyrics of Kalunga's freedom song
you,
seer of heaven's law
master of speech and nommo
snaking a circuitous path of mystery
before the gods gaping mouths of awe

how you break iron bars with combat breath?
how you make caged birds fly fearless
above the gun towers shooting blanks?
how you trap slave traders in trees
where you harbored your lion heart
earned your honorary spear of sacrifice
and saved the village

the River Congo flows clear as stars
purged of the blood of millions
purged of the minefields of decapitated hands and feet
bartered for rubber
drowning the senseless rape weapons of war
the river flows
and the lion steps forth onto the banks
wearing the Chikunga mask of royalty
poised with immanent power
you, King of the rainforest
no longer a jungle of pejoratives
your wise haired mane
holding the secrets of the Sphinx
holding the scepter of the lawgiver
in your black power fist
you, word spinner of honey and ice
judge of the hanging judge
daring the mud and water of the Mississippi

Memories of My Revolutionary Brother, Chokwe Lumumba

to mate, to procreate
to free the land of cash crop pestilence
to cultivate the lotus
cuz you knew the law of heaven
was the natural law of man
and you had a hand in bringing it home
when it wasn't no home
in the injustice system
trapped in the nets of trees
the sellers of flesh
freeze in fright
at the lion's gaze
fatal as a philosopher stone's transmutation
of evil to good
of ignorance to enlightenment
beaming through courtroom windows
giving divinity to law
like the alchemist of Chikunga
a red river runs blue
lead is gold
and gold is led away to rest
undisturbed under the cocopalm
the village is saved,
Chokwe,
the village is saved

you have earned your spear of sacrifice
you have earned your place
among the mighty Malcolm, Martin and Marcus
among the procession of holy heroes
in the ever affirming stars.

– Nubia Kai

(Flyer courtesy of Kwasi Akwamu)

CHAPTER 4
Chokwe and the Republic of New Afrika

"Change does not come on thoughts alone, because we have a revolutionary ideology and give speeches on it. It comes because you can change the material conditions of people and get people to assist in the change; be the mainstay in the change in their conditions."
– Chokwe Lumumba

Chokwe Lumumba speaking

As Chokwe transitioned from high school to college, his focus, too, shifted, from sports to academics and politics. The heinous murder of Emmett Till and other traumatic occurrences inflicted upon Black lives impacted his desire to become more actively involved in the struggle. Chokwe began his revolutionary evolution in the aftermath of MLK's assassination, the formation of the RNA, and the New Bethel Shooting in Detroit at the RNA anniversary commemoration in 1969. Chokwe attended a Republic of New

Afrika (RNA) meeting in Detroit where he heard one of the most riveting speeches of his life. It had been our brother Reggie's idea to go to the meeting after talking to his friend Chaka Fuller who was a member of the RNA. One of the RNA's founders, Anwar Pasha, who was called "Papa Wells," spoke to an audience that included Chokwe and Reggie. Papa Wells was an elder who had a long history in the movement for Black people's rights. He was one of the first ministers of the Nation of Islam and one of the first members of the Fruit of Islam. He was also one of the first one hundred taught by Farad Muhammad, whom followers believed was God in person.

Reggie was so impressed by Papa Wells's speech that he joined the RNA that day. Chokwe joined subsequently after several conversations with Papa Wells. Although Imari Obadele, president of the RNA, served as Chokwe's mentor and perhaps the most instrumental person in his political development, it was Papa Wells who convinced him to join the nationalist movement. In addition, while working in Kalamazoo helping students gain employment, Chokwe saw firsthand the disdain whites exhibited toward Blacks, the disrespect, demeaning remarks, and dehumanizing treatment Blacks received. This further propelled him to become more involved in the struggle for Black people's rights.

Anwar Pasha

In the late 1960s through the early 1970s, the United States was experiencing a revolution. Many young warriors like Chokwe Lumumba joined the struggle and armed themselves with the knowledge of their fallen leaders and the guidance of their mentors to prepare for battle. The country was in turmoil and chaos from Los Angeles to New York and they were right in the middle in Detroit. Black men and women were dying in San Quentin, Chicago, Detroit,

Watts, and all over the United States. The Black Panther Party had already formed when Chokwe joined the RNA. Chokwe admitted he began the process of joining the Black Panthers; he was impressed with their self-esteem and dedication. He certainly admired them, but the Republic of New Afrika appeared to be more politically mature. In addition, Chokwe agreed with the RNA's ideology on independence. He believed Black people in the United States needed an independent nation. In July 1969, Chokwe became a conscious citizen of the New Afrikan nation in North America and a legionnaire in the Black Legion of the Republic of New Afrika. He served over the years as minister of information, acting president, and vice president of the Republic of New Afrika.

Join the RNA are you crazy?

(Front row, left) Mabel Williams, Robert Williams, Gaidi Obadele (Milton Henry), (second row) Queen Mother Audley Moore, Imari Obadele, (Richard Henry), Chaka (Sonny) Fuller, (last row) Michael Balogun (others unnamed), (Photo courtesy of Walter P. Reuther Library)

Chockwe and the Republic of New Afrika

I was an eighth grade student at Winship Middle School, predominantly white at the time but experiencing a rapid exodus of whites subsequent to Blacks being bussed in through decentralization laws. This learning institution provided me more than academic learning; this is where I acquired some interesting and profound life learning lessons from my peers. This is where I inhaled my first cigarette in the girl's bathroom. It was with a group of white girls that I was offered and accepted a Winston cigarette and smoked it while listening to them tell sexual jokes. So many of our Black parents were fighting to have their children go to school with whites so we could obtain an equal and quality education, but look at what I was learning from the white students! If I knew then what I know now, I would have run far away from that group of white girls with their nicotine-addicting cigarettes and offensive sexual jokes. Although I was outnumbered by whites in my eighth grade class, there were more Blacks in the ninth grade, and they seemed to stick together. Apparently, there were a couple of them who were talking about Black power, and there was one girl in my grade, Yosetta, who wore an afro, and she seemed to be friends with them. However, they were outnumbered by the popular, hipper Black ninth graders. The older group appeared to be recruiting me, since one of the members was my neighbor Pam who lived at the corner of my street. Anyway, one day the Black power kids and Yosetta were talking about this organization that was something like the Black Panthers, and they wanted all the Black people to go and live in five states in this country.

Pam and her crew had a big laugh at that, including me, although that did not deter Yosetta. She continued to talk to me about the organization and even brought in a newspaper article and showed it to me. But I didn't get it. Not long after this incident, my brother Chokwe came home from college. He and our oldest brother, Reggie, began to attend meetings together. Chokwe would eventually bring our sister Itari and me to the meetings. One day, when my parents were out of town, my brothers had a meeting at our house. Our sister Itari and I were peering into the living room from the hallway corridor.

In that living room was quite an ensemble of people. Some were dressed in African clothing, some were dressed in black blue-jean attire with leopard trim and brogan shoes, some had afros, others had gale head wraps, and some were even dressed in business attire. What an eclectic group! Later I learned that this intriguing but scary group of people consisted of founding members, president, and soon to be presidents of the Republic of New Afrika: Robert Williams, Queen Mother Audley Moore, Papa (Henry) Wells, Milton Henry (Gaidi Obadele), Richard Henry (Imari Obadele), Rafael Vierra, Chaka Fuller, and others.

Chaka was the only one I knew at the time, other than my brothers. He was our brother, Reggie's childhood friend from Spokane Street. I knew him as Sonny, "Clarence Fuller." There were others whose names I cannot recall, but those who I mentioned played very significant roles in the RNA and I'm sure were on COINTELPRO's list.[20] I remember Itari telling me those were RNA members, the ones who wanted the five states. I could not believe it. The group that Yosetta and her friends were talking about was in our house! The group they were writing

Chaka Fuller

---

[20]COINTELPRO (a syllabic abbreviation derived from Counter Intelligence Program) was a series of covert and illegal projects conducted between 1956 and 1971 by the United States Federal Bureau of Investigation (FBI) aimed at surveilling, infiltrating, discrediting, and disrupting American political organizations that the FBI perceived as subversive. https://en.wikipedia.org/eiki/COINTELPRO.

about in the paper was in our house. The organization meetings our big brothers were attending was the organization Yosetta told me about. I turned to our sister, Itari and I said "Oooh, they [Reggie (Arki) and Edwin (Chokwe)] are going to get it when Mama and Daddy come back." Although, I knew that was something I would not dare tell our parents about for fear our father would "kill them" for having a group of militants in his house. Years later, Chokwe filed a FOIA (Freedom of Information Act) request to obtain his records from the police, and they had that meeting under surveillance. They also unjustly included our father as an attendee at that meeting and established a file on him.

Itari, who was 14 at this time, and I, only 13, later discussed what we had seen and what we understood about the RNA. I told her, "they must be crazy to want to live in five states." I think my reaction was the typical reaction of most Black people at the time. Itari, however, did not make that judgment. She seemed to always be more politically astute than me. Our brothers Arki and Chokwe took us to the meetings initially, but it was Chokwe who made sure we attended the nation-building classes and most of the activities offered by the RNA. It was in those classes that I began to understand the importance of the Provisional Government of the Republic of New Afrika and their work.

RNA Leadership

Over the years, the RNA had several headquarters in Detroit, Michigan. We initially met at the Black Conscious Library, Shrine of the Black Madonna, and at different people's homes, like Imari Obadele's home on Muirland and Stu and Aneb House's home on Glendale and Ewald Circle. We met at an office building on Cadillac, one block south of Warren, on the east side for a while. This building was raided by the police who took files and set the building on fire. The RNA then purchased a house, known as the UHURU (Uhuru is the Swahili word meaning "independence" or "freedom") House, located on French Road on the east side of Detroit. It was there where I received my name "Shushanna" at an African Naming Ceremony officiated by Brother Imari.

Queen Mother Moore (seated) and Nkechi Taifa (standing) (Photo courtesy of Nkechi Taifa)

In the nation-building classes, Brother Imari would often emphasize the importance of our African origin and culture. He and other leaders, including Queen mother Moore and Chokwe, taught us that our names given to us at birth are "slave names." If our ancestors had not been stolen from their native countries in Africa, we would have African names. The European slave owners stole our people, culture, religion, and eventually the precious gems off the continent and then began to occupy our land. Our RNA teachers strongly recommended that we choose an African name to feel free in our identity. In our Taliaferro family, my oldest brothers Reggie and Edwin chose the names for the family. They chose different surnames simultaneously.

Chockwe and the Republic of New Afrika

Chokwe was at Kalamazoo College when he chose the name *Chokwe*. The Chokwe are a Bantu-speaking ethnic group primarily found in Angola, the Democratic Republic of the Congo (DRC), and Zambia, Lumumba (from Revolutionary Patrice Lumumba; Congolese origin: gifted). Reggie was in Detroit attending RNA meetings with his friend Chaka Fuller when he selected the names *Arki* (Nigerian origin: warrior of the dark) and *Shakur* (Arabic origin: thankful and grateful). However, Arki was initially informed that the name *Shakur* was of Swahili origin with the meaning: one who directs the way. At some point when my two brothers Reggie and Edwin came together in 1969, they were reunited as Arki Shakur and Chokwe Lumumba.

It was great that the two eldest Taliaferro siblings had chosen free names, but it left the younger siblings in a bit of a conundrum. The next two siblings, Gregory and Denise, under Arki and Chokwe did not have a dilemma with the names because neither of them were involved in the Republic of New Afrika that inspired the name change. Itari and myself were next in line and were participating, conscious citizens of the RNA. We were in Detroit with Arki and received our names at an Afrikan naming ceremony officiated by Brother Imari Obadele.

Our sister Mildred was given the first name *Itari*. *Itari* is a female name that is of Aztec origin and means "beautiful," "smart," and "God's gift." The name *Itari* in Nigerian languages, particularly Yoruba, is a name that can mean "heart" or "beloved," reflecting a strong emotional connection. I was given the name *Shushanna* (also spelled *Shoshanna*), meaning "lily," "rose," "pure," and "innocent" (Hebrew origin with derivatives of the name, Shona a Bantu ethnic group native to Southern Africa, and Shawnee a Native American people of the Northeastern Woodlands). We both received our eldest brother Arki's chosen last name of *Shakur*.

Chokwe brought our two youngest brothers Robert and Mario into the RNA. When they were bestowed their names, they received the surname of *Lumumba*. It is my understanding that Chokwe named Robert *Jasiri*, of Swahili origin, meaning "bold" or "courageous." He named Mario *Gomvi*. The name is of Swahili origin and means "inquisitive" and "protector."

Another RNA Headquarters was the UKUUNKI House, which was really an office building located on Pinehurst and Seven Mile Road in northwest Detroit. Chokwe named the office from the seven principles of the Nguzo Saba. Although I appreciate the honor behind the name, I laughed a little with others over the pronunciation of the name. However, this was one of my favorite offices. It was close to Mumford High where Itari and I attended school, and it is where I began typing and doing clerical work for Chokwe and Brother Imari.

Brother Shipp, a muscular brother with a no-nonsense attitude, either owned the building or leased it for the PG-RNA. This is the RNA building where the police busted in, trashed the place, and arrested my younger twelve-year-old brother Jasiri and his twelve-year-old friend Sundiata Keita, all under the pretense of looking for President Imari's son who was not even there. They also arrested Chokwe and Anasa, his wife at the time. Allegedly, Imari II was involved in some crime. I believe that situation was even more frightening for Anasa. She was raised in a very conservative Black home. I believe, at the time, she was attending Wayne State University studying neural psychology. All of the movement stuff was very surreal for her.

These "suspected criminals" the police arrested that day later came to be known as Chokwe Lumumba, mayor of Jackson Mississippi; Anasa Lumumba, neural psychologist; Jasiri Lumumba, state chess champion and Detroit Public School chess coach who mentored and instructed two chess masters; and Sundiata Keita, world-renowned musician and culturalist who played with the likes of Stevie Wonder, Carlos Santana, and Alexander Zonjic. Sundiata also founded the Omowale Cultural Society, one of the first African dance and drum groups in Detroit, which taught thousands of Detroiters the art.

The RNA also met at the Paul Robeson Center located at 1130 E. Canfield and a bar on the east side belonging to a Brother Mack in the PG-RNA. Brother Mack was a bald-headed brother with a joyful disposition. Also, early on there were a few meetings at the 20 Grand (one of Detroit's most famous nightclubs). The last location where I remember RNA events occurring was at the Malcolm X Center located at Dexter and Davidson on the west side of Detroit. However, the Malcolm X Center was used mostly by Malcolm X Grassroots Movement (MXGM), the organization that Chokwe cofounded with Watani Tyehimba and Akinyele Umoja out of Los Angeles, along with other members of the RNA and the Revolutionary Action Movement (RAM). The Detroit brothers along with LA brothers cofounded MXGM and New Afrikan People's Organization (NAPO). I believe at that time Chokwe had separated from the PG-RNA but not the RNA. There had been two splits in the PG-RNA that I can recall. The first one occurred because of conflict between the Henry brothers. Milton Henry (known as Gaidi Obadele) and Richard Henry (known as Imari Obadele) were the leadership of the RNA at the time, and they had disputes over the direction that the RNA should take. Robert Williams, the first president of the PG-RNA, had returned from exile abroad, but he resigned from his position. I was not clear on what the brothers' differences were about then. All I know is that Gaidi and Imari disagreed on the direction of the RNA, and it split. Aneb told me many years later that Gaidi was concerned about the prematurity of some of the actions Imari wanted to take, like going to the land.

Chokwe followed Imari, and of course we followed Chokwe. By this time, my eldest brother, Reggie (Arki), who had also brought our siblings and me into the RNA, had left the RNA. I didn't know why at the time, but Reggie shared with me many years later that he left the RNA because he felt controlled. Reggie at one time led security for the Black Legionnaires, RNA's security forces. He explained to me there was an order given to him by Imari that he did not understand, and when he questioned Imari about it, Imari refused to discuss it with him, but he told him he didn't need to understand it and to just follow the order. This was a deal breaker for Reggie. He left the RNA.

Aneb, who served as minister of education at one time, shared with me many years later that she too left the RNA due to philosophical differences with some of the members. She believed some of the brothers did not treat the sisters equally. Aneb once told me that she disagreed with Chokwe on strategy and the direction of the RNA. "As a participant of SNCC and a Freedom Rider who fought for our rights in the South, I believed that the RNA should not concentrate on procuring land and moving south at that time. The time was not right to make that move and deal with the extreme racism there. My experiences in the South influenced my position." Chokwe and others, however, moved in that direction. Several years later when Chokwe and the others formed NAPO and MXGM, she could then see that Chokwe had come to concede her point of view.

As a teenager at the time of the split, I was not clear on what issues were involved regarding the conflict with Imari and Gaidi. I do know that the split was emotional for those involved. Of course, with brothers splitting, it would have to be. Also, Papa Wells, one of the cofounders, an elder and mentor of Chokwe and the one individual who persuaded Chokwe to join the RNA, initially went with Gaidi. The split did not last very long because Gaidi eventually stepped aside and left the RNA. He was one of the top criminal attorneys in Detroit at the time and retained that position until his retirement from law. He was the first vice president of the RNA. His friends consisted of great powerful warrior activists like Malcolm X and Kwame Nkrumah (Ghanaian president). Gaidi also became a minister of Woodward Avenue Presbyterian Church of the Covenant in Detroit some years after his exit from the RNA. He then became associate pastor at St. John Presbyterian Church on Lafayette Street in Detroit. Years later, he founded the Christ Presbyterian Church in Southfield, Michigan, where his home going services were held.

Gaidi Obadele/Milton Henry

Milton was one of several brothers of the remarkable Henry family of Philadelphia, Pennsylvania. All of the brothers worked hard and earned advanced degrees: Milton, a law degree; Imari, a PhD. I would really like to have known their parents; they instilled in their sons some excellent values. Milton's biography is long and extraordinary. He was a freedom fighter from way back. He was a Tuskegee Airman. Milton was one of the few people responsible for bringing Malcolm X to Detroit to deliver his famous speeches "Message to the Grassroots" and "The Ballot or the Bullet." He was a pallbearer at the 1965 funeral of Malcolm X. Milton was also the first vice president of the Republic of New Afrika, which sought $300 billion in reparations from the federal government for the nation's history of slavery.

One of my favorite quotes from Milton is, "Now when I said America has suffered because of the slave trade, I am saying matter of fact, America has suffered. It is a horrible monstrous place. It is a monster in the world because of the slave trade. The slave trade introduced this whole lack of regard for humanity and to the world. It characterizes the world today."[21]

My memories of Milton are all beautiful. He was one of my brother Chokwe's legal mentors. There were numerous times I heard him on the telephone with Milton discussing one of his cases. He never spoke any ill words of him, and when I discussed my desire to go to law school and my reservations about doing so, Chokwe calmed my fears by telling me there would be people there to guide me during law school and my law career. Milton's name came up in

---

[21]*Firing Line with William F. Buckley Jr.*: The Republic of New Africa. Episode 126, Recorded on November 18, 1968 (YouTube video 23:14/52:22).

that conversation as someone who guided him through law school and the practice of law.

I, too, admired Milton. He was also in the courtroom on an unrelated matter when my son Jeaco was on trial for a CCW (carrying a concealed weapon) violation in front of the hanging judge, Judge Warfield Moore. Judge Moore had a reputation for insensitivity toward young Black men and low tolerance for their alleged criminal actions. Jeaco had been sentenced under the Home Youthful Training Act (HYTA) on his CCW charge and ordered into a Boot Camp Program. While there, the boot camp officers physically and mentally abused Jeaco. According to Jeaco, they referred to him as a "murderer," referencing an accidental killing of his cousin, my brother Arki's son, Seku, in which he was charged and charges were dropped. Of course this would cause mental anguish for him. Then, Jeaco described the brutality he received once, in which an officer put his foot on his back because he repeatedly asked to go to the restroom and was not permitted to do so. He urinated all over himself.

Jeaco's opportunity to escape this abusive situation presented itself one day. Actually, it just happened to be the same day our pastor, Father Norman Thomas of Sacred Heart, had come to visit Jeaco. Father was always there for our family. Unbeknown to Father, while he was at the front desk of the facility of the boot camp registering for a visit, Jeaco was escaping through the back door, where his girlfriend was waiting in the alley in a getaway car. I'm telling you, I could not make this stuff up. It was surreal. At some subsequent point, he was picked up by the police and jailed while awaiting a hearing in front of Judge Moore, who had sent him to the boot camp. Chokwe was away on one of his cases, either in Illinois or New York. So, my friend, Chokwe's former paralegal and legal investigator who had completed law school by this time, Georgia Manzie, represented Jeaco. My daughters and I were all sitting in the courtroom waiting with clenched fists and exploding heartbeats when my child walked into the courtroom. At first, I did not recognize him. His head was bald, mustache shaved, and he had a look of pain on his face.

I recall while sitting there in anguish, praying and thinking, thinking about Judge Moore's son, with whom I had attended law school. He was a strange sort of guy but nice to me. I thought this hanging judge could hardly understand what Jeaco had been through because his kid was so square and trouble free. I recall he hadn't made it through law school at the time, just like me, and I wondered how the judge felt about that. Milton happened to be there on an unrelated matter, but he sat with us and calmed my fears. He mentioned a few things to Georgia Manzie, and I believe he intentionally let Judge Moore know he was supporting Jeaco. The court police officer was also rallying for Jeaco. We heard her tell the judge, "You don't want to give this baby a number" [meaning a prisoner inmate number]. Milton told me, "Don't worry, everything is going to be okay." Milton was right. When the judge made his ruling, he admonished Jeaco and said, "Don't come back into my courtroom. I don't want your family outside my windows with picket signs shouting. I know who your family is and that's all the more reason why you shouldn't be in my courtroom."

Another memory I have of Milton is when he was there for Chokwe when Chokwe needed his support in the media. Chokwe had been suspended from practicing law in Mississippi, and his team was organizing a national campaign for people to speak out against his suspension. In Detroit, we planned a press conference where he would notify the public of his plight. We allowed the wrong individual to spearhead the press conference (writing the release and notifying the public). She asked us to follow her lead, and I supported that initially. General Laney, an activist and a licensed gun dealer and trainer, was also working with us at the time. He argued against the "publicist's" rationalization for not wanting any of the group to spread the information on the press conference a week prior to the conference. I asked him to respect her call. He did not and mentioned it on the Mildred Gaddis Show, a local talk show. This is how Milton learned of the press conference. The so-called publicist did not notify the news until the day prior and most responded that they did not have adequate notice to send a reporter or team out. Without much notice, Milton showed up for Chokwe.

Imari Obadele/Richard Henry

Chokwe and Brother Imari Obadele

Imari Obadele, born Richard Henry in Philadelphia, was a freedom fighter, Black Power activist, reparations advocate, and college professor. He was one of the founders of the Republic of New Afrika (RNA), later serving as president of the RNA. It was Brother Imari who coined the phrase "Free the Land." Imari was Chokwe's mentor, political guide, and teacher. His many accomplishments included several books, among them *War in America: The Malcolm X Doctrine* and a book he coauthored with Chokwe, Ahmed Obafemi, and Nkechi Taifa, *A Brief History of Black Struggle in America: With Obadele's Macro-Level Theory of Human Organization*. To understand who Chokwe was, we need to understand who Imari Obadele was and where he came from.

Chockwe and the Republic of New Afrika

I remember Brother Imari as a brilliant, talented, and wise man. Where he was like a political father figure to Chokwe, he was a role model and hero to me. There were many memorable experiences Chokwe and Imari shared, but unfortunately, there were some that I believe both of them wished had not occurred. The second separation in the RNA was between Chokwe and Imari. It was not a split like Gaidi and Imari's, in which members went into two different directions, but it was conflict with leadership that impeded the organization. My sister Itari and I recall that it was incited by a few members who were sending Imari disturbing and untruthful information about Chokwe while Imari was incarcerated, subsequent to the RNA-11 event. These untruths were predicated on the premise that Chokwe, who was serving as interim vice president in the PG-RNA, was attempting to undermine Imari, who was president of the PG-RNA. While Brother Imari was in prison serving time for crimes he did not commit, these brothers took the opportunity to create divisiveness and confusion between Imari and Chokwe. These were all lies that were told to Imari. We could not understand why these brothers would do such a thing. We knew them. They had been among us for many years. Could it possibly be COINTELPRO? After all, that is their modus operandi: infiltrate a group of revolutionaries and cause division among them. That of course was one of the causes of the denigration of the Black Panther Party. Although Brother Imari and Chokwe mended their relationship from the harmful lies that were told during Imari's incarceration period, Chokwe went into the direction of NAPO and MXGM as opposed to PG-RNA. It is truly sad how some of our own people sabotage and harm each other over jealousy, greed, and/or personal aspirations; Chokwe loved Imari like a father. Imari loved Chokwe like his son. Imari sacrificed so much for the RNA, including his own freedom, but Chokwe sacrificed as well. He had to repeat his entire first year of law school because he chose to go to Jackson, Mississippi in 1970. He stayed to assist the attorneys who were fighting for Imari's and the RNA-11's freedom.

His livelihood and freedom were threatened on a regular basis by judges, courts, and the bar. His personal life and family were also threatened by racist nut cases.

Kwame Kalimara and Ahmed Obafemi recall that the conflict between Chokwe and Imari was not just with the two of them but also with several others. While Imari was incarcerated, the Code of Umoja of the RNA prevented him from presiding as president and leading the PG-RNA. Several members, including Chokwe, wanted to elect a president. Imari was opposed to this action. They did in fact hold an election and Sister Dara Abubakari was elected. She held the position until shortly after Imari's return. Imari wanted to resume his office, and Kwame recalls Sister Dara said, "If Imari wants the position that badly, he can have it." Imari then resumed his office.

Chokwe revealed the origin and resolutions for the splits in the Republic of New Afrika in an interview conducted by Owen Brooks of the MS Civil Rights Veteran on February 15, 2005:

> Milton and Imari had differences on where to gather support for the organization. Milton tended to want to organize around the Northern cities where Imari wanted to move it to Mississippi and the south.... For the most part, I think the rank and file around the country kinda supported Imari's position. But the people who, I guess you would say the periphery or the folks who—and a lot of people in Detroit—because they wanted to keep it in Detroit, supported Milton's position. Milton was kind of the popular figure... whereas Imari had kind of been behind the scenes in a lot of things....
>
> Interesting enough, because I was a law student, they had just created a RNA Supreme Court, and they put me on it, and they also put Kenny Cockrel on it, and then they did something which was very unrealistic, but in the spirit of the movement, they put a political prisoner

on it who was still in jail; his name was Martin Sostre... Of course when it came down to a hearing on this big issue, Martin Sostre was not available as you would think. Kenny Cockrel decided he was not going to serve because he felt it was too much of a political-internal issue of the RNA...so that left me as the sole judge, the young brother who was really in awe of both of them[,] Imari and Milton.

So, I did my best to weave out a decision... but the decision came down—it really didn't have to do with whether we would leave or stay.... The real issue is what I just told you. The way they surfaced the fight was around the elections, who would be elected and the way the elections would occur. Milton wanted to have elections where everyone that would come to the convention would vote, and that would mean that Detroit would pretty much decide the election, because that is where the convention was going to be. Imari wanted the election where there would be representation, and the representatives would vote from around the country for the various different units, as well as the representatives in Detroit, which would mean that the rank and file would make the decision.... I fashioned out a decision which said that if over 40 percent of what we called the conscious citizens would show up, then it could be an at-large convention, and everybody could vote.... If it was less than that, I thought it would be underrepresented and, therefore, we should vote by representatives at that point. So every area should elect a representative and try to send as many as they can....

So Milton didn't like that; so he decided no that's not going to be it.... I think, to be honest with you Milton was ending a period of his political advocacy and kind of going through some changes.... To some extent, for Milton I think this was a way out. And I don't want to try to be a psychologist, but I think to some extent it was. [...]

Prior to that time, the Provisional Government or the Republic of New Afrika was largely a loose coalition that believed in...broad objectives. We had cultural nationalists like Baraka and Karenga... H. Rap Brown, who later became Jamil Amin and any number of people. And Malcolm X's wife, Betty Shabazz. And so you can look at the initial founders of the RNA and it sounds like a long list of very astute leaders of our movement.... But because of the unpleasantries around the struggle—and by the way, we found out later the government was playing their part in it too. We can't hold them responsible, but they did their best to make it as embittered as possible. But in any event, a lot of people kind of fell away in terms of active support.... So that is what everyone calls a split and what we call the Constitutional Crisis number one.

Later on, you had another kind of a constitutional crisis.... It was a split for a little while. And that was more or less between those of us in the young leadership on the outside of the prison and Imari who was inside the prison. That occurred around the late '70s when Brother Imari had gone back to jail. And it was our view that we should be a little bit more party-like rather than government-like.... Imari always was into National Black Elections, where everyone who was Black could come in and vote for government officials. We thought that people were not ready for that and what we needed to be doing was getting involved with students and getting involved with the concrete problems people had, whether it was talking to people who were trying to do the land development thing, whether it was people who were against brutality, whatever...issue oriented and use this to help people as well as to share our views with people and to become more involved. [...]We wanted to build little people's courts where people could resolve disputes, where they could name themselves for those who wanted to change to African names, get married, and all of these kinds of things. And this would begin to build the legitimacy [of the Provisional Government] without having to pretend to have the political support of everybody behind us... But Imari's view was different. He felt we were disregarding international law and a lot of other things which he felt was important. So there was a split around that, but the People's Center Council voted...to go in the direction we had suggested, to cancel the Black elections that year, to have elections in convention, and to start to do some of this other kind of work. Imari and a few people who actually voted to do that, and some people who were not involved with us at the time who he pulled in to help him started this parallel government still called the Republic of New Afrika. So that happened in 1978, I'm almost sure. And we the RNA Supreme Court was supposed to meet around that, and it did; but the RNA Supreme Court never really resolved the issue—kept putting it off, until we ultimately resolved it ourselves. [...]

By this time the anniversary of the founding of the Republic of New Afrika began to be called Black Nation Day. Now they call it New Afrikan Nation Day... We had a big Black Nation Day Conference in March of 1983 in Detroit. Maybe five thousand people attended. Farrakhan spoke. Robert Williams came back, all the old timers came and spoke. Queen Mother Moore, Papa Wells, everybody was there. And it was at Wayne State University mainly... and Hartford Avenue Baptist Church.... Sister Dara Abubakari... was the president of what we recognized as the RNA. And Imari was the president of the parallel body of the RNA. So the Black Nation Day was designed to bring everyone together, and I was one of the architects of the event, and literally it did, because they decided to serve as co-presidents for a period of time until another election was held in '84. And the way those of us who had differences in the style and profile of the Provisional Government of the Republic of New Afrika resolved it, we decided to bring the body together because being separate was not productive. And then what we were going to do was form another organization once it was brought together that would do the kind of work we felt needed to be done without necessarily taking away from the provisional government. [...] And to the extent that Imari could find an agreement without taking away from the structure of the provisional government style of work, let it be. Our thing was that's not a major issue. . , and we could do the work we needed to do in another formation and still to be conscious citizens of the Republic of New Afrika to the extent that we needed to.

We brought the two presidents to a coalition, and we started another organization that you may call a party that would participate in the movement and would participate in the work that we thought was really important...and that was called the New Afrikan People's Organization. And really, a lot of people in the New Afrikan People's Organization had never been a part of the Republic of New Afrika. It is not correct to say we split away from the Republic of New Afrika. First of all we never left the RNA and secondly, probably more than half the people who became part of the New Afrikan People's Organization had never been a part of the Provisional Government of the Republic of New Afrika. They were new people, largely from the West Coast and some from New York and so forth, and us from Detroit. So we were able to live happily with the Provisional Government so to speak.

Kwame Kalimara, Ahmed, and I all recall that Chokwe and Imari remained very close friends and comrades to the day Imari departed this planet on January 18, 2010.

Brother Imari and Chokwe were my main teachers in the RNA. Most of the history, economics, and civics I remember came from these two great teachers. When I was in my high school economics class, I remember debating with the teacher, Mr. Burckhardt, over the different styles of government and economic systems: socialism, communism, and capitalism. I felt a need to let Mr. Burckhardt know that capitalism was not so good and socialism was not so bad. My fellow students loved it when Mr. Burckhardt and I engaged in debate. Hopefully, some of them learned from it, but I think it was because they found it occupied the entire class period, and they got out of doing work.

While working with the RNA, Chokwe became acquainted with both Milton (Gaidi) Henry and Richard (Imari) Henry. Milton Henry, who was an attorney, demonstrated to Chokwe that he could participate in the political movement as well as the Black Liberation movement. He could represent people in political cases, particularly Black people who needed help. Attorney Ray Willis further exemplified this concept subsequent to Chokwe leaving law school in 1970, after his first year, to work with the RNA in Jackson, Mississippi. Two other attorneys who impressed Chokwe and indirectly contributed to his JD degree are the late Kenneth Cockrel and Tony Axam of Atlanta.

U.S. Government Treachery

"It is not a question of whether or not you want to be in war. You don't even have a choice in the matter. You were in war from when they took the first African off the African continent."
– Chokwe Lumumba

During my involvement with the Provisional Government of the Republic of New Afrika, I quickly learned that the U.S. government exercised ongoing efforts to destroy the organization. People all over the country understood, and understand now, that the U.S. government unjustly targeted organizations like the NAACP and the Black Panther Party along with leaders of these organizations: Dr. Martin Luther King Jr., Medgar Evers, Huey Newton, Fred Hampton, and others. But many do not know what the government did to members of the RNA and the PG-RNA. The FBI and local police agencies in Detroit and Jackson, Mississippi, engaged in COINTELPRO operations against the RNA.

Once, I had the opportunity to observe my name on sign-in sheets for the RNA meetings, from when I was only thirteen years old. The green files through the Freedom of Information Act (FOIA) disclosed that governmental agencies like Detroit Police Department and some of their subsidiaries would send informants into our meetings to spy. Those records, as Chokwe and Kwame Kenyatta explained to me, revealed that at times they would have as many as two or three informants at a single meeting or event, and the informants would not even know each other. The following interviews with Ahmed Obafemi and Bilal Sunni Ali provide insight into the government's infiltration tactics and deceptive and malicious attacks on the RNA. In addition, information on the New Bethel Incident and the RNA-11 shared in this book further demonstrates the treachery of the U.S government and their infiltration tactics into the RNA.

New Bethel Incident

Among many other occurrences, an event in Detroit referred to as the Incident in Detroit demonstrated to Chokwe how urgent the need was for him and like-minded people to dedicate themselves to the struggle for Black people's rights. On March 29, 1969, the RNA was holding a convention in the New Bethel Baptist Church, of which Reverend C.L. Franklin (Aretha Franklin's father) was pastor. In a shootout between Detroit police officers and members of the RNA, an officer was killed, several people were wounded, and 142 people inside the church were arrested.

The meeting had been convened by Gaidi (Milton Henry) and Imari Obadele (Richard Henry), who were vice presidents of the RNA at the time. The purpose of the meeting was to celebrate, discuss, and commemorate the organizing of the Republic of New Afrika, an organization that advocated independence and self-governance from the United States. Imari taught the members of the RNA that they had all the elements of a nation: common culture, common language, and common people. The RNA was a nation with a provisional government—provisional because it would be modified when it acquired control of the five states that would give them sovereignty.

On the day of the convention in 1969, approximately four hundred people (men, women, and children) gathered in the church. There was a shootout between the police and the Black Legionnaires (RNA security); one police officer, Michael Czapski, was killed, and another, Richard Worobec, was wounded.[22]

New Bethel Eyewitness

One of the events that led both of our brothers, Reggie and Chokwe, to the Republic of New Afrika was the New Bethel Incident in Detroit. This event involved a shootout between the police and the RNA Black Legionnaires. Of course, the police and media accounts of this incident blamed the RNA for the occurrence of the tragic event, but members of the community who were present when the incident occurred shared their recollections of what occurred, which blamed the police for assault on the RNA and community members who were present the day of the incident.

"What is meant to be is meant to be." I could not believe what I was hearing. My friend was giving me an eyewitness account of the New Bethel Incident, and right when I was working on a book about my brother. She tried to tell me—well, she told me bits and pieces of

---

[22] Michael Czapski attended St. Theresa Catholic School with Chokwe. Richard Worobec was also involved in STRESS.

this story years before, not long after we met, when we talked about things we had in common. But, this day, I don't know if it was because I was more alert, or if she made it plainer, or if I was more attentive to the subject matter because I had just talked to another writer the night before about Christian Davenport's book on the New Bethel Case.[23] Oh my God, what was she talking about? For sure, she gave her account as if she was reliving it all over again. I had heard about the New Bethel Church shootings ever since I was in the eighth grade. Also, during my active participation in the PG-RNA, I heard it mentioned many times. My classmate, Yosetta, first mentioned New Bethel when she announced she wanted to join the RNA, and she was educating our classmates on the RNA. She actually was reading an article to us from the newspaper during our lunch hour.

Then, I remember learning about the New Bethel Incident several months later after Chokwe had enlisted my sister, Itari, and me into the RNA cadre. It was there that I learned about the New Bethel connection with Chaka Fuller and Rafael Viera. Chaka Fuller, fondly called Sonny, was my oldest brother Arki's childhood best friend. Rafael Viera was a member of the Young Lords in Harlem, New York. Although the Young Lords originated from a Puerto Rican street gang, it evolved into an organization inspired by the Black Panther Party to assist members of the community with resources in education, health care, employment, and housing. Both of these brothers were legionnaires (RNA military) at the time of the New Bethel Incident. As I understood it, they were on trial for a shooting at the New Bethel Church. Actually, during that time period of the trial, I remember going to a couple of events with my older brothers and Chaka was there. It was a time of celebration when Chaka and Rafael were found not guilty of the shootings at New Bethel. However, the celebration was short-lived. Rafael returned to New

---

[23] Christian Davenport, *How Social Movements Die: Repression and Demobilization of the Republic of New Africa* (New York: Cambridge University Press, 2014).

York, but Chaka stayed, because he lived here in Detroit. Months after the shooting, he was found stabbed to death. There was no mystery as to his assailants, but of course, the police and prosecutor never pursued the case.

During the New Bethel Incident, attendees were celebrating the Republic of New Afrika. Some indisputable facts of the case that day were the following: approximately 400 people (men, women, and children) convened in the church; there was a shootout between the police and the Black Legionnaires; police officer Michael Czapski was killed, and another, Richard Worobec, was wounded. Worobec was mysteriously later involved in other high-profile shootings through his involvement with Stop The Robberies and Enjoy Safe Streets (STRESS). Four of the Legionnaires were wounded that day. Also, while doing the research for this book, I discovered information that Czapski and Chokwe attended St. Theresa's High School at the same time. I wonder if Chokwe ever made that connection in his life.

Chokwe and classmate Michael Czpaski
(Photo courtesy of Denise Lawton)

It was somewhat puzzling to me when my friend kept saying it was horrible what they did to those young boys, and she blamed the big older one who was in charge.

"They looked like teenagers...it was horrible," she kept saying.

I said to her, "Well, it was the cops who got shot."

"I'm seeing it now, bits and pieces, but I'm seeing it now," she said.

I remained silent and just listened to her talk, as if she was in a trance describing that day.

"I saw it...I was going to the bus stop when it started. I had gone to the meeting with my husband, who wanted to work with Milton Henry. He was a law student and had assisted Milton with some legal work previously. He was interested in continuing that line of work. He eventually earned his law degree at U of D and an Accounting Degree at Wayne State University. He was a brilliant man. I was restless that day, pregnant and waddling around. I had to keep getting up and going to the bathroom.

"We eventually decided to leave. Right after we went outside to get on the bus to take us home, I saw the Henry brothers get into a car and leave. The cops pulled up fast, and one got out and was flashing a little gun. I had seen the guys marching. They were doing like a slow cadence walk and circling the building. I saw most of them like disappear around the building, when I was waddling along and I was mad at the RNA...the big guy...I'm like why did he, they have those young boys out there with those big guns.

"The RNA guys had M1 carbines, and legally they were not supposed to be loaded. Why did that big one give those instructions? Even though it was legal for them to carry those guns unloaded, the cops are looking at it like 'Blacks don't have rights, and those Blacks are getting ready to commit war on the U.S.'

"Then I saw the last young boy, when the cops pulled up, and that one cop jumped out of the car and started flashing the gun. I saw the officer on the passenger side shot. Don't know who shot first. It was stupid, he was flinging that little gun around.... They had big guns. What happened to those boys was horrible."

I could not understand why she kept talking about the tragedy of what happened to "those boys." Well, I either had forgotten or never knew that four of "those boys" were shot. When I got home, I looked up the case, and sure enough it said four of the RNA's people were shot and wounded.

When my friend and I were talking, I sure inferred that nothing had happened to the RNA legionnaires, but the cops were the ones damaged. I remember her saying, "But it's like I'm seeing it now, and what happened to those boys was wrong."

We continued to talk that day, and she said her husband wanted to be a witness, but she didn't. "He felt he had to be a witness, because they [the prosecution] had witnesses and some of those white folks lied."

I saw Rafael Viera in court, and the prosecution was trying to prove that he was one of the shooters. He was not. He was small, light brown, thin, and looked different than the one who was shooting... he was big and dark."

"Yep," I said, "and Chaka Fuller was small and thin like Rafael, and they were vindicated from the trial. All three of them were vindicated: Chaka, Rafael Viera, and Alfred Hibbit. I think they called him, Alfred 2X Hibbit."

She responded, "I don't know Chaka Fuller and the other guy."

"Wait," I said, "I have a picture of him." I pulled out my phone and showed her a picture of Chaka.

"I don't remember him. I just remember a big dark guy."

I didn't have a picture of Alfred 2X Hibbit, and I don't remember what he looked like. But, I was thinking to myself, so what if she saw a "big dark guy shoot," she could not remember who started the shooting. But she does remember it started when the cop pulled up and started waving his gun around (threatening) at them. Clearly the cops were the aggressors. The Legionnaires were not doing anything illegal. At that time, it was legal, as she said, to carry unloaded guns in the open. Now, whether or not those M1 carbines were loaded, I'll have to research the case. It could be that the big dark brother she was

Memories of My Revolutionary Brother, Chokwe Lumumba

speaking of shot with another gun on his person, and if that big dark brother was vindicated, oh well "double jeopardy." Who they need to go after is Worobec, a crooked cop, and the rest of the crooked, racist cops who have gunned down innocent Black men around this country before and since the New Bethel Case.

My friend was in the Black Panther Party at the time. She continued telling her story. "I went to the gun range with them and learned how to shoot with a long gun, but I did not complete training, and I never shot with a short gun."

I told her, "Me either," I never trained with RNA on the gun range, but I wasn't a part of security. Our oldest brother, Arki, became Minister of Defense when he joined the RNA, and he trained brothers, and with his military background, he was a good fit. Actually, COINTELPRO's investigation was focused more on Arki than Chokwe in those early days of our families' participation in the RNA. Kwame Kenyatta and this brother Kwasi Akwamu both shared the Green Files with me. Those files clearly show the emphasis on Arki in the early days of the RNA. Clearly, Arki was one of their main targets. Another target related to security training was my friend's mother, Rose Hill, Entandaji's mother.

University of Michigan conducted a study on the New Bethel Incident and reported the following findings: On March 29, 1969, the Republic of New Afrika was commemorating their one-year anniversary at the historic New Bethel Church of Rev. C.L. Franklin, Aretha Franklin's father. Chokwe and our family members had not yet joined the RNA at this time, so Chokwe was not present. The report further states while an approximate one hundred and fifty people gathered throughout the commemoration, the RNA was attacked by members of the Detroit Police Department. As a result of this unprovoked attack, one police officer, Michael Czapski, was killed, Police Officer Richard Worobec was injured, four convention attendees inside the church were injured, and 142 people were arrested and hauled off to jail, including men, women, children, and infants.

The melee began, according to the news and police reports, when two police officers drove by New Bethel Church and observed 12–14 Negroes with guns, circling the block. When they stopped to investigate the situation, they were shot by the Negroes with guns. Of course, eyewitnesses who were leaving the church at the time of the incident gave statements that contradict the media and police reports. Max Hardeman, Cynthia, his wife at the time, and Imari Obadele Jr. stated that the Black Legionnaires were circling the block when two police officers in a patrol car approached the men. Hardeman said he heard a small gun fire first before witnessing the Legionnaires shoot the officers. Cynthia reported to me that the officers stopped outside the church, jumped out of their car, and began waving the guns at the group of legionnaires. She was not sure who shot first. Then, Imari Jr. reports in his interview that the police started shooting at the Legionnaires and that they shot back at the police. Also, police and media reports indicate that the Legionnaires who were shooting at the police ran into the church, and it then became necessary for them to return fire. Numerous witnesses present at the scene inside and outside of the church gave statements that none of the Legionnaires outside of the church ran into the church. Therefore, it was unnecessary and sinister for the police to shoot into the church traumatizing and jeopardizing the lives of men, women, children, and infants. Witnesses report people scampered fearfully around inside the church finding refuge on the floors inside the pews.

Witnesses also report that police invaded the church and harassed and intimidated the attendees for a lengthy time by making them stand up with their hands on their heads for an extended period while the police were hurling insults with their guns drawn and pointed at them, before gathering them all up and taking them to the police station to be arraigned.

Memories of My Revolutionary Brother, Chokwe Lumumba

It was Representative James Del Rio and Pastor Reverend C.L. Franklin who notified Judge George Crockett Jr. of these nefarious activities that were occurring at the New Bethel Church. Judge Crockett rushed over to the police precinct and found chaos and bedlam with the police processing of 142 people they brought in from the New Bethel Church. Judge Crockett, a respected member of the court and the community, was not having it. Judge Crockett held court right there at the precinct. He also battled with Wayne County Prosecutor William Callahan regarding the arrestees' constitutional due process rights. Judge Crockett prevailed and Prosecutor Callahan promised he would stop the improper handling of the charges levied against the people brought in that day.

The following day after the arrests, the police had released all but a few individuals who were held on specific charges. Chaka Fuller, Rafael Viera, and Alfred 2X Hibbit were charged with the killing. All three were subsequently tried and acquitted. Chaka Fuller was mysteriously assassinated a few months afterwards. When I think of the New Bethel shooting, I think it is important to note that Police Officer Richard Worobec, who was involved in the New Bethel Incident, was also involved in STRESS and participated in several murders and non-fatal shootings.[24]

Coincidentally, later while still working on this book, I discovered my friend's husband's account of the New Bethel Incident. His eyewitness account was very similar to my friend's, with a few exceptions. Her husband stated the first shot they heard that day after leaving the church was from a small caliber gun (police possessed the small caliber guns, while the Legionnaires had the large guns). He next witnessed an RNA Legionnaire shoot a police officer. Also, while

---

[24]New Bethel Incident · Detroit Under Fire: Police Violence, Crime Politics, and the Struggle for Racial Justice in the Civil Rights Era · HistoryLabs Omeka S
Lonnie Saunders, Supervisor Field Investigation Division, Field Investigation Report on the March 29, 1969 Shooting at the New Bethel Baptist Church and Subsequent Events.

walking away from the scene, my friend's husband reports he never witnessed the shooter or any Legionnaires run into the church. This is an extremely important detail that contradicts the police reports. The police reported they shot into the church because the alleged shooters from the Legionnaires ran into the church.[25]

Another eyewitness account I came across is from Imari Jr., son of Imari Obadele. In 2023, he had a podcast show entitled "High Talk." Imari Jr. invited me to listen to the show entailing a discussion on the New Bethel Incident.

"My guest on the show today is Rhonda Fuller, the daughter of my father's main man Chaka Fuller, who was assassinated by the pigs."

Rhonda asked Imari Jr. if he was there the day of the New Bethel shooting. "You were there?"

Imari responded, "Yes."

Rhonda continued, "Okay, I know that one of the Black Legionnaires (RNA security) walked Milton Henry to his car.... They were approached, right?"

Imari responded, "Look, it was a set-up. Chaka, Raphael Viera, me, and Bobby Robinson was on the corner of Linwood and Philadelphia. Chaka, Rahim, and a few other brothers escorted Milton to his car. The pigs came out of the alley down Philadelphia, up Linwood, across the street and everything, from the alley behind the church.... The pigs started shooting, and Chaka and them took care of their business."

"So, they shot back," said Rhonda.

"Yes, ma'am," responded Imari.

"So that is what I wanted to know," said Rhonda. "Also, was it unclear as to whether their [Chaka and Rafael] bullets hit the cops?"

"We don't know who did the actual shooting, but...all of those brothers were shooting back at them motherfucking dogs," said Imari.

"And rightfully so," said Rhonda.

---

[25] Chris Singer, "New Bethel Eyewitness," *Fifth Estate* 81 (June 12-25, 1969), https://www.fifthestate.org/archive/81-june-12-25-1969/new-bethel-eye-witness/.

"Yeah, no respect for Black folks whatsoever," responded Imari.

"And that's crazy that it's still going on right now...and that was over fifty years ago," exclaimed Rhonda.

Imari said, "Yeah, it doesn't seem like much has changed. We are not functionally in a position to respond the way we would have fifty years ago. I'm now an old man. I'm not a leader."

Rhonda shared that she had been writing a book on her father. "Through the years...so many things have happened. Every time I get right at the door [of completion], something happens to prevent it from being published."

One time, her grandson accidentally deleted the manuscript. Although she sometimes believed it was not meant to happen, others encouraged her "to push through it" and get it done.

As the interview continued, Rhonda shared that she discovered her name on the FBI's Most Wanted List, and she doesn't understand how that happened.

Imari said, "It was there, because you are Chaka Fuller's daughter. Look, Chaka wasn't no joke, he was the real thing. When Martin Luther King Jr. was killed, you know who was out there in the aftermath of his killing, my father, your father, Chaka, and later Chokwe Lumumba. Your father was no punk, that is why you were on that list, but you should be off of it by now."

"Yeah, I could not believe what I was reading. It was a whole... operation within the FBI. The name of the operation escapes me now," said Rhonda.

"You are talking about COINTELPRO Program," said Imari.

"Yeah, they went after us."

Rhonda followed up, "I read the whole thing, they had it all laid out, what they were going to do, and how they were going to do it [dismantle the group]."

Imari responded, "I'm speechless right now because the fact that we survived is a testament to our struggle, but then I thought about

Chaka and that he did die. But he didn't die no punk, and he didn't die no useless guy."

"Yes, with my father's injuries from their attack on him, the doctor said the only thing that got him home was his determination.... Not only did he fight whoever it was off, but he got away from them, and he came home."

Rhonda told a story about a man who was a boy at the time of the incident and scared to talk. According to this man, they kept putting tickets on Chaka's car, and he had to move his car. Then he saw two of men come out of the bushes and attack Chaka, but Chaka fucked them up real quick. And then three more came, and one got him in the side, and that was the fatal wound.

Imari said he never heard these details before. "So it was more than just two pigs then."

Rhonda responded, "Oh yeah, I remember that night like it was last night."

While researching for the book, she also came across a sergeant who made a statement referring to the RNA as terrorist thugs; "he was making a statement for Czapski."

The sergeant said, "I remember you getting on the radio that day and those terrorist thugs came and attacked out of nowhere.... I know that one of them got the business at the end of a butcher knife. He signed it 'Semper fi' [always loyal, see above].... I'm like 'WOW.'

"You know, none of that surprises me," Imari continued. "All we had to do was look at the history of the dirty tricks they used on us, counterintelligence. It turned out that one of my partners, he was one of the Panther 16 in Detroit. We were around there soldiering and stuff, robbing drug dealers and carrying on; and this nigger turned out to be a FBI informant. That's just how low that they go."

Rhonda responded, "Yeah, my mom said even in the RNA, they were infiltrated, and my Dad said there were a select few, but overall he didn't know who to trust."

"That's why he and my old man was so tight. They soldiered together, so they knew each other. They trained together. My old man wasn't no joke neither; he was trained by them white folk. He was also a technical writer for the Air Force. He wrote the instructional and technical books.... They both felt the same way, I'm sure.... My old man kept me at his side, practically through everything. Even when they had their secret meetings and shit, he knew I would be outside listening. So I know a few things about a few things." Imari continued, "We had eleven acres out in Oakland County. We had to go out there and do that survival shit. I was a punk, and I didn't want to do that shit...but he carried me."[26]

It was upsetting to hear my friends Imari Jr. and Rhonda Fuller talk about the attacks made on their parents by the police, but my heart wrenched remembering that Rhonda's dad, Chaka Fuller, was killed by those police thugs. This podcast discussion also stirred up distressing memories about STRESS.

Law Enforcement Raid on the Detroit RNA Office

Our brother, Jasiri (Robert) recalls the years of the RNA with Chokwe:

> In addition to the good times with the Simba Wa Chungas, I remember a very troubling experience. The RNA had an office on Pinehurst and West Seven Mile Road, called the House of UKUUNKI. We would train, attend meetings, and conduct cultural activities in the building. One day the Detroit Police came into the office unexpectedly and arrested Sundiata and me and took us downtown. Chokwe and his wife, Anasa, were also arrested that same day. There were dozens of cops surrounding the office and throughout the neighborhood.

---

[26]Imari Obadele, *High Talk*, "Interview With Rhonda Fuller Freedom Queen, Soldier, Detroiter," August 28, 2020, podcast.

There was even a huge army tank parked across from the office. At the time, Sundiata and I both were only thirteen years of age. As two young teens, we were shocked and fearful at the same time. We didn't know why the cops were arresting us, but we were told later they had arrested us for the murder of an off-duty police officer.

They transported us to the Wayne County Youth Home, where we remained for approximately three days. We ran into Imari Jr., Imari Obadele's [president of the RNA] son, in the youth home.

When they arrested Sundiata and me, we were separated and could not communicate with each other. However, at some point we were reunited in the youth home, and Imari Jr. filled us in on what was going on. The police were alleging that when they came into the office and made the arrests, they found the gun that was involved in the shooting of the off-duty officer, a dirty cop, who was protecting a drug house. I knew that was a lie, but Sundiata and I knew exactly what firearms were at the office at the time the police arrived, and the single gun they alleged to have found was not one of them. The police interrogated us separately during the ordeal, and we did not speak to any attorney or our parents while we were in police custody.

My dad showed up on the third day of my unjust incarceration and picked me up. I don't recall ever going to court or speaking to an attorney regarding this matter. They may have just held us in juvenile without officially charging us, or Chokwe may have had the charges dismissed against us. The entire ordeal was surreal. It was one that made me have less respect for the establishment and worse feelings toward law enforcement.

RNA 11

One of Chokwe's top mentors was Imari Obadele, a man who seemed to have an infinite wealth of information that he did not mind sharing. Chokwe saw Imari as a man who spent several years in prison for trumped-up charges of which he was totally innocent. These charges were lodged against him after law enforcement agents attacked members of the RNA at their headquarters in Jackson, Mississippi, on August 18, 1971. Law enforcement swooped down on members of the RNA during the overnight hours and proceeded to shoot into the house. I believe this event was similar to law enforcement attacking Black Panther chairman Fred Hampton and his comrades in Chicago in 1969. However, there were significant differences. We lost beloved Fred Hampton and fellow Black Panther Mark Clark when police attacked Hampton's home by unleashing a barrage of gunshots in the early morning hours. Jackson police and FBI members attacked a house on Lewis Street where RNA members were sleeping. But in this case, the occupants of the house, RNA members, shot back, and a police chief, William Louis Skinner (father of Judge Bill Skinner), was killed and a police officer and FBI agent were wounded. Imari was asleep blocks away at another residence when the incident occurred. But he was charged, found guilty, and incarcerated for years, nevertheless. With the mark of a true leader, Imari did not give up or change in prison but came out of prison and received his doctoral degree, continued his activism, and remained president of the RNA and professor at Prairie View A&M University.

Prior to the August 18th shootout, Chokwe experienced what he considered a high point in his life. In March 1971, Chokwe was en route to celebrate the acquisition of what the RNA called El Malik in Hinds County, Mississippi. Chokwe was part of a caravan of people traveling from all over the country to the Land Celebration in Mississippi. At a small town called Mt. Beulah, the police and FBI had set up a roadblock. Chokwe at the time was a security leader in the RNA. It was his job to deescalate potentially threatening situations and prevent anyone from getting hurt. The FBI was continuously zooming around the cars. Fearing a bad situation, Chokwe got out of the car and approached the officer who appeared to be in charge. The officer was nervous, and it eventually became apparent that the officer was more afraid than Chokwe. The game of nerves had been played and the police lost. Chokwe and his comrades' wills were strong enough to back law enforcement down, and no one got hurt. Chokwe simply told the officer to get out of their way, and the officer simply moved. The caravan proceeded to the Land Celebration. Chokwe was exhilarated. No one could stop them now!

Ahmed Obafemi

Ahmed Obafemi *Ahmed Obafemi, Itari Shakur, and his beautiful caregiver*

Ahmed was a warrior and king of the people. He was previously married to Fulani Sunni-Ali, one of the Brink's expropriation defendants. As the former Eastern Vice President of the Provisional Government of the Republic of New Afrika (PG-RNA) and later the International Representative of the New Afrikan People's Organization (NAPO), Ahmed was a true warrior.

Memories of My Revolutionary Brother, Chokwe Lumumba

In 2019, Itari and I went to visit Ahmed in Atlanta at a convalescent home. He looked great for a brother in his eighties. Ahmed had succumbed to an illness that left him unable to use his legs. Our visit just happened to be on Memorial Day, and the facility was putting on a big celebration for the residents. The disc jockey just happened to play most of the Motown hits. The place was live and booming. The nursing staff were dancing with the patients in and out of the wheelchairs. Everyone got in on the singing (even me). It was so enlightening and uplifting to see our incapacitated seniors get down. Even Ahmed busted a couple of moves in his wheelchair. We also noticed that Ahmed was well respected at the facility, just like he had always been outside the facility. I observed the nursing staff speaking to Ahmed with compassion and seeing to his needs. Ahmed's interaction with the other residents was congenial and friendly. Prior to leaving Detroit for Atlanta, I talked to attorney Jeffrey Edison, telling him that Itari and I were on our way to visit Ahmed. Jeff said to give the brother his love. "Brother Ahmed is one of the real ones. I have always had a lot of respect for that brother."

During our visit, I shared an awful Facebook post with Ahmed about a cop bragging about Chaka Fuller's (New Bethel Incident) murder. Ahmed said we got more of them than they did of us. Ahmed also told me that when some RNA members were stopped by the Jackson, Mississippi, law enforcement barricade, one of them belligerently asked, "Who is the head nigger in charge?" Ahmed smiled widely and said to me, "I would have loved to have seen that cracker's face on Chokwe's mayoral inauguration day."

We talked about a few other RNA members the day of our visit, and their contributions to the movement, like Mutulu Shakur, a member of the RNA and Black Liberation Army. At this time, Mutulu was still serving a sixty-year sentence for his conviction in the 1981 Brink's expropriation. Ahmed shared memories of Mutulu's amazing work prior to his incarceration. Mutulu worked in the People's Drug

Program in the Lincoln Clinic in the South Bronx. Members of the Young Lords, Black Panther Party, and other revolutionaries created the Lincoln Detox program for substance abusers.[27] Ahmed said Mutulu helped introduce the treatment of acupuncture at the clinic after he found it helped with substance abusers' recovery. Also, according to Ahmed, Mutulu co-founded the Harlem Institute of Acupuncture, a school for the study of acupuncture, and the Black Acupuncture Advisory Association of North America (BAAANA) before he was incarcerated; and there are still students out there now who are working with acupuncture. Mutulu studied under this acupuncture master. When he finished, he went back and opened up the clinic. "I used to get my treatment there," Ahmed said.

Turning the conversation to Chokwe, Ahmed recalled, "Chokwe and I possibly met either at the convention in New York, but I'm not sure. I was arrested at the Democratic Convention in 1972. Chokwe was supposed to make a presentation for the 'Anti-Depression Program,' and they were trying to stop that.[28] Law enforcement had been following me and Tarik (the brother riding with me) since we left Mississippi. We were supposed to meet Chokwe down there [Miami], but he was late for a meeting. If Chokwe had been in the car, he would have been arrested also. We were distributing leaflets for the 'Anti-Depression Program.' They stopped us in our vehicle, and they arrested us and charged us with 'possession of weapons.' When they arrested us, they put out into the media that we were there at the convention trying to assassinate George McGovern.

I asked Ahmed, "Why you all would be trying to assassinate the Democratic candidate for president?"

---

[27]See also, Eana Meng, "Dr. Mutulu Shakur and the Lincoln Detox," *Of Part and Parcel*, February 20, 2020, https://www.ofpartandparcel.com/blog-2/dr-mutulu-shakur-and-the-lincoln-detox-center (accessed April 30, 2025).

[28]The RNA's "Anti-Depression Program" was essentially its blueprint for the Provisional Government to argue for and negotiate a reparations package with the United States.

He responded, "We were at the hotel, and Tarik was at the hotel to deliver the program to the Democratic Convention, so they just used that as an excuse."

I then asked, "Did the Democratic Party try to help you?"

"No," he replied. "Only Jesse Jackson and a few others put some work around it. The Secret Service and the FBI were surrounding McGovern to protect him. They knew we were not trying to assassinate him because the next day, they dropped that allegation. That was just sensationalized. They moved us from jail to jail so nobody could find us. When they finally charged us, we were able to get a lawyer and then our location was revealed. We were charged with the weapons charges, and I spent five years in prison.

"I was incarcerated in Florida State Prison from 1972 to 1976. This incarceration did not make me angry or upset at the movement because when I joined the RNA, I clearly knew what I was getting into. Their abuse of me and mistreatment was 'normal.' They jumped on me a couple of times, and I spent a few years in solitary confinement. They were trying to keep me away from mainstream prisoners and they put me with death-row prisoners. There was some difficulty with me receiving visitors because I was so far away from my home, New York. However, Fulani managed to come and visit me."

I discussed with Ahmed how I once worked with the Michigan Department of Corrections (MDOC) as a probation/parole agent and how I found it to be somewhat of a corrupt system in itself. I came to believe it was necessary for me to get out of there. Or maybe that was God's decision. I was in a bad car accident that altered my ability to do my job. Prior to that, I was told by one of my colleagues who had a reputation for being an exemplary agent that I needed to leave MDOC because I was a social worker type, and these guys did not need social workers. Most of my parolees had been in and out of prison 3–5 times. They were institutionalized in prison, and they needed my sensitive support; but they also needed a strong, unwavering, and nonsensical agent who would not be vulnerable to their cons. I eventually bought into it when confronted with the aftermath of my car accident.

When I trained to be a tether agent at MDOC, the agent who trained me for two days committed suicide. How tragic and awful a situation that was very traumatic to me. I took her death hard. Yet my MDOC supervisor insisted that I go out by myself the following day after her death and tether probationers. I did not feel comfortable or confident that I could effectively install the tethers. My feelings were unfortunately on point because the next day I found the tether-monitoring unit had violated two of the probationers that I tethered the day before and called them in to be arrested.

Subsequent to speaking to both individuals, who were both on their jobs when I contacted them, I alerted my supervisor and explained to her that I had possibly done something wrong with the tether installation process.

She said to me, "Why are you worrying about this?"

I responded, "I care because these guys are trying to get their lives in order, and I believe I may have improperly installed the tether."

She authoritatively looked at me and said, "Listen, your job is to supervise the probationer and protect the public, not rehabilitate them... Learn that!"

Chokwe, on the other hand, advised me to report my concerns to someone else in authority. He told me on several occasions that the criminal justice system is flawed and did not work in the best interest of justice. However, we had to do the best job we could in the interest of justice and fairness for our people. Despite the conversation with my supervisor, I contacted the tether unit and explained my position, and they worked with me in having the guys come in to check their tethers as opposed to arresting them. Just as I suspected, the ankle units had been installed improperly.

I asked Ahmed why he thought so many guys return to prison: "They don't have a decent chance. You have to make sacrifices and be able to get a job, especially if you are movement oriented. I was in prison before for burglary. Fulani would come and visit me and talk about the RNA. She was in the RNA. When I got out, I joined the RNA. My parole officer wanted to violate me because I was organizing. Even though organizing in itself was not a violation of my parole, associating with known criminals was. Working in the community, you are going to associate with them.

"Prison will help some people and won't help others. When you go in you should try to get involved in discussion groups and exercise and join the movement. I was conscious prior to going to prison the first time, but I had a drug problem. It is difficult to maintain a drug habit in prison. I think groups like the Republic of New Afrika and Nation of Islam are helpful with rehabilitation of substance abusers in prison. They offered rehabilitation where the prisons did not." Ahmed and Chokwe had mutual respect and trust for each other. I admired that about their relationship."

Interview with Bilal Sunni Ali by Shushanna Shakur

Bilal and Fulani Sunni Ali
(Photo courtesy of Sunni Ali family)

Chokwe shared camaraderie with very good people. Some of them were his friends, comrades, and clients. Bilal Sunni-Ali was one of the people who shared all of the aforementioned relationships. Chokwe represented Bilal Sunni-Ali and his deceased wife, Iyi Fulani Sunni-Ali, in 1983 when they faced charges related to the Brink's case. Chokwe liberated both of them from the imprisonment of their fraudulent captors. The following is an interview I conducted with Bilal in May of 2019. He transitioned on December 30, 2024:

Shushanna: Was the Black Panther Party your first participation in the movement?

Bilal: No, I was brought up in a conscious family. My uncle was a leader in the Tiger Division (Harlem) of the UNIA/ACL [University Negro Improvement Association/African Communities League]. My parents weren't members but were sympathizers and shared the same political view. So I had from when I was very small a disposition toward movement and struggle. The very first political organization I remember being in was the NAACP youth division, called the Young Turks. I was about fifteen years old then. That was around 1963. My involvement with them was primarily through my music, doing fundraisers and performing at affairs for them. We learned a lot about the mass movement, the freedom struggle in the South. It seems like the term "civil rights movement" was something that it was called later on.

S: Why did you join the RNA?

B: I was raised with that type of consciousness that we, Afrikan people, were a distinct people from the ruling society here. In my late teens in Harlem, there were several formations that spoke to that. There was the African Nationalist Pioneer Movement, an offshoot of the UNIA/ACL. Nana Oseijeman Adefunmi, King of Oyotunji Village, was at that time the prime minister of the Harlem People's Parliament (HPP). The HPP was the government over the People's Republic of Harlem. It was the time of the liberation movement in Afrika and countries that hadn't gained their independence that were nationalizing industries and institutions. This was to make them function on behalf of the people. We were learning through elders like our Nana. We were learning about this process and applying it in our community organizing. We would nationalize (some people elsewhere would call it taking over) schools, abandoned buildings, and so forth. The HPP was leading this work and linking with other formations through the Black Power conferences. This was around 1966, '67, '68. There was a national formation known as the Afrikan People's Land Partition Party, which named as our national territory nineteen states from the mid-South to the Deep South. There was a Black community formation known as the Harlem Progressive Labor Party. Bill Epton was the leader of it. So when we learned of the Black Power Conference to take place in Detroit that March (1968), we were ready for it. Before Malcolm was assassinated[,] he talked about such a conference to take place in the future, one that would form a political party, a government and even an army. The Republic of New Afrika was the result of that conference. With my experience, why would I not join? How could I not join?

S: Do you remember where you met Chokwe?

B: No. I don't have a vivid recollection of meeting Chokwe. The earliest recollection I have of him as far as I can remember is a meeting in Atlanta around October 1981. There were a few groups involved: The Provisional Government of the Republic of New Afrika. The African People's Party, and it was before the New Afrikan People's Organization (NAPO) was founded. Okay, but I think it was the National Black Human Rights Movement. So NAPO had been founded but not the Malcolm X Grassroots Movement. We, the New Afrikan Independence Movement, were developing efforts toward consolidation.

S: Did Chokwe represent you, Mutulu, Fulani, and anyone else in the Brink's case?

B: According to Chokwe's definition, and as an act of self-determination, we refer to that case as New Afrika vs. the United

Snakes of America. The state's federal system refers to it as the United States of America vs. Dr. Mutulu Shakur. The "Brink's case" historically is about a case of some white gangsters orchestrating the robbery of a Brink's truck. We always distinguished ourselves from that incident even though the media tried to label us the Black Brink's case or the second Brink's case. We even put forward definitions for our movement of expropriation, the legitimate right of oppressed people to access funds illegally appropriated by the state of the sweat, blood, and lives of oppressed Black people. But to answer your question, Chokwe represented me and Mutulu in two separate trials. I was tried and acquitted in 1983. Mutulu was tried and convicted in 1986. Chokwe always maintained that there had been no more evidence presented against Mutulu than there had been against me. The difference in the two trials was that the political climate of the country had strongly shifted to the right in that three-year period. An aspect of political climate change was that in our trial we were able to have a majority of jurors from our own community (Black and working class). However that was not the case three years later. Dr. Mutulu Shakur and Marilyn Buck were found guilty by an all-white or predominantly white jury.[29] Fulani did not go on trial but was represented in the grand jury proceedings. Chokwe was one of her legal advisors along with attorney Lynne Stewart. Lynne was also my co-counsel.

S: Did you spend any time in jail during the Brink's case? If so, how long, and what did you feel?

B. I was captured in Belize in November 1982, kidnapped by the FBI and transported to Dade County, Florida. I was transferred to

---

[29]Mutulu Shakur was released from federal prison on December 16, 2022, after serving thirty-seven years. He succumbed to cancer six months later on July 7, 2023, at the age of seventy-two. Marilyn Buck served over two decades in prison and was released on July 15, 2010. She succumbed to her cancer less than a month after her release at age sixty-two.

Miami Federal Correction Center MCC [Metropolitan Correctional Center]. I was later transported to the Southern District of New York and held at the federal lockup there (MCC) in downtown New York City, until the trial was over in September 1983. I can confidently say that I felt victorious. I had faith in the righteousness and victory of our struggle. We presented the issue of our right to self-determination and our struggle for a free and independent state outside of the jurisdiction of the corporation of the United States of America. I think it was and is the most important case in our history from an educational standpoint.

S: What were the Black Liberation Army and the Weather Underground? Do you think groups like these would be beneficial to the movement today?

B: The Black Liberation Army, in its historical sense, has been the various armed formations that, to this case, was an armed clandestine formation that was created to withstand the onslaught of the attack by the state against the Black Panther Party. The Weather Underground was a similar formation in relation to the organization known as SDS, Students for a Democratic Society. I think that such organizations would be, or are, of great benefit to our movement today. The enemy is so thoroughly corrupt and criminal that in order to advance, we need to have formations that are willing and able to do whatever is necessary to defend the people against it. For instance, we would not have found definitive information about the FBI's official counterinsurgency program known as the Counter Intelligence Program, or COINTELPRO, had it not been for units that had surreptitiously entered a federal building and found and exposed those files.

S: How long were you and Fulani married? Did you all meet in the RNA or around your music?

B: At the time of Fulani's departure from this realm of life, June 2016, we had been married for over thirty-nine years. December 2016 would've made forty years. We met in February 1972 at an

Eastern Regional Convention of the PG-RNA, held at a private Black institution known as the House of Common Sense in Brooklyn, New York.

S: Did you and Fulani perform music together?

B: Yes, we performed together a great deal as a duo and as members of the same group. We recorded in 1999, resulting in a CD called *Seven Times Seven*, which featured, among other things, Fulani on vocals doing a song called the "Harvest Song." The "Harvest Song" used the melody "Christmas Song" with substitute lyrics composed by myself that depicted Kwanzaa. It also has on it another Kwanzaa song called "Imani" about observance of the day of Imani, the seventh day of Kwanzaa.

S: Please tell me a little bit about your relationship with Fulani, her character, the lows, her illness, and the highs.

B. I would characterize my relationship with Fulani as a very holistic relationship. We were united on just about every aspect of life, on points that caused some couples to separate. We were both Muslim. We were both revolutionary nationalists. We were both connected to the struggle in our neighborhood as well as with national and global issues. We were both connected in our understanding of our embracing the mysteries of life. We were both performing artists with an artistic liturgy that dealt with history and struggle. I, above all, appreciated her principled dedication to the struggle of maintaining family life and building on family relationships. I often say we never fell in love. We grew and continued to grow in love. I was surprised that family members of hers actually came and thanked me for sticking with her throughout her illness and being hospitalized. I could not and cannot conceive of a love relationship that would dissolve over one of the partners having life-threatening health challenges. She actually stayed with me till the end pulling me back when I had thought I was checking out. But you said tell you a little. Well, that's more than a little about her; but this isn't a book about our lives. That's forthcoming, insha'Allah!

S: What instruments do you play, and what groups did you play with? How does your music define you?

B: I play or have played the B-flat clarinet, the B-flat bass clarinet, the C flute, the piccolo, the alto flute, the bassoon, the harmonica, and, of course, the saxophone, B-flat tenor saxophone, my main instrument, the E-flat Alto, and E-flat baritone. I have performed with many groups. The most long-term and most notable association was performing and recording with Gil Scott-Heron, Brian Jackson, and the Midnight Band. Before that, I performed on flute with the Simba Drummers and Dancers as part of student organizing through Simba, a political-cultural student group. Also I performed with the Sankore Nubian Cultural Workshop, the American Symphony Orchestra, and a so-called R&B group in New York City known as the Octet. Before that, I performed with various formations of the Latin, Jazz Sextet, and Latin jazz Octet and Latin jazz Orchestra. Way before that, my very first group was at twelve years old, the Symphony Seven. I lead my own group today and have done so for the past twenty years. It's called the Song of Life Ensemble. My music defines me in that it highlights and engages people in the life and struggle of Afrikan people from the ancient to the future. When you asked what groups I performed with, there are significant social, political, and cultural dimensions to each of the groups mentioned, except maybe the American Symphony Orchestra, which was part of my music education.

S: How long did they (was it Feds or police) detain Fulani during the Brink's? What was the basis for her detainment? How did they make you feel?

B: When Fulani was detained the first time, it was for about three days. The Feds apprehended her in Byrdstown, Mississippi, transported her to Jackson, and from there she was transported to

New York MCC. When she appeared before a magistrate, our brother had already gotten an affidavit up to the court. There was a Chevy dealership manager who remembered her face and the van and had sworn in the affidavit that on the day in question, she was at the dealership getting that vehicle repaired. The police and the press were harassing our brother, Lumumba Shakur. He told them that he had proof that she was innocent. When asked to show what the proof was, Lumumba flashed the affidavit. Photos and videos of him holding the affidavit went worldwide before it was delivered to the federal magistrate in New York. She was released immediately. However, immediately upon her release, she was served with a material witness summons and remanded into federal custody again. The material witness summons was scrapped and she was ordered to appear before a federal grand jury, investigating a series of robberies in New York that citizens of the RNA were alleged to have been involved with. So from November 1981 until October 1983, she was held for approximately eighteen months. During that time, she was released and rearrested several times. The basis being first as a defendant, then as a material witness, and finally as a grand jury resister because she refused to testify before the grand jury. Again, it made me feel very proud of her because of the refusal and the political position that she stood on, "No collaboration, No cooperation, and No compromise" was adopted by at least thirty other so-called unindicted co-conspirators. That was a big part of not only us winning the acquittals on over half of the federal conspiracy charges but served to disrupt the federal investigation of the movement.

S: I remember Chokwe said that there were three brothers who were tortured by the FBI in the Brink's case. I believe two of them were Sekou Odinga and Kwesi Balogun. Do you know who the other one was? He said they burned them with cigarettes and flushed one of their heads in the toilet. Ahmed Obafemi said it may have been Sam Brown, but I remember all of them having African names.

B: Sekou was the one whose head was stuck in a toilet while they repeatedly flushed the toilet. That's called waterboarding. They damn near drown you and don't allow you to breathe. Sam Brown was the third one. He had a Yoruba name, but he wasn't using it at the time. He did use the name Solomon publicly. The Feds broke Solomon's neck and continuously beat him on that broken neck. We say they broke his neck but could not break him. They forged an affidavit implicating people in the movement as being involved and broke his neck trying to force him to sign it. Whenever he appeared in court, he proudly invoked his Fifth Amendment rights and privilege. They tried to make him snitch, but he refused. Solomon had a long history in the struggle. He was involved in fighting in the resistance in Dominica. The Feds thought that if they broke him, they would break the high spirit of resistance that existed among our people at that time. Long live Solomon/Sam Brown.

S: What do you think of Kathy Boudin and members of the Weather Underground? Did Chokwe represent any of them? It seems, I remember typing some pleadings where he did.

B: I never met Kathy Boudin, but from what I've heard of her, I thought that she was a committed resistance fighter. At the time when she was identified as being involved in the operation, she had last been seen escaping from an exploding building, said to be a Weather Underground bomb factory. One of the things that this case did was show that people with a long history of struggle and resistance were deeply committed, and although unheard from publicly, they were still involved. I don't remember Chokwe representing them. As his legal secretary, you would know better than me.

S: Is Assata Shakur the biological sister of Mutulu Shakur?

B: Assata Shakur and Mutulu Shakur were not biologically related. The name Shakur, which, as you know, means thankful of the One to whom thanks is due in Arabic, was adopted by many young people in the struggle who had come under the influence of El-Hajj Salahdeen Shakur. Hajj Shakur was an associate of El-

Hajj Malik Shabazz [Malcolm X]. He was a member of both the Muslim Mosque Inc. and the Organization of Afro-American Unity. We called him Abba, which means father in Arabic. He was the biological abba of two Black Panther leaders: Zayd Malik Shakur and Lumumba Abdul Shakur. Mutulu was a youngster who grew up in the same neighborhood, South Jamaica, Queens. Although we never adopted the name, both Sekou Odinga and I were/are part of that "Shakur Family." Afeni Shakur, even though she carries the name by marriage, actually legally changed her name to Shakur because of allegiance to Hajj Shakur. Abba's influence was so highly respected that people who weren't even named Shakur were oftentimes mistakenly named Shakur on summons, indictments, and so on.

S: Was Marilyn Buck a defendant in the Brink's case, and did Chokwe ever represent her?

B: Marilyn Buck was tried in the case with Dr. Mutulu Shakur in 1986. I don't recall her ever being represented by Chokwe.

S: What is your recollection of why the second split happened in the RNA prior to the start of NAPO?

B: Although some people interpret NAPO as revenge, I don't think the split involved NAPO in any way. As I recall, there were a lot of us who disapproved of Imari Obadele's leadership. Particularly, the issue of popular elections was thought by many, including myself, to be an improper way to build a revolutionary movement. Imari Obadele was considered and declared "incapacitated." Imari strongly disagreed, of course. Sister Dara Abubakari/Virginia Collins, who had been a vice president, was elected as the first woman president of the RNA. Imari's faction declared the election illegal. The two factions that arose were those who accepted Sister Dara as president and those who went along with Imari Obadele. The split that involved NAPO was not in the Provisional Government but in the African People's Party.

S: What are your memories of Chokwe? What was his legacy to our people?

Memories of My Revolutionary Brother, Chokwe Lumumba

B: One of my memories of Chokwe is that in our opening statement, he stated that we believed that the real conspiracy in this case was that the government of the United Snakes of America had conspired to criminalize the defendants and our movement and that we wouldn't wait for the defense portion of the case to prove that. He stated that we would begin proving our case out of the testimony of the very first witness that the government called. The government called as a witness a fingerprint expert. When the witness had finished testifying under direct examination and cross-examination from all the other defense attorneys, Chokwe rose to have his turn to cross-examine the witness.

The government objected saying that the witness had not mentioned his client, me. After refuting and debunking their objection, Chokwe asked the fingerprint expert a series of related questions that brought out the fact that a set of my fingerprints had been sent from FBI headquarters to crime scenes of every major case (murder, kidnap, and robbery) on the East Coast from the year 1972 to the year 1981. They had objected to Chokwe being allowed to cross-examine the witness because they knew—or maybe they were surprised at his brilliance to be able to prove conspiracy on the part of the government from the government's own witnesses. There are so many memories.

Another memory is one from our summation. Chokwe reminded the jury of the promise he made during our opening statement to prove the U.S. government was guilty of conspiracy. He told the jury that if we were in a New Afrikan court, they could find the U.S. government guilty, but being hampered by being in U.S. court that didn't allow them to do that, they would have to come up with the next best alternative ruling and that would be to find us, the defendants, not guilty. So in September 1983, that majority Afrikan jury found me, Bilal Sunni-Ali, not guilty and dismissed the entire conspiracy indictment against me.

Chokwe Lumumba's legacy is that he became the lawyer that Malcolm would have been. He was so good at law that he actually could function as a defense attorney in the amerikkkan court system and simultaneously serve as law professor and New Afrikan Judge and make that become a reality in the minds of witnesses and jurors alike, to the dismay of the U.S. empire.[30]

They say that cat Chokwe Lumumba was a bad mother f€%¥£rr; and yes, I shut my mouth. I rest my case. Long live Chokwe Lumumba!

(Left to Right) Akbar Muhammad, Minister Louis Farrakhan, Chokwe Lumumba, Kwame Toure (Stokley Carmichael) add members of the Indigenous People

Revolutionary Leaders

If anyone wants to know who Chokwe Lumumba was, you must know of his work and beliefs. However, to get an in-depth look into this great man, you must also know more of the people who surrounded him. Who else was in his circle? Who else did he walk with? Who else did he converse with? Who else did he admire and appreciate? Who else did he love? When you learn these things about Chokwe Lumumba, then you will understand him and know him.

---

[30] This spelling suggests that the U.S. is fascist or racist. For more information, see https://en.wiktionary.org/wiki/Amerikkkan.

Memories of My Revolutionary Brother, Chokwe Lumumba

Working with Chokwe on the Black Nation Day Conference in 1983 was certainly a highlight of my life. People from all over the country attended. Many of them arrived by bus from Chicago and a few other locations. This conference was so exciting because there were some powerful speakers participating. I always admired Chokwe for his extraordinary contributions to our people but also for maintaining relationships with so many other great revolutionary leaders. I helped Chokwe prepare for the conference. My assistance consisted of my typing, reading, and printing material pertaining to guest speakers and activities. I also made phone calls to some of the guest speakers and/or their secretaries. Helping Chokwe coordinate programs and events such as these were skill-building and life-changing for me. Later, in my professional and social life, I often served as a coordinator for many events with the Teacher and Probation Officer Unions, MXGM and the Detroit Shakur Squad, Black Legacy Coalition, as well as community organizing. The skills I developed by helping my brother served me in all of the other positions.

The speakers list for Black Nation Day was awesome: Kwame Toure (Stokely Carmichael) of the SNCC; Jamil Al-Amin (H. Rap Brown), former Black Panther and SNCC leader; Louis Farrakhan, Nation of Islam leader; Queen Mother Audley Moore, one of the RNA founders; Robert Williams, first president of the RNA; Anwar Pasha, founder of the RNA; Imari Obadele, founder and second president of the RNA; Dara Abubakari, third president of the RNA; Ahmed Obafemi and Chokwe Lumumba, ministers of the RNA; Rev.

Ben Chavis, leader of the Wilmington Ten and assistant to Dr. Martin Luther King Jr.; poets Sonia Sanchez and Haki Madhubuti (Don Lee); and others. The guest speakers at this event all had an extraordinary biography and repertoire of activism:

Stokely Carmichael (Kwame Ture) was most memorable to me because of his leadership with the SNCC and his challenges to Dr. Martin Luther King Jr. and his nonviolent movement based on his Pan-African beliefs. Stokely believed our strategy of protest should be one of self-defense and self-determination (like Malcolm X) as opposed to nonviolence and passive resistance. Stokely, one could say, was the father of the "Black Power Movement," or at least he helped popularize the slogan "Black Power."

H. Rap Brown (Jamil Abdullah Al-Amin), former minister of justice of the Black Panther Party, served briefly as the fifth chairman of SNCC. However, I remember him best for coining the phrase "burn, baby, burn" during the rebellions of the late 1960s that occurred all over the United States in Black neighborhoods. Subsequent to his heavy organizational work in our communities, in 1970 he was placed on the FBI Most Wanted List for a firearms charge. He disappeared but was later arrested, stood trial, and sentenced to five years in prison. Brown converted to Islam in prison and changed his name to Jamil Abdullah Al-Amin. While he was serving as an imam in Atlanta, he was arrested. In 2000, Al-Amin was charged with murdering a Black police officer and injuring another outside the convenience store he owned. In 2002, Al-Amin was convicted of the murder and other charges and transitioned while serving a life sentence.

Dr. Maulana Karenga is one of the signers of the Declaration of Independence of the Republic of New Afrika and its first Minister of Culture, but he is best known by many people throughout the world as the founder of Kwanzaa. Dr. Karenga and others in his Us Organization created Kwanzaa as a celebration of Black Nationhood. It is not a religious holiday, as some people originally thought, but it is a time for Black people to celebrate our Blackness and beauty.

Chokwe made Kwanzaa part of our family life and celebration beginning in the early 1970s. However, family members who were in the PG-RNA had been celebrating Kwanzaa and practicing the Nguzo Saba (Seven Principles of Black Nationhood) since the late 1960s. Our siblings, parents, children, and extended family members gathered annually for our family Kwanzaa celebration. Our celebrations were similar to the community celebration but more intimate. Chokwe would lead us all in the lighting of the candles, always giving a preface of the meaning of Kwanzaa. He eventually would go around the room, and family members and friends would give their understanding of the principles. He would also encourage family discussion that would become very private and in-depth at times, especially for the young adults. He would encourage them to discuss their personal life goals, the reasons for them, and how they planned to achieve them. In Detroit, the Alexander Crummell Center through Mama Malkia Brantuo, Mama Imani Humphrey, and Mama Aneb House; the RNA; the Shrine of Black Madonna; and the Pan African Congress were among the first community groups to celebrate Kwanzaa. Mama Imani continued the traditional celebration through her African-centered school, Aisha Shule, after the Crummell Center closed. Chokwe and Kwame Kenyatta continued the traditional celebrations through the Malcolm X Grassroots Movement after they became inactive in the PG-RNA.

Nubia, Chokwe's wife, added a beautiful touch to each event from the very beginning of her participation in our Kwanzaa celebrations,

Chokwe Lumumba and Maulana Karenga

with both family and community. When my husband, children, and I lived upstairs from Nubia and Chokwe, Nubia would make sure everyone would receive one gift a day for seven days during the candle-lighting ceremony. This tradition continued in our family until Nubia's earthly transition. I recall delivering some of her Kwanzaa gifts years after her passing that were tucked away in my closet. They were intended for individuals in Detroit who were not present at the last Kwanzaa celebration she attended, and because she was returning to Jackson, she asked me to deliver them. The gifts represented African cultural values, from the handmade dolls, jewelry, and African attire to books and music written and performed by Black people. Nubia also introduced the Kwanzaa song and some activities during the extended family and community celebrations, and she decorated the celebratory space with beautiful authentic African patterns and art throughout the room.

(Photo courtesy of Freedom Archives)

NAPO/MXGM and Other Activism

"I only came to the movement because of King and he was killed. I only stayed in the movement because of Malcolm and he was killed. Then I became a leader."
– Chokwe Lumumba

Chokwe was involved in several activist organizations, including PG-RNA and Detroit Human Rights, and he was very much a part of the anti-apartheid movement of South Africa when he was

Memories of My Revolutionary Brother, Chokwe Lumumba

living and practicing law in Detroit. Chokwe was also a member of the minority of Black leaders from the beginning of the movement who shared an anti-apartheid/U.S. divestment stance on South Africa. Although he was aligned with Black Nationalists, the Negro Leader Regime had not caught up to their progressive positions; Detroit Mayor Coleman Young, who in 1974 became Detroit's first African American mayor, was among this group. It took some time before Young decided to participate and protest apartheid in South Africa, despite numerous attempts by concerned Black citizens and nationalists in Detroit, like Chokwe, to bring him on board.

Some time prior to Nelson Mandela's historic visit to Detroit in 1990, there was an anti-apartheid rally held at Hart Plaza. I was with Chokwe this day. I can't recall if we were coming from Frank Murphy Hall of Justice or if we rode over from his law office on West McNichols. But, I do recall this; we were going to attend a rally that was apparently organized by Mayor Young's people. Chokwe had received a call that the mayor wanted him to speak. We were rushing to get there on time. Just like when I was a little girl, I could not keep pace with my Brother's long, quick legs; mine were too short and not fast enough. Also, just like when I was a little girl, I didn't want him to know, so I ran some and walked some as we made our way across Jefferson and up to where the rally was being held. Out of breath but on time, we made it only to be blocked. After a little runaround from security and the ushers, Chokwe was advised that he was not on the program and not scheduled to speak. Wow...that blew my mind. Of course, Chokwe and other nationalists had criticized Young and other members of government for not getting involved and committing to protest apartheid in South Africa, but weren't they supposed to? I thought that Young was going to do the right thing, the appropriate thing and give a platform to someone who was fighting this thing long before him and the other Johnny-come-lately folks.

Now, I am not trying to trivialize Young and the others' late participation, because it certainly helped in the battle. However, I get so sick and tired of seeing the original "OGs" thrust to the side and given no credit. Like with the Reparations movement, Queen Mother Moore, Robert Williams, Imari Obadele, Reparation Ray Jenkins, and Congressman John Conyers were all staunch activists fighting for reparations from the beginning, but their names are barely mentioned today. Unfortunately, this would not be the first time that this type of exclusion would happen to Chokwe, nor would it be the last. The doorkeepers would not even allow us to enter through the stage area. Frankly, I don't remember much after that. I was so hurt, angry, and upset about the treatment of my brother. I do remember this though. He did not disparage Young or anyone else. We went home.

I learned early in my life that my brother was not a hater, gossiper, or petty individual. As a matter of fact, I don't ever recall my brother expressing hatred for anyone. I remember he spoke often of injustices committed by systems and the people who operate those systems. He spoke of opposing, protesting, and fighting those people to change the oppressive systems they are operating. My brother spoke the truth and consistently took actions to make revolutionary changes. Just because he loved his people and oppressed people did not mean he hated the people who were oppressing them. It only meant he did not like what they were doing, and he not only spoke against them, but he took actions against them. Ironically, when Chokwe passed away, Coleman Young Jr. attended his service at Fellowship Chapel. He was one of the first people there, and he wanted to share a few words. Due to time constraints, I had to gracefully announce to Senator Coleman Young Jr. that he would not be able to speak. Kwame Kenyatta shared with me, several months prior to his own death, that Chokwe and Coleman Young had mended their differences. I was so grateful Kwame shared this information with me. It is always positive to see one's heroes unified. Coleman Young and Chokwe Lumumba are both heroes of mine.

From the late 1970s through the mid-1980s, I lived upstairs from Chokwe and Nubia. During the latter years of my living in the house, Chokwe was organizing with Watani Tyehimba, Akinyele Umoja, and other founders of NAPO and MXGM. Watani and Akinyele were living in Los Angeles, and they were members of the African Peoples Party and House of Umoja at the time, but they later relocated to Atlanta and established the main headquarters for NAPO and MXGM. Many RNA members like Ahmed Obafemi, Kwame Kalimara, and Bilal Sunni-Ali became members of NAPO and MXGM. These brothers also relocated to "the land," namely Georgia, Alabama, and Mississippi. I also recall typing documents and information for Chokwe for the organizations. Similar to how my siblings and I joined the RNA, we joined NAPO and MXGM. However, my oldest brother, Reggie (Arki), was not involved at this point. When he left the RNA, he went into another direction in life, one of religion. Our sister Itari and I and our younger brothers worked with Chokwe and the organizations. Itari traveled with Chokwe a lot and attended NAPO conferences out of state. I was in college and law school during the early days of NAPO and MXGM and was not very active. However, I continue to provide clerical services for the organizations. When Chokwe moved to Jackson, Mississippi, in 1988, I became his representative in Detroit and took on a lot of the organizing and leadership work with Detroit MXGM.

MXGM Founders (front row): Chokwe Lumumba, Akinyele Umoja, Kwame Osagyefo Kalimara at a press conference at the Bureaus des Avocats Internationaux (BAI) in Haiti (Photo courtesy of Akinyele Umoja)

As one of the cofounders of NAPO, Chokwe served as chairperson for over a decade. His leadership helped NAPO to establish an office and organizational presence in Detroit and Jackson, Mississippi. As NAPO chair, he organized a campaign against police terror and joined with others to stop the Ku Klux Klan march in 1990. As a member of NAPO, Chokwe led and/or participated in the organization's community youth programs, anti-crime patrols, political education forums, legal service clinics, and various other community service activities. He also participated in political action campaigns against racist institutions, the U.S. bombing of Libya, and many other acts of economic exploitation, racism, and international lawlessness.

Prior to his involvement with NAPO, Chokwe was a cofounder of both the National Black Human Rights Coalition and the Detroit Black Human Rights Coalition. He actively participated in the effort to build a National Human Rights Campaign. On November 5, 1979, Chokwe and two other national leaders presented a statement charging the United States with human rights violations to the president of the UN General Assembly, Salim Ahmed Salim. This presentation was part of a demonstration by 5,000 Black people at the United Nations on Black Solidarity Day.

Our sister Itari recalls traveling with Chokwe many times for the Republic of New Afrika and NAPO work. Itari shares the following memories of her travels with Chokwe:

On one trip to Chicago, she remembers meeting with a group of white activists. "They called themselves the John Brown Anti-Klan Committee. There were also members of the white activist group the Weather Underground there. I accompanied Chokwe and his security to the meeting, where I was supposed to be an observer. We arrived at a white community center. I was sitting where I could see anyone who came near Chokwe or by him, but I did not see anything strange.

The second time I traveled to Chicago was during the New Afrikan People's Organization days. Chokwe was aligned with the Palestine Liberation Organization. I remember Chokwe was flying back and forth from Chicago to Detroit when he was working on the Pontiac 16 case. During that period, his lung collapsed, and I believe it was also around the time of the death of Mayor Harold Washington. They loved him like we loved Coleman Young.

I also accompanied Chokwe once to a protest with the John Brown Anti-Klan Committee. We drove from Detroit to Lexington, Kentucky, to protest the twenty-three-hour lockdown of prisons. If the men refused to work for a couple of dollars a day, they had to stay in their cells. During these lockdowns, the men could only come out of their cells for exercise one hour a day. My son Oronde, my daughter Kenya, nephew Ra-Redding, and I accompanied Sister Rosie Lewis, her family, and Brother Zaribu and his wife, Lavenia. Brother Zaribu, who was forty-one years old, challenged my son to run. He was in such good shape, he beat my seventeen-year-old son Oronde, who was captain of the basketball team. Brothers Kwame Kenyatta and Kamau Daaja Ra were also there. We met at the Malcolm X Center. We were all on the bus, while Chokwe's wife, Nubia, was singing songs about the "Black Child," and it was then I realized Nubia could sing.

The John Brown Anti-Klan Committee came two busloads deep. There were also reporters from Palestine. The Israelis were killing millions of Palestinians at that time. The reporters came in to report their side of what was going on with the Israelis. The only white people who were allowed to come into the Malcolm X Center for the press conference were the white liberal reporters. We had a policy at the Malcolm X Center that white people were not allowed into the center. That policy was enacted because we believed that white people could not be trusted. Malcolm X once said, "Do not let them into your ranks, because they have pretended, and they are actually your adversaries." When we approached the prison in Kentucky, their security angrily told us to leave.

Then, when we went to Marion, Illinois, I became scared to death. The road was very wide, as wide as Woodward Avenue in Detroit. It was a dirt road leading to this prison. There were guards in towers with assault weapons pointing at us. Their security also had tanks riding down the road. I had seen National Guard tanks in the streets of Detroit during the riots, but these tanks were a lot bigger with huge tires. I also remember seeing nasty hogs in the ditches along the road. The guards in the towers got on a speaker and threatened us. They told us to turn around. They started to become more and more aggressive. We were not doing anything, but we did retreat.

Chokwe opened the Malcolm X Community Center for Black Survival on Dexter Avenue in Detroit. This was a center that provided programs for the Republic of New Afrika and the Malcolm X Grassroots Movement (MXGM). I was working there as the receptionist for the center and Chokwe's legal clinic located inside the center. The center eventually housed programs for the youth and outreach for senior citizens and the community, including a food co-op. MXGM staff would find resources to assist the community with numerous issues, including utility shutoffs. Everyone seemed to understand that Chokwe was courageous and meant business; he did not play. He said what he meant, and he meant what he said. He exemplified this sentiment at the center, in the courtroom, and really everywhere he went. He was not afraid of judges, prosecutors, police, or any of his many adversaries.

Once, Minister Louis Farrakhan said when introducing Chokwe, "You can't be a punk to run with Chokwe." That was a very accurate statement. Not only was Chokwe brave, but his comrades, associates, and friends were brave too.

(Left to Right) Chokwe, Milton Henry (Gaidi Obadele), Reparation Ray Jenkins, Hodari Akinyele (back row)

Reparations Struggle

Chokwe was one of the first individuals in the United States to take legal steps regarding "reparations." He worked with Raymond "Reparations Ray" Jenkins, Imari Obadele, Attorney Nkechi Taifa, Congressman John Conyers, and Councilwoman JoAnn Watson of Michigan in founding the National Coalition of Blacks for Reparations in America (N'COBRA) and pursuing reparations for Black people in America. Ray Jenkins, a strong crusader and proponent of reparations, contacted Chokwe, Conyers, and others to bring this issue to the forefront. As a result Conyers introduced Bill HR 3745, to establish a commission to examine the impact of slavery on living African Americans; the bill was ultimately defeated. Chokwe lectured all over the country on college campuses, in churches, and at community forums on "reparations." Massachusetts State Senator Bill Owens actually introduced the first legislation for reparations in the U.S. Our beloved Civil Rights leader Rosa Parks worked at Congressman John Conyers's office on the reparations issue and other issues of liberation for our people. Chokwe and others who were among the first to work on reparations continued the work of Queen Mother Moore and other ancestors who were among the very first people in the United States to take reparations for Black people seriously.

Chokwe, Sen. Bill Owens, Adjoa Aiyetoro, Imari Obaele

Chokwe and Nkechi Taifa (Photo courtesy of Nkechi Taifa)

Chokwe was also a cofounder and a member of the Malcolm X Grassroots Movement. While leading this organization, he and Kwame Kenyatta developed numerous needed programs for Detroiters at the Malcolm X Community Center, which served as a home for MXGM activists working for the betterment of Black people. The center also provided numerous youth programs: New Afrikan Scouts, summer jobs, Students Against a Violent Environment (SAVE) (founded by my son Jeaco Hill, nephew Oronde Taliaferro, and several Mumford High School students), tutoring and creative writing workshops, camping, and cultural and educational forums for all. It also had a free legal clinic, a food co-op, and utility resources for residents with low income. MXGM also hosted speakers to go to various locations to discuss the numerous issues the Black community faced, as well as Kwanzaa and Malcolm X Day Celebrations, accompanied with programs including African Naming Ceremony for KWANZAA directed by Kwame Kenyatta.

Memories of My Revolutionary Brother, Chokwe Lumumba

Chokwe and his partner Adam Shakoor had developed an affidavit that allowed an individual to legally change his or her name. Some of the participants in the naming ceremony would elect to utilize the affidavit. However, some participants would change their name for symbolism only. We also provided poets and African dancers and drummers at these events. Kwame continued organizing MXGM events after Chokwe left the city of Detroit.

Kwame's organizing roots came from his involvement in high school in the Black Student Movement, of which he was a leader, and as a member of the Pan Afrikan Congress (PAC), under the tutelage of Kwame Atta and Mwalimu Ed Vaughn. Kwame began performing nation-building with Chokwe towards the end of Chokwe's work for the Provisional Government of the Republic of New Afrika and the inception of NAPO and MXGM. During this time, Chokwe and Kwame were a dynamic team.

Kwame often provided security for Chokwe, along with my ex-husband, Jeaco, and Kamau Daaja-Ra. One time when Chokwe, Kwame Kenyatta, and Kwame Kalimara went to Battle Creek, Michigan, without the rest of the security team, they were arrested. Attorney Gerald Evelyn, who was providing legal assistance to Chokwe on this case, was also arrested. They were working on a case against a group of activists called the "Coalition to End Police Brutality and Racism." This particular day, there was a hearing on the lead defendant, Larry Guy, who was charged with planting pipe bombs. The racial climate was very contentious and volatile. The judge was racist and wanted to hold both attorneys in contempt. Chokwe called the judge out and the judge retaliated by ordering arrest for all of them. Gerald Evelyn told me the contempt convictions were rescinded later.

Kwame Kenyatta, co-director of Detroit-MXGM and director of the Malcolm X Center, was in leadership of the organization until he went on a hiatus to become involved in the political scene in Detroit. Kwame served more than fifteen years in three elected offices. He was elected to serve on the Detroit Board of Education to implement an African-centered curriculum in 1992 through 1997. He was elected to

Chockwe and the Republic of New Afrika

the Wayne County Commission in 2000. He ended his public service in Detroit as a City Council Member from 2003 through 2005, after it was clear that his power on the council had become useless because of the state takeover. Kwame then moved on to Jackson, Mississippi, to assist his comrade and friend Chokwe Lumumba with his victorious mayoral election, and Kwame served on Mayor Lumumba's administration as a Compliance Officer for the city of Jackson, Mississippi. After Chokwe made his earthly transition, Detroit MXGM began the State of the City Community Conferences where the community gathered to discuss, plan, and become more informed on significant issues. This was a brainchild of mine and Kwame Kenyatta in honor of Chokwe Lumumba.

Chokwe's political and activism growth and development in the Republic of New Afrika inspired and equipped him to organize and fight on many critical issues, including *anti-apartheid*, *human rights*, and *reparations*. His years with the RNA also enabled him to build similar organizations and coalitions, including **NAPO, MXGM, NCOBRA,** and **Human Rights Coalition**. The Republic of New Afrika played an important and perhaps the most significant role in cultivating the Revolutionary Chokwe Lumumba!

(left side): General Rasheed, Shushanna, Brother Jumante, Michael Balogun,
(right side): JoAnn Watson, Aneb Gloria House, Nkechi Taifa,
Brother Jumante's mother, Maynard Henry

Memories of My Revolutionary Brother, Chokwe Lumumba

Watani Tyehimba and
New Afrikan Scouts
(Photo courtesy of
Watani Tyehimba)

(Left to Right) Akinyele Umoja, Tupac
Shakur, Watani Tyehimba, Asinia Tyehimba
(Photo courtesy of Watani Tyeimba)

(Back row) Double K,
Jeaco JC Hill, Kwame Kenyatta

(Left to Right) Chokwe, Kamau
Daja-Ra, Kwame Kenyatta

(Left to Right) Malik Yakini, Kamau
Daaja-Ra, Kwadwo Akpan,
Kwame Kalimara, Chokwe
(Photo courtesy of Malik Yakini)

(Left to Right) Malcolm Lewis, Ikemba
Agulu, Kwasi Akwamu, Jamal Wright,
Akinyele Umoja, Shushanna,
Anemashaun Bomani, Itari,
Khary Frazier, Yusef Shakur (kneeling)

CHAPTER 5

Heartbeats

"Love plus the power of God...plus the people's power equal progress."
– Chokwe Lumumba

Chokwe and family

Chokwe, like all of our brothers, was a handsome, intelligent man. Through the years, he dated some equally beautiful and intelligent women. Most of his teen and adult life he was involved in monogamous relationships, with beautiful love stories behind them. However, there was a time of uncertainty in his personal relationships when he was a "free agent." It seemed that the more popular and public Chokwe became, the more women pursued him. That was manageable when he was single, but when he was in a committed relationship, this created a life-changing dilemma for him.

Even through his struggles with marital fidelity, Chokwe's love for his children ran very deep. His oldest son Kam's battle for his life matured Chokwe. Raising his daughter, Rukia, and his youngest son, Chokwe Antar, helped him evolve into a good father. His wife Nubia was perhaps the strongest force and guide for helping Chokwe become an attentive and involved father and husband in his family. Chokwe's activism and legal work required him to travel extensively and work extremely long days and nights. It must have been difficult to learn how to navigate his life schedule, but he managed. In my mind, Chokwe's love and support for each of his children resulted in the biggest accomplishments in his life.

Chokwe's Loves

Martina

Martina was Chokwe's high school sweetheart. She was different from the other women he loved in many ways. Martina was a tall, melon-complexioned, beautiful young lady with long legs. She was also loving, compassionate, and intelligent.

Growing up in a household with seven brothers and sisters meant that it was difficult to have any privacy. Whenever anyone had "company," they would take them into the living room, and during that visit, the living room was off limits to everyone else—everyone else but me, I concluded. Lucky for me, at 4888 Spokane and 4762 Spokane, the couch in the living room was positioned where I could scoot behind and conceal myself. Boy did I get an earful and an eyeful. It was like being at the drive-in movies. I saw a few kisses and heard some mushy love stuff. I remember once my brother Greg was playing some sad song while breaking up with one of his girlfriends. I didn't like my brother Greg that day because he made the girl cry, and I remember after she left, he played the Contours' song "First I Look at the Purse."

I didn't see or hear any ridiculous stuff coming from Chokwe. He just had nice G-rated (general audience) stuff going on. Everyone loved Chokwe and Martina being a couple, even the parents. I thought they would get married, but that was not in the cards. I guess when they graduated from high school, their lives going in different directions ended their relationship. It's surprising how things turned out. Chokwe went on to be a revolutionary activist, and Martina became a Catholic nun and then left the convent and married a white man.

Anasa

Chokwe and Anasa

When Chokwe married Anasa, his first wife, in the late 1960s or early 1970s, the ceremony was held in a Christian church and people were dressed in African attire, but there were no genuine cultural traditions at the ceremony. Anasa was a beautiful caramel bride with lovely sparkling eyes. Although Chokwe and Anasa's marriage was short-lived and without children, they appeared happy and loving to each other.

Both of them were aspiring young people attending graduate school programs: Chokwe was in law school and Anasa was in medical school.

However, Chokwe's activity in the movement might have contributed to the dissolution of their marriage, as well as the fact that he had a son, Kam, from a relationship outside of their marriage. Although Anasa was quiet, reserved, and somewhat distant, she formed a warm relationship with our parents. Chokwe admired and respected her, not only during their marriage but in later years as well. Chokwe asked me to try to contact Anasa for two significant events in his life, when our mother died and when he was inaugurated mayor of Jackson, Mississippi. I tried but was not able to locate her until shortly after Chokwe died.

Chokwe and Nubia

4 HAIKU FOR NUBIA

telephone wires sang
Her voice over
soft sister laughter.

You held us
with summer stained
smiles of love.

I hold you
breath today..... You sail
home across the ocean.

I see you Nubia
walking your Mississippi Road
God in your hands.

– Sonia Sanchez

Nubia appeared one day with Chokwe, a beautiful, fashionable, spunky young lady. Chokwe introduced the petite, caramel, curly haired sister to us as "Pat." Her name was Patricia Dejesus. Although our family loved her, a couple of us wondered whether she'd fit into his life as a revolutionary; she seemed to be on a different page than Chokwe. When Chokwe heard that Itari and I had been discussing their relationship behind his back, he was not pleased. As it turned out, Nubia adjusted to Chokwe's revolutionary lifestyle and became a revolutionary herself.

Chokwe was smitten by Nubia and she by him. She was a flight attendant for Northwest Airlines; she and Chokwe met when he was a passenger on the airline. Nubia said when she waited on Chokwe for the first time, "I looked over and saw him...that tall drink of water." The rest was history. They dated and eventually married.

In 1978, Chokwe decided to participate with the Pontiac 16 legal defense team.[31] His work with this case resulted in many life-changing situations for himself, his family, and his law partners. The trial was lengthy, and he had to relocate the family to Chicago. The move appeared to provide some real benefits for Chokwe and Nubia's relationship. Although they were a couple and living together prior to leaving for Chicago, it was there they decided to marry. Several members of our family went to Chicago to participate in the ceremony, as well as a couple of Nubia's family members from Washington, D.C., and several of Chokwe's friends and comrades from Detroit. King Sundiata Keita officiated over the African marriage ceremony. It

---

[31]See chapter 6 for the details of the Pontiac 16 case.

was a beautiful occasion, much different than Chokwe's first African wedding.

Chokwe and Nubia's ceremony was cultural, from the African garments to the exhilarating and rhythmic, entertaining African dancers and drummers to the rituals. First, a member from each family had to give permission for the couple to marry, only after the bride and groom expressed why they should be married. Greg served as our family member to give permission for Chokwe to marry, even though he was Chokwe's younger brother. Nubia's handsome nephew gave his permission for Nubia to marry. The next ritual involved the participation of the bridal party. The bridesmaids had to taste goat's milk (symbolizing fertility in the marriage), cayenne pepper, and several other items to bless the wedding. The drummers, dancers, King Sundiata's remarks, and the happy, celebratory spirit of the attendees symbolized a successful marriage. Nubia was officially welcomed into our family and Chokwe into hers. Through their union, they were blessed with two children: their beautiful daughter, Rukia Kai, and handsome son, Chokwe Antar.

King Sundiata Keita performed cultrual wedding for Chokwe and Nubia Lumumba, also pictured is Rukia Lumumba, Greg Taliaferro and Jeffrey Edison

Nubia was inspirational and supportive. My family lived upstairs from Chokwe and Nubia and their family, so we saw each other a lot and spent a good deal of time talking. Unfortunately, after Chokwe and Nubia were featured in *Essence* magazine, Nubia and I had a falling out. Although our family was initially excited that they would be featured in a magazine, this soon turned to dismay when we realized the article highlighted Chokwe's infidelity and the shortcomings in their marriage, primarily Chokwe. In addition, Nubia stated in the article that she had learned about one of his affairs from one of her sisters-in-law; she was referring to me, as I had mentioned a woman I'd met at law school who had offered to babysit my baby for me, not realizing she was involved with Chokwe. Apparently, Nubia had figured it all out but did not share it with me. I was angry with Chokwe for what he had done to Nubia. Even though Chokwe was my brother, I felt pain for Nubia. She was angry with me for expressing my dismay that they would reveal the shortcomings of their marriage in such a public way and place all the blame on Chokwe.

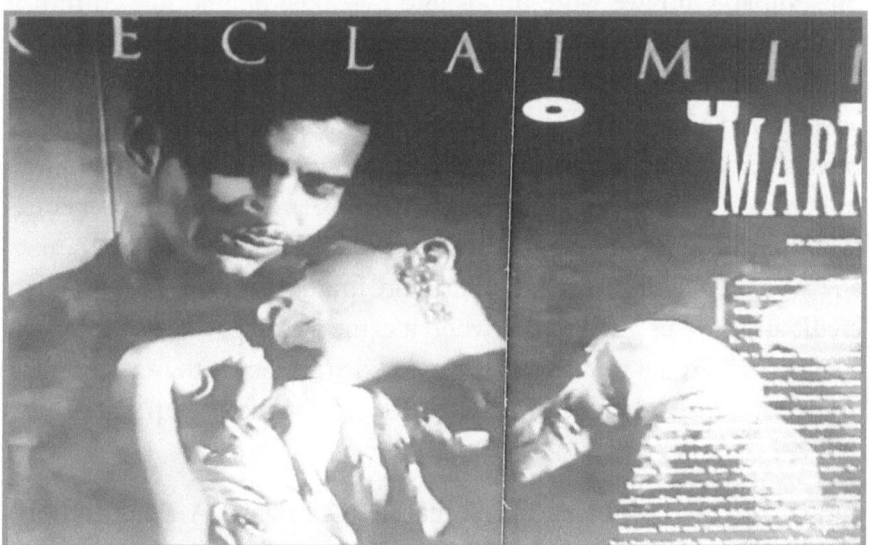

Chokwe and Nubia in Essence interview

Chokwe and Nubia were a united front, however. Chokwe said to me, "Nubia and I chose to share our personal issues with other Black couples with hopes they can get something from our mistakes. The article was not about our marital problems in general, but it's about infidelity, and I'm the one guilty of that. Unless you know about Nubia committing infidelity in the marriage, then you should not have any issues with what she did." Unfortunately, I still did not see things the way Chokwe saw them. Nubia and I, then, became distant from each other for several months.

Chokwe and Nubia separated for a time; it crushed Chokwe that Nubia asked him to leave their home, but he did so until they eventually reconciled. When they reunited, Chokwe became more family oriented, helping out a great deal more in terms of caring for the children when Nubia was away on her work trips with the airlines.

Nubia was like a big sister and friend to me. She was wise where I was not, and I often sought advice from her on finances, clothing styles, and just life in general. Nubia was smart, fashionable, savvy, and I enjoyed her company a lot. She taught Chokwe how to dress: pre-Nubia, Chokwe wore floods and dashikis; Nubia dressed him in handsome suits. She never just criticized for the sake of criticizing. She used to help other Black women who designed, made, and sold clothing, jewelry, and accessories. Nubia would sell their merchandise during her travels throughout the world. She and Itari would often barter and sell merchandise for these African and African American entrepreneurs.[32] Another thing I admired greatly about Nubia was how well organized she was personally, professionally, and financially. She had excellent credit and gave us good advice when it came to things like home buying. She convinced me to move to the east side of Detroit to buy a home as an investment and helped my husband and me every step of the way.

---

[32]Itari managed Mahamadou Sumareh's Authentic African Imports, Djenne Beads & Arts, and before that Itari worked at Nezza Tashary Bandele's African imports shop called Alkebulan Art.

Nubia was a hardworking mother and wife. She put many tireless hours into raising her children with discipline and love, supporting her husband's work while creating a home whether it was in Detroit, New York, or Mississippi. She did that always. You could not help but admire Nubia. She was abrasively truthful and honest, but everything was said out of love not hate. Nubia loved our family and was an integral part of it. When we gave our parents a surprise fiftieth anniversary party, it was Nubia who worked along with me and our niece DeLisa to make that phenomenal occasion happen. Nubia also helped prepare food for many family occasions and community events. Nubia and I were a team; I depended and relied on her often. I certainly missed her during our separation.

Nubia and I were able to reconcile in 2001. Things often occur in mysterious ways. Like the Bible says in John 11:32-37, "God does not always come when you call him, but when he comes, he is right on time." Subsequent to my and Nubia's falling out, Chokwe was invited to speak in Detroit at a National Black United Front event. One of the event organizers asked me to introduce Chokwe. As I took the stand and looked at my brother, I made one or two remarks about his dedication and work for the community. Then, I looked over at Nubia, and I dedicated almost the entire introduction to her:

I have seen my brother courageously go up against the Supreme Court, white racist police, and I know of him going up against the Ku Klux Klan, but I have never seen any fear in him dealing with those situations. However, the only time I saw fear in him in my life is when he thought he was going to lose his wife and family. You see Chokwe can do great things, but not by himself. The old adage is the woman behind the man makes him great, but in Chokwe's case, it's the woman beside the man who makes him great. I want to thank my sister-in-law Nubia for helping to make my brother great.

Chokwe and Nubia looked at me with love on their faces; that little speech brought me and my sister-friend back together again.

Gloria

Several years after Nubia died, our family learned that Chokwe had a girlfriend. We had heard rumors about this, but Chokwe never confirmed it. However, one day in 2012, he mentioned her name to me and later gave me her phone number "in case," he said, "you need to reach her if something comes up." This was surprising and a bit confusing. I eventually met Gloria, a beautiful caramel sister with a friendly disposition, when our mother died, prior to her funeral. Gloria offered to help our family in any way she could; her kindness and generosity touched my heart. About eight months later, when Chokwe ran for mayor, I went to Jackson to help him with the campaign. Gloria and I became better acquainted then, and it was apparent to me how much she loved my brother and he loved her, too.

Chokwe and Gloria

Several months later, at Chokwe's funeral, Gloria's name was not mentioned. Toward the end of the service, I told my niece Rukia and nephew Chokwe that it wasn't right that Gloria wasn't mentioned. They encouraged me to say something; I went up to the pulpit and whispered in the pastor's ear, asking him to allow me to say a few words. And I did:

Chokwe was such a great man and loved so many people and so many people loved him. When Nubia left, it was God that called her home. It was not because of anything that Chokwe and Nubia did, and the love still remained with Chokwe so strong. But Chokwe was a man and Chokwe lived on. There was a really special person to Chokwe who took his hand and walked by his side and helped this man along. That person is Gloria, and I would like to say to Gloria thank you for loving my brother and being there for him.

Chokwe's Children

Kambontope Lumumba

Chokwe and son Kam
(Photo courtesy of Asinia Tyehimba)

Chokwe's first child, Kam, as we call him, was born in 1971 prior to his marriage with Nubia, but Nubia helped care for Kam when he lived with them. Although Kam's mother, Chris, had custody of Kam, Chokwe cared for Kam financially and physically. Chokwe's love for his first child was unwavering.

Kam is funny, smart, and very people oriented. He went through a rebellious period with his father. He would often do childish things to get Chokwe's attention or act out over his resentment for his living situation (having to live in two separate houses). He wanted his parents to be together. One time, Kam took Chokwe's wallet and passed out ten- and twenty-dollar bills to kids in the neighborhood.

One of the parents discovered Kam's generous deeds and brought it to Chokwe's attention.

That was a rough time, and things got worse when Kam became a teenager. He lived with his mother for a great deal of that time, and he unfortunately got involved in the street life. At some point, Chokwe brought Kam to Jackson to get him away from the street life in Detroit. Many other families had that same idea; however, the street life was already thriving in Jackson. One horrible evening, Kam was shot in the head while sitting in a car with another individual. Kam survived, but he remains paralyzed.

I remember having an in-depth conversation with Kam about what had happened to him and what had happened to my son, Jeaco, who was also shot in the head but did not survive. Kam helped me move forward just in that one conversation, which occurred about ten years after my son's death. Kam allowed me to express all my rage and sorrow about my son's murder, about the people who were involved in his murder, and the police and prosecutor who refused to hold the murderers responsible. Kam told me that those responsible for his shooting had never been caught either and that he wasn't angry: "My God is a mighty God, and I thank him and my Grammy for my life." He said he was thankful to the person who had shot him for changing his life: "I want to tell him he slowed me down. He changed the course and direction my life was going." Kam was only twenty years old when he had been shot and paralyzed. Today, he is a beautiful spark of inspiration for everyone he comes into contact with. He makes each person feel as if they are the only person in his life. He has a positive, radiating spirituality. He lives with our nephew Mark and his family and is well cared for.

Chokwe once said about Kam, "I am happy to have been able to move my oldest son, Kambontope, out to Mississippi to watch him mature and develop." Chokwe was right because, even according to Kam, Mississippi is where he grew into his manhood. At an event in

Detroit that Kam attended, Chokwe said, "Kam is one of my heroes. Yes, Kam is my hero."

And Kam said of his father in a poem:

There is no doubt that my Dad
was a king of a man

He conquered his goals
And he made history

My Dad was a very strong
and good man

There will never be
another one like him

He loved
His People,

and he definitely
laid out a blueprint
for the People

to Free the Land
by any means necessary

My Dad, Chokwe Lumumba
did this!

Rukia

Chokwe and daughter Rukia

When Rukia was born in 1978, I was living upstairs from Chokwe and Nubia with my husband and children. When I went downstairs to see the new baby, I witnessed a beautiful sight. Short, petite Nubia was standing over tall and lean Chokwe as he sat on the bed with their beautiful, tiny baby girl. They both had heavenly expressions on their faces. That precious baby girl was the size of a football in Chokwe's hands. Nubia adjusted to motherhood easily; she was a natural mother.

Rukia was a sweet and loving child growing up. She was always agreeable and got along well with her multitude of cousins. In Detroit, she had twenty-four first cousins whom she saw on a regular basis through family gatherings and cultural events. Even when their family began to relocate to Chicago, New York, and Jackson, Rukia continued to visit her cousins.

As Rukia grew up, she became involved in many activities inside and outside of school, including the Malcolm X Grassroots Movement (MXGM). When Rukia was at Tougaloo College, she was very active with organizing events there. Like her father, she seemed to be involved in educating people about injustices and oppression. She organized events for Freedom Fighters to visit Tugaloo, like Geronimo Ji-Jaga Pratt. Apparently, her fellow students and the school thought highly of Rukia, too. One year, she was chosen as Ms. Tugaloo. She also studied abroad in South Africa. After college, Rukia moved on to Howard University Law School. It was clear that she was walking in her father's footsteps.

Rukia was the big cousin to the younger cousins in Detroit. One year, she collected all of the kids between the ages of nine and twelve, rented a fifteen-passenger van, and drove them from Detroit to Alabama to Camp Pumziko, MXGM's summer camp. When they arrived, they were in for a culture shock, especially the girls. Camp Pumziko was a real naturalistic experience: the campers stayed in the woods on campgrounds and had to catch their food and cook it.

Years later, after several of her older cousins began to have children, Rukia had a beautiful caramel baby son whom she and his father, Chaka, named Qadir. He reminded us of his grandfather Chokwe. He was quiet and content playing solo.

Rukia is her father's daughter. She has become an activist, organizer, and leader in her own right. She is the executive director at People's Advocacy Institute and serves on the Electoral Justice Project of the Movement for Black Lives Matter, fighting unjust incarceration and prison conditions, among numerous other activities.

Chokwe Antar

Chokwe Antar was born in 1983. It seemed when we had children in our family, there would be a group of girls, then a group of boys, then a group of girls again. However, Midda, as we called him, was just one of a few boys born following a group of girls, and he was the only boy his age. So, while he was still in Detroit, his parents had to be innovative with activities for him. That wasn't for too long because they moved from Detroit to Jackson, Mississippi, when Antar was five years old. In Jackson, he was able to acclimate to groups of boys in school and in the neighborhood and to MXGM/NAPO children from Atlanta and southern chapters that would organize many activities for the children.

Chokwe and son Chokwe Antar and daughter Rukia

When Midda was in his teens, Chokwe sponsored an AAU basketball team, the Jackson Panthers. Midda was one of the players on the team. Chokwe brought his Jackson Panthers to Detroit to play in AAU tournaments, so our family was able to spend time with him as well as see him play basketball. He had become quite a handsome young man. He was very smart and respectable and able to talk with adults easily. Chokwe Antar and his teammates seemed to have good relationships, and they got along well with others. Midda and Chokwe told me later that a couple of the young men on the team went on to play professional basketball and overseas basketball, including Maurice Williams of the Cavaliers.

After Nubia died, Chokwe and Chokwe Antar grew even closer. Whenever they visited Detroit, it seemed as if they were inseparable. My most memorable time of Midda and his father was during the worst time in my life, at my son Jeaco's funeral; just like no one really prepares you for motherhood, certainly no one prepares you for the death of your child. There is not a class or book that can prepare you. When my first born and only son Jeaco was murdered, I didn't have a clue of what to do, but I just did. My daughters and husband were there to help as much as possible, but they were enduring a lot of grief, which limited their help. Our father was already gone, and our mother had Alzheimer's. Mainly, our niece DeLisa, who had worked with me in making final arrangements for others in the family, took care of a lot of the arrangements. However, the day of my son's funeral of course was the most difficult for me. When I was walking from the family car into the church, I did not have a clue of what I would do or say to people. When I looked up inside the church, the first thing I noticed was my big brother Chokwe and his son, Chokwe Antar, standing there welcoming people and shaking their hands. So it then was a no-brainer for me. I just stood beside them with a smile on my face, welcoming people and shaking their hands.

When Chokwe died during the seventh month of his mayoral term (he was sworn into office on July 1, 2013, and died on February 25, 2014), Chokwe Antar wanted to know what his uncles and aunts would think if he ran for his father's mayoral seat to complete the term. There was not much time to consider the move because the seat had to be filled in a special election within two months of Chokwe's death. Each of his uncles and aunts gave their blessing, thinking it would be the right thing to do for the people of Jackson and Chokwe's legacy. However, our oldest brother Reggie expressed some reservations. Although he agreed with the rest of the family that the reasons for Antar's run were good ones, he pointed out a couple of concerns, particularly the fact that Chokwe Antar and his wife, Ebony, had recently been married and were expecting their first child. In addition, Chokwe Antar would be dealing with the loss of his father. Chokwe Antar did run, and the family rallied around him just like they did when his father had run for his mayoral seat. With the help of Chokwe's close attorney friends in Detroit, Gerald Evelyn and Adam Shakoor, we organized van loads of people to journey to Jackson, Mississippi, to canvas for the campaign. Family friend Attorney John Royal, president of the National Lawyers Guild (NLG), was also able to assist with procuring funds from NLG attorneys to take a bus full of campaign volunteers to Jackson to campaign for Chokwe Antar.

Unfortunately, Chokwe Antar lost the election to fill his father's seat, but three years later when his father's term was over, time allowed him to adjust to his new family life and deal with the loss of his father. When Chokwe Antar ran the second time for mayor, Rukia became his campaign manager, and there was more time to prepare and fundraise for his campaign in both Jackson and Detroit. After a hard-fought campaign, Chokwe Antar became Mayor Chokwe Antar Lumumba. We are so proud of him and his sister Rukia.

CHAPTER 6
Devoted Defender of the People

*"Special change comes when you get the right
people, at the right place, at the right time.
We are the right people.
We have earned the right to change.
We have suffered from the past.
We have learned from the present.
We are ready for the future.
We are the right People."*
– Chokwe Lumumba

Chokwe expressed on numerous occasions that he wanted to be the attorney that Malcolm X could not be. During his legal career, he accomplished this goal. He became the revolutionary attorney who worked for the people to fight against oppression, false incarceration, and injustices. Like Malcolm X, Chokwe worked to promote the people's aspirations and goals.

Chokwe worked on thousands of cases during his lengthy career, both as a deputy defender and in his private law practice. Some were more memorable than others, but they were all important to him. Most cases were resolved in dismissals before trial or negotiated pleas or sentence bargains. Chokwe began his legal career under the supervision of Attorney Myzell Sowell, former director of the Legal Defender's Office on Gratiot in Detroit. Chokwe represented his indigent pro bono clients as if they had paid the big bucks. When Chokwe was assigned a case the Recorder's Court, judges knew they were in for a long haul. Chokwe tried each case like it was the most important case.

Chokwe eventually gained the respect of most of the judges. Even the ones who disliked him had to admit they respected him. Also, even the judges who held Chokwe in contempt appreciated his dedication and integrity. However, judges all over the country understood that Attorney Chokwe Lumumba did not hold back.

On several occasions, Chokwe told a judge politely but directly, "Your honor, I motion for you to recuse yourself off this case."

"On what basis?" the judge would ask.

"On the basis that you are a racist, sir, and you are unable to preside over this trial fairly or impartially."

The Wayne County Prosecutor's Office would gear up for a "Chokwe Lumumba case," so much so his cases would generally be the talk of the office. Some of the prosecutors feared him, some disliked him, but almost all of them knew and understood Chokwe Lumumba was no one to mess around with. He was a good advocate and, more often than not, a winning advocate. Chokwe won over 80% of thousands of his legal cases he handled during his early twenty-one-year history as a lawyer in Detroit. Prior to leaving for Mississippi, Chokwe won complete acquittals for 180 out of 200 cases in Michigan. He practiced law in many courts and many states, as a member of the state bar or on a pro hac vice basis. He even practiced outside of the United States (see Appendix 1).

Devoted Defender of the People

After beginning his law career at the Public Defender's Office, he opened his law firm with his partners, Earl Ashford and James Cannon. The law firm expanded several times to include the following attorneys: Jeffrey L. Edison, Adam Shakoor, Harry Davis, Ernest Jarrett, and Naomi Ottison, with Juanita Christian and Norma Dotson as associates. Chokwe was also an active member of the National Conference of Black Lawyers and a senior attorney of Lumumba and Associates in Jackson, Mississippi, and Counsel to the firm of Curtis and Edison in Detroit, Michigan.

Chokwe the Dedicated Lawyer

While Chokwe was in private practice in Detroit during the late 1970s through the early 1980s, he worked briefly on the case of Assata Shakur, a member of the Black Liberation Army who was convicted for killing a state trooper on the New Jersey Turnpike in 1977. She escaped from prison in 1979. He also represented Geronimo Pratt, a Black Panther wrongly imprisoned for murder. Both cases are discussed later in this chapter.[33] During the 1980s, there was a marked increase in the number of imprisoned African Americans in the United States, due in part to mandatory sentencing guidelines. Chokwe became interested in organizing to demand reparations for the damage done to the generations of African American slaves, which he believed had contributed to contemporary problems of Blacks in the United States. In September 1987, Chokwe addressed a conference sponsored by the National Conference of Black Lawyers at Harvard Law School. At that time, he was a cofounder of the newly formed National Coalition of Blacks for Reparations in America. He discussed the constitutional neglect of the needs of enslaved persons.[34]

I cannot count the times I saw Chokwe sitting at his office desk pondering and calculating while writing—whether drafting an

---

[33]https://mississippiencyclopedia.org/staff/colbeck-chris/.
[34]en.wikipedia.org/wiki/Chokwe_Lumumba

appeals brief to the higher court with objections of the injustices that occurred at the lower court level, a motion to set aside a defendant's case, an opening argument he would soon deliver that would set the tone for the trial, or a closing argument that he had to deliver like it was his last one, as he knew each closing argument he delivered would oftentimes mean the difference between his client either walking out the courtroom to their family or spending the remainder of their life incarcerated. Chokwe actually poured his brain, heart, and soul into his work. He treated his clients with respect and fought vehemently for acquittal on each of their cases. He treated them equally; pro bono, assigned, and paying clients all received the same consideration and defense from Chokwe. I believe he treated each of his clients like "movement figures...political prisoners." He believed each client's vindication and acquittal were critical for them to return to their families. Just as he believed Mutulu Shakur's acquittal was critical for him to return not just to his family but to the movement.

Did he ever represent a client that he knew with certainty was guilty? Did he ever defend a person who broke the law? I don't know the answers to those questions, but I do know the Sixth Amendment of the U.S. Constitution affords every citizen a right to counsel in a criminal proceeding. I also know Chokwe understood the hypocrisy of the law as much as he respected the intent, rationale, and reasoning for most laws he was sworn to uphold. It was amazing to see Attorney Chokwe Lumumba at work in his office, sitting tall in his black leather chair, deep in thought, flicking his mustache. He had a way of tinkering with his mustache; that's when I knew he was really deep in thought. He would sit in that chair building his arsenal of words, preparing for a legal battle in the courtroom. He would sometimes sit in that black leather chair for twelve out of twenty-four hours, from 5:00 p.m. to 5:00 a.m., preparing a defense for his clients.

I witnessed this on numerous occasions as his secretary. I often assisted him, and I remember one such occasion in November of 1980 when this happened. This particular memory stays with me because I was seven months pregnant with my third child, Little Shushanna. Chokwe was working on a brief appeal for the Michigan Supreme Court. He wrote on his yellow legal paper and then after completing two or three pages, he would hand it over to me, and I would type the pages. This went on until approximately 5:00 a.m. Each hour, I thought he would stop, but he just kept going, going, and going. We did have some food delivered, but even then, he continued to write. At one point, as I was waiting for him to pass on some more pages for typing, I became very restless and began talking. I did that a lot. I talked about all kinds of things: my children, our parents, our siblings, political issues, and my then-husband and some issues we were having. The entire time, he was writing and I was talking. In times like these, he displayed his photographic memory. Although it seemed like it would be impossible for him to have heard what I was saying, he did in fact hear every word of it. Whatever issues and problems I brought up in that one-sided conversation in his office that night, days later he commented on each one of them and suggested some resolutions. As remarkable as he was at work in his office, he was more amazing in the courtroom. It was like seeing an award-winning film. As the firm filing clerk, as well as secretary, I often would stop by the courtroom where Chokwe had cases. Whenever the opportunity arose, I sat in on his trials. There was one time when I was filing papers at the courts in the City County Building when I decided to drop by the courtroom where Chokwe was appearing on the Hayward Brown case.

Hayward Brown

The media describes Hayward Brown as a "radical black activist who assaults police officers." The community described Brother Brown as a "soldier protecting his community." Yet the streets would describe Hayward as a "raider, robbing drug houses for his own benefit." In Detroit in the 1970s, Hayward was part of a trio: the other two were Mark Bethune and John Percy Boyd. Police Chief Nichols dubbed them "Mad Dog Cop Killers." Many said at the time that they were self-acclaimed vigilantes protecting the community from the ruthless, racist, destructive actions of Stop The Robberies and Enjoy Safe Streets (STRESS). This controversial police tactical unit was created to stop crime before it occurred in the city of Detroit. The dynamic attorney Kenneth Cockrel initially represented Hayward Brown when he was arrested subsequent to his capture by Detroit Police. Hayward was captured in the aftermath of one of the largest manhunts by the Detroit Police in history. Unfortunately, Bethune and Boyd were killed in a shootout with the police at Clark College in Atlanta, where they had fled. Chokwe inherited Hayward Brown's cases in 1997 when Kenneth Cockrel became the youngest person to become a Detroit City Council member.

Our brother Greg, an associate of many street people at the time, cautioned Chokwe about Hayward Brown. Greg's sources had advised him that Hayward was into the drug life in the streets. Chokwe defended Brown on charges of possession of a concealed weapon in the virtually all-white suburb of Dearborn, Michigan. When a jury of nine Blacks and three whites could not reach a verdict, Lumumba declared, "The Wayne County prosecutor has chased Haywood Brown relentlessly from jury to jury, from judge to judge, and from court to court with trumped-up charges. Not only are his human rights being violated, ours are likewise. They are using our tax dollars in their endeavor to silence another freedom fighter."[35]

On my way to the courtroom located in the City County Building, I filed into the elevator with several other people. Oddly, there was a small couch on the elevator. Two white men standing near the couch were engaged in a conversation. Right before I exited the elevator to

---

[35]KeyWiki Contributors, "Chokwe Lumumba" *KeyWiki,* https://keywiki.org/Chokwe_Lumumba#Hayward_Brown_case (accessed April 15, 2025).

take care of my filing, I heard one of the two smiling men say, "Wait until he gets a load of this!"

The other replied gleefully, "I can't wait to see his face."

I proceeded to exit the elevator and went on to the Clerk's Office, Probate Court, and the Register of Deeds Office. I had to file in various places because I did the filing for most of the attorneys at the firm. After I finished in the City County Building, before going to the other buildings where I had to file documents, I decided to visit Chokwe, who was in trial in one of the courtrooms. I went to the courtroom where Chokwe was representing Hayward Brown. I arrived during a recess and people were up and walking around the courtroom. I spotted Chokwe and went up to him and asked, "How is the case going?"

He responded, "Okay."

I chatted with him for a minute and then proceeded to leave the courtroom because I had more filing to take care of at Recorder's Court and 36th District Court. Chokwe said they were on a thirty-minute recess. I figured I didn't have the time to court watch and get all my filing done.

On the way out the door I noticed a lean, white man in a gray suit with red cheeks. Something clicked in my mind. I didn't get what, but I went back up to the front of the courtroom and I asked Chokwe, "Does this case have anything to do with a couch?"

He answered, "No."

As I began to walk away, I said, "Okay I'll see you back at the law office."

"Shushanna wait, why did you ask me that?" he said.

"Well, I was on the elevator and these two white guys had what looked like a small couch or loveseat on the elevator."

"Really? Could it have been a car seat?"

"Yep, it could have been." I also repeated to him what I heard the white guys say on the elevator.

He smiled and said thanks. "I'll see you back at the office."

He informed me later that the prosecutors had brought in the car seat to use as an exhibit to demonstrate how they believed Hayward Brown had concealed a gun. I don't know if the information I gave him helped him win the case or not, but he did win, and the prosecutor's surprise was definitely foiled by little old me. However, the next round with the prosecutors didn't go well for me.

On another filing trip, I went to the twelfth floor of Recorder's Court to the Prosecutor's Office to file a motion for adjournment on the Hayward Brown case. The usual procedure was to go to the reception desk in the Prosecutor's Office and drop the motion off. I just had to deliver it, and the receptionist would stamp my copy, signifying that it had been delivered. This time, she got on the phone, and a white man came out of the back and asked me to step behind the reception area.

He asked me, "Are you an attorney?" Then looking at my brown brief folder, he asked me if I was a law student.

I don't know why he was asking these questions, but I answered them, "No."

Then he directed me to follow him and one other white man out of the office and onto the elevator.

They proceeded to ask me, "Why are you delivering the motion and not Attorney Lumumba?"

"Attorney Lumumba is in trial in another case."

Then they proceeded to talk in a demeaning way about Chokwe. The taller one in the blue suit said, "Lumumba is a coward. He got you doing his dirty work."

The shorter one in the brown suit with the ugly tie laughed and said, "He would not have the guts to come down here with this" (slapping the motion that I was attempting to file in his hand).

I just listened and did not respond, but I did not like it one little bit. How dare they talk about someone whom I admired very much? How dare they talk about my brother that way? How dare they attempt to humiliate and disrespect me? But I had learned long before that it was best not to reveal my relationship with Chokwe in certain venues. It was more helpful to him. I did, however, finally ask, "Where are we going? And why didn't the receptionist stamp my copy?"

"We are going to see the judge," said Tall Blue Suit. "It will take more than a stamp receipt for this motion."

I was confused and thought perhaps there was something I should know to do but didn't. I recall the first day Chokwe trained me to file in the courts. He took me to various courts like Recorder's, Circuit, and 36th District and showed me the filing procedure, and then he cut me loose the next day. His law partners also took their turn taking me into the courts. Mostly everything was on-the-job training. At the time, I had not had one day of law school or study of the law, and this situation made me very uncomfortable.

We finally arrived at the courtroom of the judge. The court bailiff announced the judge and everyone stood. "Court is in session," he said.

Then, Brown Suit Ugly Tie told the judge that "Attorney Lumumba has failed to appear for this court hearing and the state moves that his motion for adjournment be denied." He then followed up and said, "Ms. Bernadette Hill is representing Attorney Lumumba today."

I was flabbergasted. The judge then instructed me to come forward and be sworn in. "Young lady, what is your name?"

Nervous and frightened, I came forward and responded, "Sir, my name is Bernadette Hill, but I am not representing Attorney Lumumba, I am not an attorney, I am not even a law student. I just came down to file these papers for Mr. Lumumba and the prosecutors brought me in here."

The courtroom audience broke out in laughter.

I must have sounded like a scared little girl rambling off my response to the judge.

He said, "Ms. Hill, the court is not trying to hold you liable for representing Mr. Lumumba, but you can tell Mr. Lumumba his motion is denied."

I couldn't wait to get out of there and go back and tell Chokwe what they had done. Also, I think something in me that day decided that I would never be so vulnerable again. Although it was four years later when I decided to practice law, I think it was that day that I conceived the thought of becoming a lawyer but pushed it to my subconscious. It was so unfair what they did in that courtroom. That was not justice. Chokwe told me later he went back to the judge and got the decision reversed. No harm, no foul; but he said no one in the prosecutor's office would own up to their actions. Chokwe ultimately won that case for Hayward Brown, too!

My interactions with Hayward were all positive. Both Hayward and his mother reminded me of my family. His mom was a caramel-complexioned, chubby woman with a round, lovable face. Hayward had the same lovable face and soft demeanor. Looking at his stocky stature and lovable face and feeling his softness, I could not imagine that he was guilty of the cop's allegations. But then, there were the street's allegations. Was it possible that he had joined ranks with Boyd and Bethune to become vigilantes against the STRESS cops for the people?

I saw Hayward occasionally in the courtroom or at Chokwe's office. One particular day, Hayward walked into the office and came up to the receptionist desk where I was sitting. As usual, he was polite and friendly.

"Hayward, Chokwe is in a meeting, but it won't be too long."

He responded, "That's okay, I have nothing but time (smiling). How are things going for you?"

It was then that I noticed a long, ugly, discolored wound on his neck. "Oh my God, Hayward what happened to your neck?"

He responded, "The Pigs tried to kill me."

"What? That's awful!"

"Yep, they keep trying," he said. "They tried to kill me on some train tracks, too."

Oh my God, I thought, *they are still hanging us!* I had never heard of that happening in that time period (1970s). Unfortunately, what happened to Hayward in jail was not so rare, and Chokwe went on over the years to work on several jail house hangings. Tragically, those young men did not survive as Hayward did, for the moment, anyway.

I didn't know how to respond to Hayward at that awkward moment. Thank God Chokwe called for Hayward to come into his office. Chokwe told me later that Hayward was found hanging in jail. The police claimed he tried to commit suicide. I believe that Chokwe, and Kenneth Cockrel before him, believed Hayward over the police.

Attorney Kenneth Cockrel

Kenny Cockrel was a community activist with a Marxist-Leninist philosophy. He was a yellow melon–complexioned, tall, lean, handsome brother with arrogance, intelligence, and courage. He talked like a speed speech debater, and he walked like an African warrior. He had earned widespread popularity and respect in the movement and the courtroom. The community held him in high esteem. He later became a city councilman and remained on the council until his death at the age of fifty. I loved this man's swag. I remember observing him in the courtroom once. With all the court cases and attorneys I have observed in the courtroom, and there are many, I had never experienced one like Kenneth Cockrel. Where Chokwe, Cornelius Pitts, Milton Henry, and Elbert Hatchett all were among the giants in court, Kenny presented a style that was undeniably unique.

During one particular case, I watched the white, dark-haired, slender, Saks Fifth Avenue suit female prosecutor along with her white, male, black suit co-counsel battle Attorney Cockrel in the courtroom. It was not much of a battle. It was what in the boxing world would be called a TKO. The female prosecutor presented a long laborious closing argument, while Cockrel sat silently with his long lanky legs crossed. She vehemently went on and on about why the defendant should be found guilty, and Kenny continued to sit, but he swiveled in his chair and rolled his eyes repeatedly without saying a word. After she finally finished what seemed like hours, it was the defense's turn to render their closing.

Attorney Cockrel stood up and in minutes in his rapid speaking voice walked over to the jury and succinctly, chronologically, and emphatically disputed everything she had said. It was as though he cut up everything that came out of her mouth during her perhaps thirty- to forty-minute closing in less than ten minutes. What I saw was remarkable! Next, the white, black suit male came back with the rebuttal for the prosecutor's side. He was not as lengthy as the female, but neither was Kenny. From a lay perspective, the jurors did not appear impressed with black suit male's rebuttal. It appeared to me that Kenny had inflicted a devastating blow during his closing, where the closing and rebuttal arguments from the prosecution could not recover.

Cockrel represented the majority of political grassroots cases prior to Chokwe Lumumba. Kenny was active in politics and left-wing progressive movements. He cofounded the League of Revolutionary Black Workers and the Labor Defense Coalition. He helped found the law firm Philo, Maki, Ravitz, Pitts, Moore, Cockrel & Robb, which specialized in representing individuals and organizations brutalized by social and political injustices. He gained nationwide acclaim when his coalition brought down the powerful STRESS unit. He was a brilliant advocate for the common man, helping to expose and demolish racial and social injustices wherever they would raise their ugly head, thus uprooting and changing the entire criminal justice system in Detroit. He was extremely popular with the citizens of Detroit, and he was expected to run and be elected as mayor after Mayor Coleman Young, but his life was cut short too soon when he died suddenly after suffering a massive heart attack at age 50. Perhaps Chokwe was inspired by legendary attorney Kenneth Cockrel to call judges out in some of his court cases because that is exactly what he did on numerous occasions. In a Mississippi case, Chokwe told Judge Marcus Gordon he had the temperament of a barbarian and that he was operating a "kangaroo court." In New York on the Brink's expropriation case, Chokwe told the judge to recuse himself from the case due to his racism.

Kenneth Cockrel was certainly an inspiration to Chokwe Lumumba and paved the way for him in the courtroom and his community work. I, too, admired Kenny. Attorney Cockrel and Chokwe both successfully represented Hayward Brown and defendants connected to STRESS cases.

After Hayward Brown was hanged in jail and survived the hanging, Chokwe went on to work on numerous jail house hangings that many in the movement coined "jailhouse lynchings." At one point in Chokwe's legal career, he and others were investigating forty-nine similar cases. One of these was the murder of Andre Jones.

Andre Jones

I recall seeing an episode of *Unsolved Mysteries* that, at the time, I had no idea Chokwe was involved in. When Andre Jones was murdered, Chokwe was living in Mississippi, and I no longer had the familiarity with all of Chokwe's law cases that I had when he was in Detroit and I was working with him. He, however, would keep me abreast of cases in which he needed my assistance. The show did not mention Chokwe at all. After Chokwe's initial work on the case, Minister Louis Farrakhan's lawyers took over. I recall from watching the episode that this was a horrific situation. One night, Andre, an

18-year-old young man, and his girlfriend were stopped by police at a sobriety checkpoint and Andre was arrested and hit with a slew of charges: driving a vehicle whose identification numbers had been altered, driving with false plates, driving with an open container of alcohol, and possession of a .38-caliber gun that police claimed Andre threw out the window prior to stopping. Andre was driving a vehicle of his friends that was later to be found stolen.

However, Andre's girlfriend Tanisha Love provides an account that is quite different from the police report. According to Love, Andre did not throw anything out of the vehicle, and the police immediately shackled and handcuffed Andre after he told them he didn't have his license. At about 2:00 a.m., Love called Andre's parents. The police transferred Andre from one facility to another and when Andre's mom was finally able to locate her son, she was told that he had committed suicide by hanging himself in jail. The Jackson Medical Examiner found Andre's death to be a suicide and said his wounds showed it was possible for him to hang himself with his Air Jordan shoelaces. "The imprint around the neck matched the size and imprint of the string," Simpson County Coroner Bobby Williams said. "In suicide cases consistent with Jones's, victims bend their knees and put pressure on the rope around their neck," Williams said. "This cuts off the air supply and renders the victims unconscious, and from that point, the circulation is cut off," Williams said. Andre's parents contacted Chokwe.

Jones's parents hired Chokwe to file a wrongful-death suit. Chokwe believed, along with Jones's parents, that Jones had been murdered and had not committed suicide. According to the *Clarion-Ledger*, "Lumumba said, [that] 'the theory of Jones hanging himself with a shoestring is not one we think is credible.' Also, he said he doubted that no one would have heard noises from Jones." Authorities said that Andre tied his own shoelaces to an iron grate above the shower head and hanged himself. Chokwe procured a medical examiner from Chicago to conduct another autopsy. Dr. James Bryant reviewed the remains and he said he believed Andre was strangled. "In a usual case of suicide by hanging, the ligature mark is alongside the neck and doesn't go all the way around. Where, in Andre's case, the ligature mark went along side of the neck and all the way into the back and criss-crossed in this fashion." Dr. Bryant's report also revealed bruising elsewhere on the body that the official State autopsy report did not reveal. In addition, a jail house inmate stated he heard an officer ask Andre, "Do you know what happens to niggers for stealing a white man's truck?" The police and media could not find any gang affiliation or criminal record on Andre. Contrarily, Andre was scheduled to begin college that fall. Andre's parents went on to sue both the State of Mississippi and the Federal Government, but both cases were dismissed.[36]

Also important to note: Oct. 25, 1998—In the period between 1987 and 1993, at least 48 people, including 22 Black men, were found dead from hangings in Mississippi jail cells. In each and every case, the authorities declared the official cause of death to be "suicide." One of the 22 Black men was 18-year-old Andre Jones. Chokwe was also involved in some of the other "jail house lynching" cases. In addition to the jail house lynching cases, he rallied to expose and fight for some form of justice for the families. He was involved in numerous death penalty cases from Illinois to Mississippi.

DeWayne Boyd

Chokwe's compassion for our people was infinite. He utilized his law skills and knowledge to represent a large spectrum of people involving an array of legal issues. I recall when he represented

---

[36]"Andre Jones," *Unsolved Mysteries*, https://unsolved.com/gallery/andre-jones/& sa=D&source=docs&ust=1746090962076898&usg=AOvVaw0kouh2hgNT7phbL skq5sIc (accessed May 1, 2025).

DeWayne Dewey Boyd, a native Detroiter, a civil rights activist, and a Black Land Development activist who was fighting against government theft of Black people's land. He always believed in food sovereignty and supported Black ownership of grocery stores in food deserts. He worked with farmers in this country and numerous African countries to realize Black food sovereignty. In 2019, DeWayne was named the Minister of Agriculture for the State of the African Diaspora, Sixth Region, an official position under the auspices of the African Union. According to Chokwe, "DeWayne was involved with the Florida International Trade and Cultural Expo where he played an important role coordinating African, especially Congolese, participation in this foreign trade network of over 70 nations in the Caribbean, South America, Africa, Asia, and the USA."[37]

DeWayne also personally experienced the attempted theft of Black land in this country. He held the lease to his grandmother's land in Starkville, Mississippi, when white hunters and farmers claimed to have leases to this land. One of these men was falsely receiving large government subsidies on the land. During this period, DeWayne was hired as the first Black Meat Inspector of the State Department of Agriculture in Mississippi. While DeWayne was complaining about the white men's theft of his property, the men were bringing charges against him of stealing crops and committing arson on the land, and they also went after his job while he was in his 90-day probation period. DeWayne hired Chokwe, who offered his protection to Boyd while he was in Mississippi trying to prevent the illegal expropriation of African American-owned land. They were victorious in DeWayne's case. Chokwe won an acquittal for DeWayne, who was framed on arson charges after discovering and reporting dishonest schemes by white farmers to control and profit from DeWayne's family's land in Starkville, Mississippi.

---

[37] Earnest McBride, "The Passing of a Great Man: DeWayne 'Dewey' Boyd Sr.," *Jackson Advocate*, November 4, 2024, https://jacksonadvocateonline.com/the-passing-of-a-great-man-dewayne-dewey-boyd-sr/ (viewed April 28, 2025).

Devoted Defender of the People

In addition, DeWayne worked with Congressman Conyers' administration on special projects to procure better trade agreements between African farmers and the USA. Conyers released DeWayne from this position when funds were lost. DeWayne did not hold any resentment towards Conyers's position, but he maintained that FBI informants were working in Conyers's office and falsely claimed that he embezzled the money. Chokwe and DeWayne continued their relationship evolving around the protection of Black Farmers' land.[38]

Geronimo Pratt

It was admirable that Chokwe made himself available, mostly pro bono, to work on cases of our warrior brothers and sisters in the movement. These warriors were struggling for the liberation of our people, and Chokwe was struggling for the liberation of our people and the soldiers in the struggle. Geronimo Pratt, also known as Geronimo Ji-Jaga, was definitely amongst these warrior soldiers that Chokwe represented. According to sources, Geronimo was a leader of the Black Panther Party and a decorated military veteran. He unjustly spent twenty-five years in prison. Reportedly, the Federal Government targeted Pratt in a COINTELPRO operation in the early 1970s. "Geronimo was falsely charged with murder and kidnapping in 1972. He was finally released in 1997 after it was established that the FBI had withheld exculpatory evidence from the defense. After being released from prison, Pratt dedicated his life to working for those wrongfully incarcerated." Reportedly, he moved to Tanzania with the daughter

(Photo courtesy of Freedom Archives)

---

[38]Ibid.

of Eldridge and Kathleen Cleaver, and that is where he passed away on June 2, 2011.[39]

Elliot Culp

Chokwe was involved in numerous death penalty cases from Illinois to Mississippi. RBG Street Scholar reported, "In July 1995, thirteen-year-old Elliot Culp was one of several witnesses to the murder of a white woman by a white man. Although Culp had reported what he saw to the police, they chose not to investigate the perpetrator but to arrest Culp instead. The teenager spent one year in prison charged with capital murder before Chokwe won his acquittal and release. Chokwe said at the time of Culp's release, 'This verdict is a triumph over thoughtless narrow-minded advocates for wholesale execution and wholesale incarceration of our children.'" [40] If Chokwe had not won, Culp would have been facing the death penalty. He was the youngest person ever tried on capital murder charges in Mississippi.

Pontiac Illinois Case

In 1978, Chokwe joined a team of attorneys in Chicago. While representing his Detroit law firm, he successfully defended the Pontiac Brothers—sixteen prisoners who were charged with the murders of three prison employees in connection with a riot at Pontiac Correctional Center in Pontiac, Illinois. On July 22, 1978, inmates at the maximum security prison in Pontiac, Illinois, rioted to protest violations against prisoner rights, including unsanitary living conditions, cramped quarters, cold, insect-infested food, lack of medical treatment, and guard brutality. Many prisoners were

---

[39] Geronimo Pratt - Wikipedia/ Geronimo Pratt (1947-2011) Posted on April 1, 2012, contributed by Eric Greve.
[40] RBG Library, "A Biography of New Afrikan Attorney Chokwe Lumumba," 5.

injured, and three guards were killed in the riot. Twenty-eight African Americans and three Latinos were charged. Sixteen of the accused, known as the "Pontiac 16," faced murder charges and a possible death sentence if convicted. Lumumba agreed to defend Ozzie Williams, whom he perceived to be one of the most political of those charged in this significant case. Eventually, all charges against the defendants were dismissed. Lumumba said at the time, "The Pontiac Sixteen Trial is the type of case that I got into the legal profession to deal with." At trial, ten of the Pontiac Sixteen were found not guilty; all charges against the other defendants were dismissed.[41]

The Johnnie Griffin and Scott Sisters Cases

Chokwe's biographical sketch as of 2007 reflects he represented Black workers in numerous racial and sexual discrimination cases in Mississippi, including cases against Frito-Lay, the Jackson Housing Authority, the Specialty Foods Corporation, and the Anderson Tully Company. In 1991, Chokwe also won a lawsuit for the family of a civil rights activist named Johnnie Griffin. The family filed a wrongful death suit because "a self-avowed segregationist police officer shot Griffin to death at his home in front of his four children. Chokwe and attorneys Brunetta Brandy of Detroit, Michigan, and Everett Sanders of Natchez, Mississippi, won $250,000 in compensatory damages for the family."[42] The case was reminiscent of the Medgar Evers assassination, inasmuch as both activists were fighting for the freedom of Black people, and they were shot down and killed in front of their families.

---

[41]"Biographical Sketch of Chokwe Lumumba as of February, 2007, 3" https://l.b5z.net/i/u/6075908/i/Chokwe_Lumumba_s_Bio.pdf ; KeyWiki Contributors, "Chokwe Lumumba," *KeyWiki*, https://keywiki.org/Chokwe_Lumumba (accessed November 24, 2025).

[42]Ibid.

That same night, [Medgar] Evers returned home just after midnight from a series of NAACP functions. As he left his car with a handful of t-shirts that read "Jim Crow Must Go," he was shot in the back. His wife and children, who had been waiting up for him, found him bleeding to death on the doorstep. "I opened the door, and there was Medgar at the steps, face down in blood," Myrlie Evers remembered in *People* magazine. "The children ran out and were shouting, 'Daddy, get up!'"[43]

"In the 1990s Chokwe increasingly specialized in cases where racial prejudice and political power combined to produce biased investigations, unjust arrests, and excessively punitive sentences. In a landmark case for Mississippi, he won the acquittal of George Little, a young African American charged with murder for defending himself against an attack by a white man."[44]

However, Chokwe's most well-known case in Mississippi was his defense of Jamie and Gladys Scott. The two sisters were convicted of armed robbery in 1994 and received double life sentences. Their alleged co-conspirators, three teenagers known as "the Patrick boys," took plea bargains and testified against the sisters in return for lesser sentences. The boys all served no more than three years in jail.[45]

The sisters appealed their convictions in 1996. Chokwe played a major part in the fight for the sisters' release from filing court appeals to appeal to Governor Haley Barbour of Mississippi for a pardon. Chokwe said that Jamie Scott's condition (she needed a kidney transplant) cast a pall over their future: "If she should die, it's going to cost (the state) thousands of dollars to defend it, and if they lose, it could cost them a million dollars," Chokwe said. I recall assisting

---

[43]"Murder of Medgar Evers," Medgar Evers College, https://www.mec.cuny.edu/about/history/murder-of-medgar-evers (accessed November 24, 2025).
[44]KeyWiki Contributors, "Chokwe Lumumba."
[45]Ward Schaefer, "Tragic Case of the Scott Sisters," *Jackson Free Press*, November 3, 2010.

Chokwe with disseminating information and gathering petitions to support a plea for a pardon from Governor Haley Barbour. Our organization, the Malcolm X Grassroots Movement, like with many of Chokwe's political cases, spearheaded a national petition drive to free the Scott sisters. We worked diligently in Detroit and around the country to assist with this venture. This case, like most of his political cases, evoked empathy in me; however, this one especially touched my heart because of the cruelty in imprisoning young women for 16 years over an alleged theft of between $11 and $200. And one of the sisters was in need of life-saving medical attention. This to me was incredible!

On November 24th, Chokwe delivered to Barbour's office a stack of papers bearing the names of 24,000 people who signed an online NAACP petition for the sisters' release. He also carried another 1,500 letters of support that he received personally at his law office. Among the new crop of supporters was Hinds County District Attorney Robert Shuler Smith, who reviewed the sisters' case and pledged his support in a separate letter. "The Scott sisters do not have a previous criminal history, which is at least a hint that they were most likely law-abiding citizens for most of their adult life," Smith wrote. "Consequently, they do not have the profile of those who exhibit predatory behavior or aggressive conduct towards criminality."[46]

The Scott Sisters case put Mississippi in the national spotlight. Gladys and Jamie Scott were released from prison January 7, 2011, after serving sixteen years behind bars. All along they maintained their innocence, but it was a grassroots movement that helped them gain their freedom. Upon their release, the sisters arrived at the Masonic Temple for a press conference. There, they received cheers, songs, and tears. With their attorney, Chokwe Lumumba,

---

[46] In a December 30 press release, Barbour announced his decision to suspend the sentences, effectively granting the Scott sisters parole for the 1993 armed robbery that they allegedly masterminded.

they answered questions about their release but not the crime they were given two life sentences for. Chokwe said he would continue to work for a pardon to wipe the Scotts' record clean. "You're not going to criminalize us, you're not gonna make us criminals, so we're going to resist and we will resist everywhere we go because we will tell you that we are not guilty of the crime that you charged us with," Chokwe said.[47] Gladys Scott responded to a question regarding her giving a kidney to her sister as a condition for the release from prison. Jamie Scott was diabetic and needed a kidney transplant.

"Whether I was, you know, released because I had to give her a kidney, I was going to give it to her anyway if I had to give it to her in prison," said Gladys Scott. "We couldn't have made it in that prison being bitter. You know we couldn't have done it. It wouldn't have worked. We don't hold grudges against anyone. They have to pay for their actions and placing me and my sister in prison for a crime we did not commit," Jaime Scott said.[48]

Shakur Family and Brink's Expropriation Cases

Assata Shakur aka Joanne Chesimard

Assata, who was on the FBI's Most Wanted List, had been reportedly living in Cuba under the protection of the government since 1984 after she was rescued by fellow Black Liberation Army (BLA) members from incarceration in 1979. Chokwe assisted National Conference of Black Lawyers (NCBL) attorneys Lenox Hines and Lewis Myers Jr. in representing Assata on a murder case

---

[47]"As they left the Central Mississippi Correctional Facility in Rankin County Jamie and Gladys Scott prepared for their first day of freedom since they were 21 and 19 years old. Maggie Wade of Rankin County, Mississippi WLBT, "Scott Sisters Released from Prison," January 8, 2011, https://www.wlbt.com/story/13806902/scott-sisters-released-from-prison/ (accessed May 26, 2025).

[48]Maggie Wade, WLBT 3, "Scott Sisters Released from Prison," January 8, 2011.

in 1977 that was dismissed. Assata is also the godsister of Mutulu Shakur, who is accused of being the mastermind of the Brink's expropriation. I recall when Donald Trump was elected president during his first term, he said he was going to go after Assata and bring her back to the United States. Assata Shakur is synonymous with the great sheroes of our history: Harriet Tubman, Sojourner Truth, Fannie Lou Hamer, Ida B. Wells, Ella Baker, Angela Davis, etc. She fought tirelessly and selflessly for our people like our great warrior sisters. She was beaten, abused, and falsely incarcerated like Fannie and Angela. She was hunted like an animal like Harriet. Like Sojourner, Ella, and Ida, she persistently preached and taught our people to fight for our liberation.

In 1977, Assata was falsely convicted of killing a state trooper on the New Jersey Turnpike in 1973. Thank God, brothers from the Black Liberation Army broke Assata out of the hell of a prison where the U.S. Government left her to languish. Instead, she went into exile and remained in exile in Cuba until her transition in September 2025. Asante Sana (thank you) Fidel Castro and Cuba! Chokwe went on to represent Assata's godbrother Mutulu Shakur in the aftermath of the Brink's expropriation. He also represented his son Tupac Shakur in a case that involved the police.

Dr. Mutulu Shakur

Chokwe first spoke of Mutulu Shakur to me when he was defending him in the Brink's case. Mutulu was accused of masterminding the Brink's expropriation in 1981 and other attacks on armored trucks. He was also charged with the escape of Assata Shakur. Although Chokwe was successful in gaining the acquittal of Bilal Sunni Ali in 1981 and the dismissal of charges against Fulani Sunni Ali and others in the Brink's case, he failed to get the same outcome in Mutulu's case. In 1983, Mutulu was convicted of all charges against him and spent thirty-seven years in federal prison until his release in December of 2022. Mutulu's conviction impacted

Chokwe deeply, and I believe it hurt his heart. Bilal Sunni Ali explained to me that Chokwe did not fail in Mutulu's case. "When I was tried and acquitted, it was a different time. However, the political climate in this country had changed and shifted to the right when Mutulu was on trial."

In recent years, I watched a wonderful documentary on Mutulu Shakur titled *Dope is Death*, and I learned why Chokwe was so invested in fighting for the freedom of Mutulu. Mutulu had spent his adult life prior to his incarceration involved in movement organizing. He was a member of the Republic of New Afrika, Black Liberation Army, and the Revolutionary Action Movement. He also worked closely with the Black Panther Party. Actually, I learned from this film that Mutulu was only 17 when the New Bethel Incident occurred (see chapter 4) and he was present in the church. In recent years, I heard Mutulu and a sister who was present in the church at the time of the shooting give an account of what occurred in the church. According to them both, Mutulu was inside the church when the police shot over a hundred rounds into the church. Mutulu and others were directing people to safe places in the building. At one point during the incident, Mutulu said he shielded a sister with his body from the barrage of bullets that were penetrating the church. In 2023, our organization, MXGM, hosted a Malcolm X Day Celebration at the King Solomon Historic Church in Detroit, and a sister whose name I cannot recall shared that same story with me and added that she was the woman whom Mutulu shielded from bullets.

Mutulu Shakur
(Photo courtesey of Freedom Archives)

Mutulu proved to be a man of courage and integrity, a leader and protector of the people consistently throughout his life.

The documentary film *Dope is Death* details Mutulu's and others' heroism, selflessness, and courage. In the late 1960s, there was a heroin epidemic running rampant throughout communities of color, Black and Brown people. Members of the Black Panther Party and the Young Lords, including Mutulu Shakur, opened up the Lincoln Detox Center in the Bronx, New York, and began treating substance abusers and other members of the community in need of medical attention with acupuncture. Many of us in the community believed Dr. Shakur was a healer, not a killer.

Mutulu was denied parole nine times. Diagnosed with stage 3 multiple myeloma, a blood cancer that destroys the immune system, bones, and kidney, the father and mentor to the late Tupac Shakur was finally granted parole by the U.S. Parole Commission due to his terminal health condition. He was released from the Federal Medical Center in Lexington, Kentucky, on December 16, 2022. He was able to spend several months with family and friends subsequent to his release. "He was one of the longest held prisoners of war in the U.S., having been held for 37 years on a 60-year sentence," said Jackson attorney Ishmael Muhammad, spokesperson for Camp One Rootz. "He finally gained his release after years of being inside the walls suffering torture and humiliation at the hands of the prison."[49] Our warrior brother Dr. Mutulu Shakur transitioned from this planet on July 6, 2023.

Shakur Squads had organized all over the country, including in Detroit, Michigan, to procure petition signatures and letters requesting Dr. Shakur's compassionate release. The Detroit Squad was able to raise $10,000 to contribute to Dr. Shakur's release and after-release medical care. Our Squad was made up of members of

---

[49]Earnest McBride, "Dr. Mutulu Shakur given special honors after prison release," *Jackson Advocate*, January 31, 2023.

Malcolm X Grassroots Movement and Moratorium Now. The two groups came together and combined efforts and energy. Moratorium Now was working on the prison release of Warrior Mumia Abu-Jamal and MXGM was working on Dr. Shakur's release. Coordinating our organizing efforts of Verbena Lei, Sarah Torres, Heather McNeilly from Moratorium Now and Ikemba Agulu, Camille Jackson, Kwasi Akwamu, Nubia Monique Wardford, Itari Shakur, Anemashaun Bomani, Nguvu Mark Strong, and myself was genius. We held weekly petition drives and letter-writing events, presented educational forums, and hosted film fundraisers: *Dope is Death* is about Dr. Mutulu Shakur's acupuncture work and *Mumia: Long Distance Revolutionary* is about the life and unjust incarceration of Mumia.[50] Several years later after Chokwe represented Dr. Shakur in the courts, he represented his son Tupac Shakur.

Tupac Shakur

Tupac Shakur is considered by many people to be one of the greatest rappers in history. Tupac was raised in a revolutionary family. His mother, Afeni Shakur, was a Black Panther. His father Mutulu Shakur, who raised him, was a member of the Republic of New Afrika. Tupac was a member of the New Afrikan Scouts, a youth group of Chokwe's

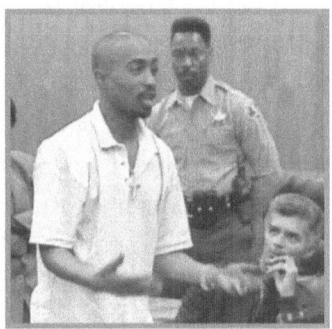

Chokwe and Tupac Shakur

---

[50]Mumia Abu-Jamal is a freedom-fighter journalist who has been incarcerated by the U.S. for over 40 years. He was a former Black Panther, a veteran, a writer, a father, and an activist; a victim of racism and police violence, target violence; and a target of government war on Black liberation activists. He was framed and wrongfully convicted by Philly's racist injustice system in 1982, sentenced to be executed. The people's movement forced the state to take Mumia off death row in 2011, but he still faces Death by Incarceration. Hundreds of people signed the petitions for Dr. Shakur's release, including congressional representatives we solicited for help. Congresswoman Rashida Tlaib was the most supportive in giving her assistance to our efforts.

organization, New Afrikan People's Organization. I guess Tupac could not help developing into a revolutionary. He carried the principles of the movement with him, and you could hear them pronounced in some of his rap lyrics and during his interviews and speeches. Of course, he did not always promote revolutionary principles in his lyrics. He once said, "You have to meet the people where they are to bring them those messages," and that is exactly what he did. Tupac retained trust in some activists in the movement when many in the music and entertainment industry had deserted him. Watani Tyehimba, co-founder of the New Afrikan People's Organization, was Tupac's manager when he entered into the rap industry. He kept Watani close for most of his rap career. I often think that if Shug Knight had not gotten to him in prison and convinced him to join Death Row, Tupac would still be with us today. In 1993, Chokwe served as counsel and national legal coordinator for Tupac. He was successful, along with Atlanta attorneys Ken Ellis and Tony Axam, in winning dismissals of assault charges arising from allegations that Shakur shot at two off-duty police officers in Atlanta. "Huey P. Newton was a target. Angela Davis was a target. Marcus Garvey was a target. Tupac is a target," said Chokwe Lumumba, Shakur's Atlanta counsel, who says his client fired in self-defense. "Anybody who basically has been a person who the police don't like becomes a target."[51] Tupac died on September 13, 1996.

Brink's Expropriation

When my brother was working on the Brink's case in New York, those were some very difficult and challenging times for everybody. His wife Nubia and the kids had to relocate to New York. They had already relocated once before to Chicago to work on the Pontiac 16 case. The Pontiac Brothers were up for the death penalty if found

---

[51] Malcolm Gladwell, "The Rappers's New Rage," *Washington Post*, December 16, 1993.

guilty. It was difficult for his law partners because they basically had to cover much of his share of expenses at the law firm. It was difficult for me, too, because I had started my first year of law school, and I looked forward to his brilliant guidance. Once, I was at a study group session at Wayne State Law School, facilitated by Leroy Soles of the Black Legal Alliance (BLA), a program that Chokwe and his classmates initiated to help first-year law students. I was hoping I could get tutorial assistance there, as it was not available to me at University of Detroit Law School. One of the senior students in the session was an old classmate from St. Theresa.

Terry was very smart, and she knew it. She was also extremely competitive, and I did not like those attributes about her. However, now we were grown up, and we were in this small room together, and she asked me, "Why are you here?"

I told her, "To see if I could get some tutoring." She reminded me that this program was for Wayne State students when she discovered I was a U of D Law student.

"Besides, why can't your famous brother help you?"

I became incensed at that point. "My famous brother is out helping others in the Brink's case in New York, and he does not have the time to help me right now."

She was like a great advocate who would not let up on her position, or a dog with a bone that refused to let go. She then said, "He is a great attorney and all, and he is capable of helping many people, but you are his sister. Aren't you more important than the others in New York? Don't you need him now?"

At this point, I was livid. "No, I am not more important. My brother is doing work that will help all of our people, not just one of them," and I rudely walked away from her.

The irony of that situation is that my classmates at U of D Law School who knew Chokwe Lumumba was my brother assumed he was helping and even doing my class work. Once, Professor Goffney, my Torts professor, used my brief outline for an example to show the class how to write a good brief. I heard the rumbles and accusations of several students: "Her brother probably wrote that for her or had someone else write it for her." How insulting; that was what some white students were accused, and I would say guilty, of doing. Actually, Jill (Attorney Sophia Elijah), one of Chokwe's paralegals, showed me how to brief a case. No, she did not—absolutely did not—write that brief; I wrote the brief!

I saw Terry numerous times after that encounter. She was a practicing attorney, and I was the filing clerk for Chokwe's firm, and I would run into her at the courts. Neither one of us ever mentioned that situation again. I believe she knew she had offended me. Also, I realized I was so hurt inside because deep down I desired to have my big brother home helping me. But I certainly did understand why he couldn't. Besides, when I really needed something, Chokwe's partners—Earl, Harry, and Jeff—were there for me during his absence. Harry Davis, the youngest partner, actually spent time listening to my moot court preparation and instilling confidence in me then and throughout my law school experience. I appreciated them all so much.

(Photo courtesy UVA Library)

The Brink's case also had some difficult challenges for Chokwe. In 1981, several people carried out an expropriation of an armored Brink's truck that left a security guard and two policemen dead in

Nanuet, New York. Later, several members of the Black Liberation Army and Weather Underground were arrested and charged with these crimes. Chokwe was practicing in the state of New York on a pro hac vice basis: this is when an unlicensed attorney in the state makes a request for the court to allow him/her to practice in the courts on a limited term. An attorney is licensed to practice law in the states where they have passed the bar and gained admission.

The court hearing the Brink's case did not want to allow Chokwe to represent his clients. The defendants were made up of members from what the state determined were radical groups: Black Liberation Army, Republic of New Afrika, Black Panther Party, and Weather Underground. The court's position was that Chokwe was a risk and danger because he was a member of the RNA. At the onset of the Brink's case, Judge Irving Ben Cooper of the Federal Court in Manhattan barred Chokwe from representing Fulani Sunni Ali (Cynthia Boston) because of his political affiliations and beliefs. John J. Martin, U.S. Attorney of the Southern District of New York; Kenneth Gribetz, Rockland County District Court Prosecutor; and Justice Harry Edelstein, State Supreme Court justice, all supported the position that Chokwe should not be allowed to represent any defendants in this case. However, prosecutors Martin and Gribetz later withdrew their oppositional motions to have Chokwe barred, purportedly due to trial expediency.[52]

There were many memorable major incidents during the Brink's trial. At the beginning of the trial, Chokwe filed a motion for

---

[52]"In barring Mr. Lumumba from Federal Court, Judge Cooper cited Mr. Lumumba's political ideology, his writings, his values as a lawyer and his behavior on the witness stand. Mr. Lumumba is general counsel to a group that calls itself the Republic of New Afrika. The group says it seeks to establish nationhood for Black Americans in five southern states. Therefore in interest of a 'Speedy Resolution, Attorney Chokwe Lumumba was allowed to proceed with representation of his clients.'" Glenn Fowler, "Prosecutors in Brink's Case Drop Opposition to Lawyer," *New York Times*, December 12, 1981.

recusal (removal) of the judge on the case. The judge asked him, "Mr. Lumumba, what is the basis of your motion?" Chokwe responded, "On the basis that you are a racist, Sir." The judge, flabbergasted, held Chokwe in contempt but deferred the penalty until after the trial was over.[53]

Chokwe was nearly arrested for the deferred contempt charge by the judge in the New York case. One day, I was sitting at the receptionist desk at Chokwe's law office (one of the many hats I wore at the firm), and two of the largest and tallest white men I had ever seen entered the office and approached the desk. They must have been around six foot seven or taller.

I asked them, "May I help you?"

"Yes," one of them responded while showing me his badge. "We are U.S. Marshals, is Mr. Lumumba in?"

"No," I nervously responded. "May I give him a message?"

"Yes, tell Mr. Lumumba we came to arrest him, and we strongly suggest that he turn himself in."

I later found out they were there to arrest Chokwe for the deferred contempt charge by the judge in the New York case. Jeff Edison, Chokwe's partner, accompanied him to turn himself in. The judge sentenced him to 350 hours of community service.

Chokwe said, "I completed those hours with pleasure for Mother Waddles, helping her establish her nonprofit." Mother Waddles was an iconic figure in Detroit who was known for providing for the poor and homeless.

---

[53]"Detroit attorney Chokwe Lumumba was sentenced in New York Monday to perform 350 hours of community service for repeatedly accusing the judge at the federal Brink's robbery trial of racism. Lumumba had called the trial judge 'a racist dog.' The sentencing judge referred to 'total disrespect' shown by Lumumba, who also was placed on three years' probation. Lumumba said his case was aided by letters of support from many black lawyers and two U.S. congressmen, John Conyers and George Crockett, both Detroit Democrats. Lumumba, 36, had represented Bilal Sunni-Ali, who was acquitted." "Brink's Trial Lawyer Sentenced," *Detroit Free Press*, November 30, 1983.

During the Brink's case, many people rallied behind Chokwe and the brothers and sisters on trial. I recall the efforts to raise money for Chokwe to defend against suspension from the Brink's case and help with expenses on the case that he was virtually doing pro bono. Several well-known Black attorneys like Elbert Hatchett, Cornelius Pitts, Milton Henry, and Gerald Evelyn contributed financially to support his political cases. In addition, several Jewish attorneys, including William Goodman and Ken Mogil, also supported Chokwe. One of the fundraisers was at the home of my high school comrade Llenda Jackson. Her father, Murray Jackson, was a well-respected poet, author, academician, and civil rights activist. He hosted one of the fundraisers in his beautiful home in Sherwood Forest, a high-income subdivision in Detroit. It was a very pleasant and sociable occasion. People came and went throughout the event, all leaving a check or some type of donation. It was amazing to see that many of the guests who arrived with a check were Jewish attorneys. When I inquired as to why they were so supportive of the Brink's expropriation case, and many other of his political cases, he explained: "Some Jewish people have always been involved in civil rights struggles throughout history. Many of them acknowledge and remember their assimilation and struggle into this country. Also, they know if the courts are successful in preventing me from representing my clients on the Brink's case that will set precedence for others, them included." I then gained a newfound respect for many Jewish attorneys.

However, what was most memorable about this event is when I entered the basement and a group of women were gathered, involved in what appeared to be a philosophical discussion. One of the women, tall, big-boned, with a beautiful afro, seemed to be leading the discussion, and she looked so familiar.

I said, "Who is that sister? She looks like Angela Davis."

Llenda smilingly responded, "That is Angela Davis."

I could not believe I was in the same room with my shero Angela Davis!

Llenda asked, "Do you want to meet her?"

Did she really need to ask that question? When there appeared to be a break in the women's discussion, she took me over to meet Sister Davis. Llenda told her I was Chokwe's sister.

She said, "Pleased to meet you, your brother is phenomenal, and we are all pulling for him."

I was like a fan-struck little girl. I graciously thanked her, but looking back I should have told her, "You have been my hero for so long. Llenda and I, along with our fellow Mumford High students, supported and protested for you while you were wrongfully incarcerated. We shouted 'Free Angela! Free Angela Davis!' and marched around the school rocking our big, beautiful afros, holding our clenched fists up to make the Black Power sign while someone waved the red, black, and green flag." I read her autobiography twice, once when I was in college and again when I began teaching high school. I became teary-eyed many times during my readings, but especially when I read about her mistreatment in prison, like when they wouldn't give her her glasses, and she could not read or see clearly. If I ever see her again, these things I will tell her.

There were indeed other instances in the Brink's case where Chokwe would often share events of his cases with me. I would sometimes initiate these conversations by raising inquiries after reading about the cases in the newspaper or reading legal pleadings on the cases I was typing for him. However, there were times when he would initiate a conversation with me, and that was when he was very troubled and disturbed about things that were happening to the defendants in the cases.

This happened more than once with the Brink's case. He shared with me how the FBI and police had physically abused Sekou Odinga, Kuwasi Balagoon, and I believe the third brother's name was Sam Brown. He said while the FBI and police were interrogating the brothers, they burned cigarettes into their bodies, and they forced one of them to put his head into the toilet while flushing it. I later learned that that heinous tactic was called "waterboarding." He told me, "Shushanna, these brothers are true warriors for our people. To endure what they have endured is remarkable and honorable." He referred to the police and FBI members who were involved in these incidents as cowards and animalistic. I could feel my brother's outrage and hurt for these brothers. I knew that these types of incidents were what kept him up for twenty-four hours at a time writing, researching, and working for his clients (the people). This is also why he remained so active in the human rights and Black Power movements.

Sekou Odinga

Chokwe did not represent Sekou Odinga in the Brink's case. Sekou actually represented himself, but Sekou was one of Chokwe's comrades in the Republic of New Afrika. I recall that Chokwe spoke of Sekou Odinga as a warrior soldier who sacrificed his life for our people. I recall Chokwe, with pain streaming from his eyes, sharing with me details of how "law enforcement" tortured our brother Sekou while incarcerated. I will always remember that Brother Sekou was a warrior soldier his entire time on this planet, and I would like to think of Brothers Sekou, Chokwe, Mutulu, Imari, Malcolm X, Kwame Toure; Sisters Fulani Sunni-Ali, Betty Shabazz, Queen Mother Moore; and so many of the other warriors as resting peacefully now in a place called Revolutionary Heaven.

Fulani Sunni-Ali

Chokwe's client/comrade in the Brink's case that personally impacted me was Fulani Sunni-Ali. I knew, loved, and respected her. She was one of my heroes. Fulani was a beautiful, cocoa brown–complexioned sister with a soulful voice. She was always adorned in African attire, rocked her natural hair, and was just so genuine. I first met Fulani when she was married to Ahmed Obafemi. They were both members of the PG-RNA. I recall her father, Alajo Adegbalola, was a close comrade to Brother Imari Obadele and held several positions in the PG-RNA, including first vice president and minister of defense. Brother Alajo was a strong older warrior with a warm, kind heart who facilitated our couples' relationship classes, where my first husband, Jeaco, and I participated with Fulani, Ahmed, and others.

Chokwe and Fulani (Photo courtesy of Fulani Sunni Ali Family)

Years later, in 1981 after meeting and working with Fulani, Chokwe represented Bilal Sunni-Ali, Fulani's second husband, during the Brink's' case. Fulani was arrested, jailed, and separated from her children, while pregnant, all because she would not give erroneous information on her husband. The government wanted to convict Bilal Sunni Ali in the Brink's case, so they concocted some underhanded scheme to charge her and keep her detained. But she refused to comply and was a hero to many people, particularly Black women. Using silence as a means of resistance, Fulani and other grand jury resisters refused to provide information to government officials. For this she was jailed again. Fulani Sunni Ali was finally released a year and a half later on October 19, 1983. Throughout this time, I found the things Fulani experienced reprehensible and they cut though my heart. I, like Fulani, was pregnant at one point during this trial.

Chokwe successfully got all charges against Fulani dropped, and he victoriously won the acquittal of Fulani's husband, Bilal, on all counts charged against him in the Brink's trial on September 6, 1983. Because of what happened to Fulani in the Brink's case, I was so inspired to include her in my poem "Respect Me Black Man." This poem is about great Black women who have fought our battles. The women named in this poem are looked upon as heroes to so many of our people.

> Respect me Black Man
> For I am a Queen
> For I freed hundreds of women, men and children
> By way of the Underground Railroad
> For I am Harriet Tubman
>
> Respect me Black Man
> For I am a Queen
> For I courageously stood up
> And then tired and limp sat in the front of the bus
> Where we were forbidden
> For I am Rosa Parks
>
> Respect me Black Man
> For I am a Queen
> For I educated our children
> Despite all odds
> For I am Marva Collins
> I am Mary McLeod Bethune
>
> Respect me Black Man
> For I am a Queen
> For I refused to give in
> Even when hunted and sought by the FBI
> For I am Angela Davis
> Respect me Black Man
> For I am a Queen
> For I endured the pain of being

Devoted Defender of the People

Separated from my children, to
Free you, to free our people
For I am Fulani Sunni Ali

Respect me Black Man
For I am a Queen
For I carry your babies and
Bear the unbearable pain

Respect me Black Man
For I am a Queen
For I fight battles when you sometimes won't
Respect me Black Man
For I know of your pains and sorrow
And the obstacles in your path

For I know how you struggle
And how he "the white man"
Holds you back, how you endure and
Persevere and they still won't let you win

So don't mistreat me Black Man

For I am truly a queen
For I am a Beautiful Black New African Queen

I am your queen!

– Shushanna Shakur

Fulani went on to lead a productive life raising her children along with her husband, Bilal. They relocated to Atlanta, and they visited Belize often. As a matter of fact, Fulani was in Belize when I attempted to contact her for an interview regarding Chokwe, subsequent to his death. She attempted to contact me back, but we missed each other. Unfortunately, my sister in love and struggle became ill afterward and made her earthly transition in 2016.

I am so proud of all of these revolutionary warrior brothers and sisters. They all had unimaginable courage and a great love for our people. These warriors were known to be members of one or more of the following organizations: Black Liberation Army (BLA), Revolutionary Action Movement (RAM), New Afrikan Independence Movement (NAIM), Provisional Government of Republic of New Afrika (PG-RNA), and the Black Panther Party (BPP).

CHAPTER 7

Injustices from Jackson to Detroit

"Anyone who allows themselves to be abused and doesn't do anything about it really deserves the abuse."
– Chokwe Lumumba

Chokwe ran into "Mississippi injustice" again and again. One of his first encounters with this adversary was when he traveled to Mississippi to work with Imari Obadele and the Republic of New Afrika. Several RNA members traveled to the land they had acquired in Jackson, Mississippi, to advance the RNA objectives of procuring five states for Black people and remaining independent from the United States. Of course, they were met with negativity, antagonism, and racial hatred by belligerent law enforcement. Then, in 1971 while Chokwe assisted Attorney Ray Willis and others in the representation of RNA President Imari Obadele and the others known as RNA-11, he again experienced the impact of southern Mississippi racial disdain and hatred.

Years later after the RNA-11 travesty of injustice, Chokwe made a life-changing decision, and he returned to Mississippi. In 1988, he and his wife, Nubia, packed up the children and moved their lives to Jackson, Mississippi. They were about to embark on a journey that would alter and modify their lives from most things familiar to them; some things for the best and of course a lot for the worse. Some people wondered at the time why he was moving to a place that had such a dreadful history. Of course, he knew that Mississippi was among the main states in the union that enslaved, raped, lynched, segregated, and abused Black people. He must have had some fear of the remnants of those egregious practices. However, I believe that is exactly why my brother chose to defend our people in Mississippi.

Chokwe and Nubia were able to find a fabulous home right there in the city of Jackson that Nubia absolutely loved. The children went to good schools and were happy and adjusted well, and these were significant factors influencing their decision to move to Jackson. Also, they joined a beautiful community that supported them through everything. I think Nubia's feelings about their home in Jackson are exemplified in the following haiku written by poetess Sonia Sanchez, a friend of Chokwe and Nubia. Ms. Sanchez wrote a poem for Nubia when she made her earthly transition: "I see you, Nubia, walking your Mississippi Road God in your hand" (see chapter 5).

Perhaps the bouts with "Mississippi injustice" that took place in the courtrooms were some of the most challenging for Chokwe. He was a brilliant attorney who was respected by prosecutorial and adversarial judges in Michigan. Even though they resented him, they respected him. He was stiff competition who courageously opposed them in representation of his clients. Unfortunately, this was not the case in Jackson and surrounding counties in Mississippi. Judge W. Swan Yerger of the First Judicial District of Hinds County, Mississippi, filed a bar complaint against Chokwe, alleging professional misconduct. This action was a result of Chokwe's dissatisfaction with Judge Yerger's (who was known as a self-proclaimed segregationist) dismissal of *Robert Tims et al. vs. City of Jackson et al.* on December 6, 1999. This case involved the violation of an African American man's constitutional rights by Jackson City officials and the fraudulent misrepresentation of a white Jackson City police officer who failed to give mandatory information to Tims (Chokwe's client) regarding a car accident where he was hit. On September 13, 1999, the city filed a motion to dismiss. On December 6, 1999, Judge Yerger granted the dismissal. Chokwe then filed a motion for reconsideration of the motion to dismiss. This motion was overruled June 27, 2000, after the case languished in court for over three years.[54]

Later in 2000, the Mississippi Bar publicly reprimanded Chokwe for speaking out against Hinds County Circuit Judge Swan Yerger. Chokwe announced Yerger dismissed the case without just cause because it was a lawsuit filed against white policemen by a Black client of Chokwe's. When Chokwe challenged Yerger's actions and charged him with making racially discriminatory decisions, Yerger held him in contempt and complained to the Mississippi Bar. Later, the Mississippi Court of Appeals ruled that Yerger's dismissal of the lawsuit was wrong and reinstated it.

It was rumored during the case that Judge Yerger was a cousin of Byron De La Beckwith, the sinister Ku Klux Klan member who murdered civil rights activist Medgar Evers. Medgar's wife, Myrlie Evers, mentioned years later at Chokwe's funeral services that Chokwe assisted in De La Beckwith's conviction in 1994. After two previous acquittals, De La Beckwith was tried and convicted in 1994, with the conviction upheld by the state Supreme Court in 1997. He was imprisoned and died in 2001.

Chokwe's Suspension

After Chokwe began practicing law in Detroit in 1969, there were incidents in the courtroom at Recorder's Court or Wayne County Circuit Court where he was admonished by a judge or two for a variety of issues, from wearing a dashiki into the courtroom to speaking up to judges in defense of his client. The dashiki incident where the judge advised Chokwe he was improperly dressed for the courtroom was an easy fix. Chokwe just snapped on a tie with his African dashiki attire and nothing more was said. Speaking up or back to the judges was not

---

[54]For the case, see *Tims et al vs. City of Jackson et al*, https://law.justia.com/cases/mississippi/court-of-appeals/2002/conv12386.html

as easily remedied. Judges would often hold on to their resentment for Chokwe in subsequent cases; one judge repeatedly threatened to hold him in contempt for not appearing in her courtroom when he had conflicting scheduled trials and/or hearings in another courtroom. Judges in Michigan usually just threatened Chokwe with contempt, but there were a couple of rare occasions where he was actually held in contempt. He also was held in contempt and sentenced to perform numerous hours of community service in the New York Brink's case. However, it was in Mississippi where they felt a need to hold him in contempt, fine him, incarcerate him, and then suspend him.

I can recall when Judge Gordon actually jailed and held Chokwe in contempt and then filed a complaint with the Mississippi Bar to suspend him. The judge said Chokwe was disrespectful to the bench when he was trying to make a point about inappropriate jury instructions that might have led to the conviction of his client. I found this out when I called him one day and asked him how he was doing. "I'm doing better now that I am out of jail." I thought I heard him wrong. "You mean your client is out of jail." "No, me." Then I thought he must have run into a judge who actually sent him to jail for contempt but only for a few hours. "What happened? What were you doing in jail?" According to Chokwe, his client was before the court for a new trial on arson and robbery charges that was granted by the Mississippi Supreme Court. Chokwe was trying to show that the jury had been compromised and wanted to bring in some of the jurors on behalf of his client who would be able to speak to that assertion. However, the presiding judge, Gordon, was denying everything Chokwe put in front of him. This compelled Chokwe to speak up and question the judge about the unfairness of the process, and the judge retaliated by fining Chokwe $500 and sending him to jail for three days. After he explained to me what had occurred, I was angry. How dare that idiot judge jail him for speaking up for his client!

In 1996, Leake County Circuit Court had convicted Chokwe's client Henry Payton of bank robbery and arson. The Mississippi Supreme Court overturned the decision and sent the trial back to Judge Marcus Gordon for a second round. The court found Payton guilty again, though Chokwe said Gordon had been openly hostile to Payton. In 2001, Chokwe filed a motion for a new trial, based on some jurors' opinion that they had been compromised due to Gordon's instructions to continue deliberating until they had a decision. At the hearing, Gordon cut off Chokwe's selection of potential jurors. The judge also allowed Payton to be led to the court in chains, possibly influencing jury opinion against Payton, and he interrupted Chokwe during his opening statements.

Chokwe told *Clarion-Ledger* reporter Jimmie Gates that Gordon "had the judicial temperament of a barbarian." Gordon held Chokwe in contempt for his claim of Gordon's unfair handling of the case, which began a chain of events, culminating with Chokwe being removed from the courtroom amid challenges from him that he was proud to be rid of Gordon's presence. He was jailed for three days and fined a combined $800.

In 2001, a statement Chokwe made to Judge Gordon got him in more trouble: "Look, Judge, if we've got to pay for justice around here, I will pay for justice. I've paid other judges to try to get justice, pay you, too, if that's what is necessary." Gordon cited Chokwe for contempt, fined him $500, and ordered him to serve three days in the county jail. According to an Associated Press story written at the time, Chokwe was referring to the fine itself, meaning that he would happily pay the fine if it meant justice for his client at the time, Henry Payton.[55] A 2003 tribunal recommended a public reprimand for Chokwe, but the bar sought a harsher punishment.

---

[55] R. L. Nave, "Lumumba's Close Call with Disbarment," *Jackson Free Press*, May 16, 2013, https://www.jacksonfreepress.com/weblogs/politics-blog/2013/may/16/lumumba-close-call-with-disbarment/ (accessed May 8, 2025).

The Mississippi Bar wanted to suspend Chokwe from practicing law for an unspecified period of time. The court ruled that in addition to the fines Chokwe had been ordered to pay, his law license would be suspended for six months.

Although Chokwe was suspended from practicing law in Mississippi, he was still licensed to practice law in Michigan. Fortunately, given the relationships Chokwe had formed with his law partners, Jeffrey Edison, Ernest Jarrett, and several other lawyers and judges, he was able to financially survive the unjust suspension by the Mississippi Bar. Chokwe was able to commute back and forth from Jackson to Detroit during his suspension to practice law and represent clients. He was already an associate to attorneys Jeffrey Edison and Paul Curtis, so he had an office available in Detroit, along with many connections.

As they had during the Brink's expropriation case, people all over the country rallied around Chokwe during this period to help him fight the suspension in the appeals process. His supporters in Detroit organized a petition drive and speaking events for him, as well as approaching news outlets, radio stations, community activists, and members of the legal community (including judges and lawyers) to solicit monetary donations.

Chokwe was humble enough to solicit varying perspectives from people with less knowledge and learning than himself. Apparently, that was one of the components that constructed his brilliance. Also, he had enough sense to reach out to colleagues and mentors for assistance and advice on many issues. He was constantly in touch with Dr. Imari Obadele of the RNA throughout his life, as well as Milton Henry, Albert Hatchet, and Cornelius Pitts on numerous occasions regarding clients he was representing. And, of course, he mulled over many of his criminal cases with his law partner Jeff Edison. And he contacted the other partners for guidance on some of the civil cases, including Earl Ashford, Adam Shakoor, Ernest Jarrett, Harry Davis, and Naomi Ottison and his friend Gerald Evelyn.

When Chokwe was suspended, it was both traumatizing and remarkable. I recall an extraordinary, surreal incident involving me. As I said earlier, while Chokwe was suspended and appealing the court's decision, petitions were circulated all over the country to contest his suspension. As his liaison in Detroit, I spearheaded the collection of thousands of these petitions, and I also solicited and collected letters from the various organizations contesting his suspension. With the help of my pastor, Father Norman Thomas, I had arranged to attend a meeting of the Catholic Pastoral Alliance at Sacred Heart Church. The meeting had been pre-scheduled about two months in advance. The time of the meeting was at 1:00 p.m. Earlier that day at 1:50 a.m., my son, Jeaco Hill, was murdered on the streets of Detroit. I don't know how I did it, but I know why I did it. I attended that meeting and procured a pledge for an official letter from their organization and a signed petition by all attendees.

Of course, I explained to the meeting attendees what had just transpired that morning. They appeared to be in amazement and wonderment at my attending that meeting. I knew that the meeting was set up for the purpose of me giving a presentation about Chokwe's situation and our request for help. When I look back, I don't understand how I made it to that meeting, but I knew I had to help my brother in his critical situation. I knew that my brother accomplished all types of remarkable things for people despite the personal situations he was undergoing, and I could do the same for him. The Pastoral Alliance did in fact send a letter later and also persuaded a couple of other organizations to send a letter and submit petitions. Chokwe's suspension case resulted in Mississippi Supreme Court reinstatement of Chokwe to the bar in 2007 with an 8 to 1 decision.[56]

---

[56]Ibid.

Chokwe Encountered Mississippi Injustice Outside the Courtroom

Youth Rally sponsored by Jackson Human Rights Coalition in Jackson, Mississippi!

Chokwe always had a special place in his heart for our youth. He organized with young adults when he was in college. He guided youth in organizing for their rights to a quality education in the 1970s. He actually guided our student leaders at Mumford High School, where Itari and I attended high school. Then again in the late 1990s and early 2000s, Chokwe came to Detroit to organize attorneys to represent Parent, Teacher, and Student protestors who were targeted and arrested for organizing and protesting against the state takeover of our Detroit schools.

During Chokwe's early years with the RNA, he worked closely with the youth, teaching us in Nation Building classes, organizing us to stand up for our rights and beliefs. I recall myself and other young teenagers spending our Saturdays selling RNA newspapers. Chokwe taught us the importance of educating and informing our people of the truth of our condition. We understood, because we as a group made a concerted effort to sell each paper before returning home.

When Chokwe moved to Mississippi, he continued to organize youth through the Malcolm X Grassroots Movement. He also founded an AAU basketball team in Jackson. Chokwe addressed the youth with the following message.

Free the land! Free the land! Free the land! What that means brothers is this: Where do y'all play ball, right here at this court right? [*Crowd shouts back "Right!"*] If somebody else owns the court when they say it is time to go you got to go and you can't play no more basketball then can you? If somebody else owns the basketball and takes it away then you can't play no more basketball can you?

Injustices from Jackson to Detroit

Somebody else owns the colleges and that's why there are so few people who are getting into college nowadays. It's not like it used to be, and you can't play ball like you used to, and they got all these different rules preventing you from playing ball the way you want to. We must understand certain things when we are going after justice. We started out in Africa and the reason you got medicine today is because we created the medicine. Just like Dr. J created the glide at the top of the key, we created the law. We created the streets. We built the first universities, and it is a darn shame that we are around here now and don't own nothing. You almost can't go to a store where one of us owns the store. Now tell me where I'm wrong now. [*Crowd shouts, "You right!"*] And right now we are surrounded by the police. The police ain't out here to support us. They are out here, because some redneck mayor sent them out here. What it is about is doing something for ourselves so we can do something for everybody. We are out here now because a couple of brothers got cattle prod. When something like that happens we need to respond to it. We need to do something. Today, Black youth, the world is yours! All you got to do is stand up and take it. So what we are saying is we have to stand up and learn something and start doing for ourselves.

Watching Chokwe speak to the youth of Jackson, Mississippi, was heart-warming for me. Chokwe has cared about our youth since I was a youth. He was one of my greatest teachers and mentors at home, in the RNA, and in his law office. He educated me and my fellow teen comrades about our history and rights in this country. He taught us that we deserved to have fair and just treatment and we needed to stand up and pursue our rights and freedoms. When he was speaking to the group of youth on the basketball court in Jackson, he was educating them and inspiring them to move forward. He strategically chose to approach these young people on the basketball court and reach them where they were. He shared basketball analogies with them because that was the language they understood. I also know that he cared about those youths on that court because he started coaching youth in Jackson on the AAU team he founded. It is admirable that Chokwe found time in his busy life as an attorney and revolutionary activist to educate and mentor our young people.

Chokwe and Activists Protest in the Streets of Jackson, Mississippi!

Chokwe and protesters from the Jackson's Human Rights Coalition marched the streets chanting, "Whose streets, our streets!" while the Klan—fully clad in Klan attire armed with their Nazi flag, a symbol of hatred—marched. Chokwe spoke to the crowd who came out to protest the injustice of what was occurring in Jackson that day. He highlighted the injustice of allowing the Klan to march freely in the streets of a place where they had a history of burning homes, beating defenseless individuals, and executing Black lives through lynchings:

> The crowd shouts "No Justice No Peace [*helicopter sounds muffles out the chants*]!" Chokwe responds, "Look who they got caved in? They don't have the Klan caved in. They don't have a helicopter flying over the Klan. They got the helicopter flying over you and then they are going to call you a criminal [*helicopter muffles out Chokwe*].... We are going to continue to say what we got to say! We want everybody to be on notice why we are here today. The only reason why is because we stood up against the people they are protecting. Look, it's no sense to us just standing here preaching to the converted, so we have to say something to people who obviously don't know no better, Right!"

Chokwe spoke to the *Jackson News* about the Ku Klux Klan:

> The news reporter reported Chokwe's group criticized the six men who were arrested with weapons and ammunition as they arrived in Jackson. Chief of Police

Bartlett of Jackson Police Department stated the five men from Texas and one from Alabama who were stopped were released after the investigation showed the weapons were not illegal or concealed, but the vehicles' guns seized. The Committee to stop the Klan said their work was not done yet. They planned to reveal some of their next projects at city hall on Monday [...]WJTV Chokwe stated to the crowd of protestors:

They think the police are some kind of savior because they stopped the Klan because they arrested a few people. Perhaps in a staged event but certainly in one, where the people they arrested were released allegedly carrying automatic weapons yet they were released shortly after they were picked up shows there were no serious efforts to protect us or to prosecute anyone who was intending to violate us.

These people who stand between us raped our women, killed our babies in Atlanta. The only reason these clowns are on the police forces is because we marched.[57]

All types of emotions were aroused when I watched the news footage of my brother, Chokwe Lumumba, leading brothers and sisters from Jackson, Mississippi, in a protest march against the notorious Ku Klux Klan. Resentment and disdain for the Klan is ever present when I hear, read, or think about them. Our people, Black people, African people forced into slavery in Amerikkka, were harassed, tortured, and even lynched by the KKK throughout decades in this country, and not much if anything was done about their barbaric and cruel actions. But this day as I watched, I felt joy and tasted victory in 1990 as Chokwe and the other brave and courageous protestors marched against the

---

[57] *Jackson News* Reports about the Ku Klux Klan (protest about 5 Klansmen who confronted Black protesters in Jackson, Mississippi).

white-clad inhumane beings with hatred in their hearts and racial venom spilling out their mouths.

I knew, and many learned, that he loved our people, and he would fight for our people. Chokwe reached out to the youth of Jackson because he cared about them and their future. Chokwe protested against the sinister Ku Klux Klan because again he cared about his people; he also knew that you stand up against wrong, you stand up against people who cause harm, and you stand up against evil. I believe events like speaking to the youths on the basketball court about their futures and marching with the people in Jackson inspired him to become involved in politics and serve as a city council member and ultimately the mayor.

My Brother Never Left Me and He Never Left Detroit

There were several jobs and several times that my big brother Chokwe came to my rescue. One of those times I recall was when I was working at the Boys Club in Detroit as a typist/receptionist. One day I was given a pink slip that was really white and told to finish the day out. I couldn't understand why this was happening to me. My supervisor, the assistant director of the Boys Club, was a well-educated man. He was constantly telling me I need to be doing more with my life than working at the club as a typist. He was constantly giving me books like Nietzsche and Victor Frankl's on existentialism. Then he would sneak in quizzes during our discussions. He would tell me "Bernadette, you are overqualified for this job." He knew it and I knew it, but as a young mother without a degree at the time, that job was the best I could do. His impression of me made me more puzzled as to why I was being let go. He told me he couldn't discuss it with me and that something had occurred in the office. He further said I would find a better job, and I didn't need to be working in this environment. That was the most I could get out of him. His boss, a white woman and the director over the club, called me in the office a few days prior to my expulsion and asked me some questions about things that I did not have any answers to, like where certain records and documents were located. I didn't have a clue because I didn't have anything to do with any of that stuff.

I remember being confused and crying about the situation. When I shared my experience with Chokwe, he visited the club and came back with some answers for me. It appeared that some money had come up missing at the club and they fired everyone working in the office but the director and assistant director. Chokwe told me that the employees were not unionized and it was best for me to just look for another job. He also told me that my supervisor had resigned. Chokwe was in law school when this incident happened. But a couple of years later when he became a lawyer and opened up his law firm, I was the first employee his firm hired.

When I was in the eleventh grade at Mumford High School, I came close to going to jail. One ordinary day of school, the activist students at Mumford got word that the white students at Henry Ford High were attacking the Black students. The grapevine said the white students were beating the Black students with baseball bats and they had even cut one Black girl's hair. This of course angered and incited us, and we loaded up in cars of the students who had them and caravanned over to Henry Ford, which was located a few miles from Mumford. On the way, we learned students from Mackenzie High, another school in our area, were also on their way there. In our car ride over, we talked about how the white students outnumbered the Black students like 3 to 1. Their demographic population was unlike Mumford and Mackenzie schools. Our schools only had a dozen white students at that time. The majority of the white and Jewish kids at Mumford and Mackenzie had moved from the city to the suburbs back in the 1960s. The biggest migration from them occurred, I believe, right after the rebellion in 1967, and it was completed by the time I graduated from Mumford in 1973.

The first thing I noticed when we arrived at Henry Ford High was a large group of white boys on one side of the street with baseball bats, broken bottles, brass knuckles, and other objects in their hands. Further down, the other side of the street was lined with police. However, before we could even get down the street where either party was located, we were threatened by a white couple. Henry Ford High sits on one side of Evergreen Street, and parallel on the other side of the street are residential homes. Once we got out of the cars, we were walking on the side of the street with the houses. A white woman with hair rollers came out of her house angrily shouting obscenities at us and tells us to get off her f------ property. She was met with obscenities right back at her, "b----, f--- you." Then, her husband came barging out the house so quickly it startled me. He pointed a gun at my friend Emory who was returning the obscenities that his wife had thrown out. Almost immediately several cops approached, and we attempted to tell them this man was threatening us with a gun. Instead of the cops listening to anything we had to say, they started harassing Emory, asking him for his identification and name and stuff. Then, one of those pigs started writing Emory a ticket. Emory tried to object and asked how the guy could pull a gun on him and get away with it. One cop responded, "Because he is an off-duty police officer." It was then that I said to the police officer ticketing Emory, "You know you are wrong. If you are going to write him a ticket, then you are just going to have to write all of us a ticket." Well, I almost got what I requested. All of them did not get a ticket, but Emory and I walked away with tickets.

After we walked away, no one seemed to know what we were going to do. That is when Sly, a female friend of mine, and I walked away pledging we were not just going to stand there. As we walked a little further, we were confronted by a group of white girls, laughing and poking fun at us. One of them called us "spades" and the others laughed. I don't know who threw the first blow or hit, but I was engaged in a fight with a white girl. Someone pulled me off of her and said, "The pigs are coming. Let's get out of here." As we ran, I recall slowing up and saying, "I didn't do anything wrong. Why should I run?" It was then that the police ran up on us, and one of them grabbed my arm. A couple of the students, who happened to be my cousins Marco and Mario Davis, grabbed my other arm, attempting to pull me away from the police. I was shouting in pain, "stop, let go!" My cousins let go, and I fell on the ground. The cop literally dragged me all the way across the lawn of the school to the street where the paddy wagon was parked and threw me in the vehicle. They arrested my cousins and a couple of other students and threw them into the van also.

While piling us in the paddy wagon, about three pigs were in a ferocious altercation with a well-built, muscular, fudge-complexioned Black boy. We later found out his name was Richard. Apparently, Richard was not having these pigs. He was beating the s--- out of them. He was holding them off and getting his blows in until they piled up on him. At one point, Richard became dazed like a prize fighter who had just received a knockout punch, and he was unstable on his feet. Two of those pigs held onto him while one of them beat his head against the paddy wagon. We were shouting and screaming, "STOP!" Not listening to us, but eventually one of those pigs ordered the others to stop and they threw Richard in the wagon with us. On the drive to the police station, they refused to roll their windows down and we repeatedly told them we could not breathe. One of the pigs was a Black man, and we repeatedly asked him for air. He told us to shut the f--- up and don't refer to him as brother. "I am not your brother."

When we arrived at the precinct station, they piled the boys in a cell. I was told later by my cousins Marco and Mario that they were in the cell right next to a collection of white boys they had hauled into the station, too. We heard them discussing what to do with Sly and myself. We were the only girls they brought in. Ironically, the white girls were never apprehended. They eventually allowed us to sit in their office space and wait for our parents. One of the officers tried to intimidate and scare me and told me I was going to be in big trouble with my mother because I was now a criminal. Not to my surprise, but to his, my mother was more concerned about what had happened to me and whether I was hurt. The officers gave my mother a court date for me at Juvenile Court and released me into her custody. I learned later that one of the Baker sisters, either Janis or Alice who were activists at my school, had gone over to my house and informed my mother what had occurred at Henry Ford High School. My mother called Chokwe and allowed them to explain to him what happened. Chokwe told me he and RNA legionnaires rode up to Henry Ford High, but the place was cleared out by that time. I liked the thought of my big brother coming to my rescue with his army. I smiled about that for a long time. All the way until right before my court date at Wayne County Juvenile Court, I began to worry about getting locked up and sent to a state facility like Imari, Jr. (son of the president of the RNA) and others for protesting. It was years later when I learned Imari, Jr. was sent away for more than protesting. Fortunately for me, whoever the referee or judge was that I appeared before dismissed the charges of trespassing, loitering, and disturbing the peace. I don't remember him, but I do remember what he said to me. Go back to school and get your education and don't come back before me again, or I'll lock you up. "Yes, sir," I responded. Who would have known, who could have predicted that I would be back to Wayne County Juvenile Court not as a defendant but as a probation officer?

When I grew up, one of the career jobs I landed was "Juvenile Probation Officer." I was a probation officer assigned to monitor and supervise juvenile offenders when they violated their probation. I would write reports, make recommendations, submit reports to the court, and often testify in court. One case landed me in a world of trouble—the Che Lark case. This young man received a new charge of breaking and entering an occupied dwelling, which was a probation violation, along with a few other charges that were unrelated. During my investigation into Che's school, home, and police report, I discovered that the building he was accused of breaking into was not occupied, contrary to the charge the prosecutor had levied against him. The dwelling was a house owned by an elderly woman who was not living in the house but had been residing in a nursing home for some time. I talked to her son, who said the house was empty, and the kids did not do any damage. He did not want them to get locked up because of some shenanigans. I, in turn, relayed this information to the defense attorney, Arthur Bowman, who brought it up in court and asked for a dismissal of the case, which he was granted.

The prosecuting attorney along with a particular referee, Referee Lily, teamed up and sent a letter to the head of the probation department requesting that I be removed from my position after the case. The letter stated that I was unethically assisting the family and contributing to the delinquency of a minor. The prosecutor claimed I was engaging with the family in laughter and disrespect in the court room. Although Referee Lily acknowledged he did not have any connection to the Che Lark case, he alleged he had seen me behave inappropriately with my juvenile probationers in several cases in front of him. I remember him stating, "Ms. Hill is acting as if she is the defense attorney when she is a probation officer. It is not her job to represent and/or defend the probationers assigned to her caseload." In addition to this letter, my supervisor Helen Surrel, head of the probation department, and I were not on good terms. In fact, I did not like her, and I don't think she liked me. Surrel did not care for my union-organizing. At that time, I was the secretary of AFSCME Local 1905. We were speaking out on better pay for employees and resources for our probationers at the court. So, I'm thinking she is not going to defend me against their ludicrous charges. Therefore,

I ran to my big brother, who was a practicing attorney at this time. He came up to the court and met with Ms. Helen Surrel. I'll never forget Chokwe said, "I don't know what problems you are having with Ms. Surrel, but she didn't mention any. I think she is okay, and we had a good conversation. As a matter of fact, she told me that she was in the process of responding to the prosecutor and referee's letter in support of you." Surrel also shared with Chokwe that she had personally spoken to Judge Lacey. The Che Lark case was conducted in his courtroom. Judge Lacey was known as the toughest judge on the bench at Juvenile Court and he certainly wouldn't tolerate the behavior the prosecutor described I exhibited in his court room.

There were also a couple of other times Chokwe came through for me. I would primarily get in trouble in school or on a job because of standing up and speaking out on racism and discrimination. I often wondered if Chokwe felt responsible for my actions because he brought me into the movement and taught me how to stand up and speak out.

Detroit Recorder's Court

Although Detroit Recorder's Court was admired as one of the most effectively run criminal courts in the country, the state saw fit to merge it into the Wayne County Circuit Court in 1997. When I was in law school, our law professors used Recorder's Court as a model criminal court in illustrating the operation of a criminal court. The cases were handled in a fair and expedient manner. The court cases of Detroiters from a predominantly Black city who were facing criminal charges were processed and executed at Recorder's Court by mostly Black judges and juries. White radical racists who were upset with the convictions of two white cops, Walter Budzyn and Larry Nevers, fought for this merger and got it. Budzyn and Nevers were dirty, racist white cops who murdered a Black male, Malice Green, who was suspected of concealing heroin in his hands. These white supporters and the state of Michigan dismantled an exemplary court system because the court correctly prosecuted and convicted two white, murderous cops. Since the merger, many predominantly Black defendants go before white judges and predominantly white jurors, since the judge and juries are now elected countywide. I found it admirable that Chokwe, who was highly admired for his work at Recorder's Court but was living and practicing law in Mississippi at the time, still found a need and the time to give his support to the fight to save Recorder's Court.

Detroit Public School Protest

The most significant time when Chokwe came to my rescue was related to a protest situation that resulted in my going to jail as an adult and being placed in a cell. In the late 1990s, Detroit Public Schools (DPS) experienced a governmental takeover. It actually began under a democratic governor, Jennifer Granholm. White Republican legislatures were after the revenue from the Detroit Public Schools, and she, in my opinion, assisted them in getting it. She was the first one to bring Robert Bobb in for the Detroit Public School System. She called him an Emergency Financial Manager. Interestingly, hough, Detroit schools were in the black.[58] If my memory is correct, this action by the governor occurred subsequent to a few white private charter school owners offering to open up several charter high schools in Detroit. The Detroit Federation of Teachers rightfully rejected this offer, and it was ultimately rejected by the district. Somewhere in the hijacking of the Detroit schools and subsequent to Detroit residents passing the largest millage in Detroit history and in most cities of similar demographics, we passed a mileage of $1.5 billion for the building and

---

[58] Manon Steel, "The Empire Strikes Back: State Takeover and Education in Michigan," Perspectives on Urban Education 17 (Spring 2020), https://tinyurl.com/3sp7xwh6. See "Governor Appoints Robert C. Bobb Emergency Financial Manager for Detroit Public Schools," Jan. 26, 2009, State of Michigan, https://tinyurl.com/2pp6vd92; "Takeover of Detroit Schools Show Few Intended Results," Mackinac Center for Public Policy, Jan. 19, 2006, https://tinyurl.com/yk59fmxu; Elena Herrada, "A School Board Member in Exile on the Decline of Detroit's Public Schools," Workers World, https://tinyurl.com/pc68wbwa.

renovation of our school buildings. Unfortunately, the predominantly white Republican Legislature believed the predominantly Black city of Detroit was not responsible, astute, or intelligent enough to govern over that amount of money. So they conspired to take it from the city moving forward.

These efforts ended in the dilution, dismantling, and theft of resources from the Detroit Public Schools. Under Robert Bobb's supervision of the Detroit Public Schools, schools were merged and closed. Then, charter schools for private pay were opened throughout Detroit. With the closing of Detroit schools and the opening of the charter schools, many students left and went to the charter schools and the government funding followed them, thereby diluting and diminishing funds for the education of Detroit Public School students. Also, what is important to know about this sinister act of manipulation and theft is that Detroit Public Schools was not financially bankrupt, like most school districts when there is a government takeover. DPS was in the black. So they had to concoct another angle, another strategy to take over the system, and this they did. Dan Degrow, a white state representative from Port Huron, Michigan, a Michigan school district smaller than Detroit's, proposed that the state take over the Detroit schools due to test scores and poor grades. He proposed this even though his whiter district was in the same shape. His proposal passed and gave them a passageway to take over and put emergency managers in just about every single Black school district in Michigan, and it resulted in shutting down many of the schools and sometimes the entire district in the Detroit area: Detroit, Benton Harbor, Inkster, and Highland Park. This whole takeover resulted in millions of dollars unaccounted for from Detroit by the State of Michigan and the charter schools primarily performing lower than the Detroit public schools. What did they care? They got control of the money. Over a decade later, after a long-protracted fight from grassroots activists, DPS was in the red and had to be restructured according to the thieves in order to survive.

Throughout this ordeal, I was giving Chokwe, who was then in Mississippi, updated reports on what was happening with DPS. Chokwe got involved from the inception. I was attending meetings of Keep The Vote No Takeover, headed by fearless educational warrior Helen Moore, who has been fighting for the educational rights of our youth for over fifty years. Chokwe put out a call to the legal community in Detroit to come together and assist in this protracted struggle of saving the Detroit Public Schools from the Republican vultures. Helen arranged the meeting at the Dexter Elmhurst Center and Chokwe flew in from Jackson, Mississippi. There were several grassroots organizers present like Kwame Kenyatta, who was also on the School Board at the time, Lamar Lemons, Richard Clay, and several others, including myself. However, there were only a few from the legal community who appeared. I later learned from meeting with some of them that they were not clearly convinced that a state takeover was a bad thing. They were thinking it could provide more options and improve the educational system. I hope they recognized how much that way of thinking cost us. Not only did it lead to the takeover of the Detroit schools but also to the takeover of the whole city of Detroit. It is important to note Mark Fancher and the National Conference of Black Lawyers joined our fight.

However, the attorneys who did show up that day consisted of George Washington, Jeffrey Edison, and Sharon McPhail. If there were any others, I apologize for not including you. From that meeting, Attorneys McPhail and Washington organized to take the lead on pursuing legal matters against the DPS takeover. Chokwe attended several subsequent meetings and forums in this fight held at the Fine Arts Theater and Sacred Heart Activities Building. At that first meeting, I recall Chokwe mentioning that people would go to jail and we would have to be prepared. Kwame Kenyatta reminded me sometime later that he recalled my saying that we should not protest inside the meetings.

This is important because at one of our regular meetings at the Fine Arts Theater, Chokwe was referenced in the discussion. I really don't recall the point. But I recall Sharon McPhail saying something like, "It doesn't matter what Chokwe said, he is not going to be there." Yes, she said that in my presence and it incensed me. *Of course he would not be there; he lives in Jackson, Mississippi. However, he organized your involvement* (I was thinking but did not say). A few days later, most of our group was outside of Finney High School, not far from my home at the time. We were passing out literature to all of the attendees going into the building. At some point, this one sister named Rose was talking about going inside the meeting. I reminded the group that the strategy we decided on at our meeting was to stay outside and leaflet. This sister became loud and irate, even confrontational, telling me in so many words, "You don't call any shots." She was so loud that a cop who I had seen Rose talking to just a short while earlier came over and the group members disbanded. Most of them went into the building.

I don't know exactly what it was; peer pressure, I guess. I knew what the strategy was supposed to be, and the group had abandoned the strategy. However, it was something clawing in me about Attorney McPhail's words, "Chokwe isn't going to be there." So I made my decision to go into the building where a DPS Board meeting was in session. The heated topic was about hiring David Adamany as CEO of Detroit Public Schools. Our group wanted no part of this appointment. Amongst many reasons was our opposition to them appointing a white man to govern over a school district that is over 80% Black when there are plenty of qualified African Americans to do that. The people in the district pushing his nomination believed he was particularly qualified because he was the former president of Wayne State University.

Helen Moore was at the front of the room attempting to interject the truth as she always did. People were demanding more time to speak as they always did. Then, something unusual happened. A sister named Hakika, who was sitting next to Malik Shabazz, a self-professed Black Panther and community activist, kept screaming and shouting offensive remarks like, "Who wants a faggot over their kids?" David Adamany was an alleged homosexual. Freeman Hendrix, deputy mayor at the time, was warning her repeatedly that she was out of order and to refrain from that behavior. Although Freeman and I were on separate sides of the appointment, I understood his point. Freeman is married to my best friend from childhood, and I respect him even if he was assistant to Mayor Dennis Archer, whom I was totally disappointed in and did not respect. However, I assessed what was going on and I felt that I could help. Our group and people from the audience were moving toward Helen, who had posted right next to the sister who had been shouting. Police were gathering in the aisle toward the forming crowd.

Malik Shabazz, who stands over six feet, four inches tall, was grandstanding to the Board members on stage and telling them that they had not properly warned the sister. It had been just a few days prior to this when we were at the court building for a hearing on this matter when I was able to calm Malik down. So I guess I thought I could advise him that day to take the sister out of the meeting. At some point before Freeman Hendricks shouted, "Officers, remove her from the meeting," I was reaching up with my right hand trying to get Malik's attention when suddenly and painfully someone from behind pulled my left arm and dug their nails into my left hand. I didn't know who or why, but I reacted physically. The next thing I remember is being on the ground with hands all over my body. At some point I was forcibly yanked up from the ground, and there was a police officer bending my right arm behind my back and another cop bending my left arm behind my back. And if that wasn't enough, a huge six-foot Black female pig had her arm around my neck. The entire time they're pulling me. And I'm screaming, "Why are you doing this to me?

STOP!" A female officer who had just maybe fifteen minutes prior to this melee asked me for a pen, responded, "You are resisting. Stop resisting!" It was at that point in time that I learned from firsthand experience that when criminal suspects say they were not resisting or fighting with the police they probably were not. The news footage that I looked at later has the police, in my opinion, pulling me around like a rag doll. HOW IN THE HELL COULD I HAVE BEEN RESISTING ANYTHING with both my arms and neck in their ferocious locks?!

Shortly after, I was arrested, hauled off in a police car, and ended up in jail. This turned out to be the most humiliating experience in my life. The young officer who arrested me rejected my pleas not to handcuff me for "disorderly conduct." At the time, I was still employed by the Michigan Department of Corrections as well as the Detroit Board of Education. I explained that to the young officer, who was about my son's age, and I said, "I know you can use your discretion in putting on the handcuffs. Please don't put them on me. Would you want your mother in handcuffs?" He very promptly and politely responded while placing the cuffs on my wrists, "My mother would not be in your situation." On the way to the police precinct, I was mulling over in my head what name to give them. Do I use my entire name Bernadette Taliaferro-Cain or just Taliaferro? I was thinking that my in-laws, who were not part of the progressive grassroots movement, would not want people to see their daughter-in-law (carrying their name) on the news. My father-in-law at the time was a professor at Wayne State University. No problem, the name situation was resolved for me. When I arrived at the precinct, the arresting officer said, "Ms. Hill (Hill was my first married name), what are you doing here?" I'm looking at her in astonishment and thinking I did not say my name is Hill. She continued, "Ms. Hill you were my English teacher at Martin Luther King High School." *Great, I'm thinking, my former student is processing me.* She continued to take my fingerprints. She and her partner took good care of me during their shift. It was too bad for me that I stayed there past their shift.

As I was placed in the jail cell, I got a look from the other side. As a parole/probation officer, I had been on the other side of the jail cell numerous times. However, this side of the cell was more atrocious than the side I would frequently visit from. The smell that emitted was a cross between menstrual blood and urine. It was horrible. The cell was old, cruddy, and of course excruciatingly uncomfortable. I recall four of us being in that cell. There was one woman who was arrested for manufacturing drugs. According to her, when they came and arrested her, she was in her kitchen cooking crack cocaine on her kitchen stove. There was another woman who was in there for felonious assault. She said she hit her husband on the head with a large object and he was in the hospital. Then, there was Hakika, the sister who started the melee, and me. I remember looking at her like I wanted to cuss her out.

I made my call from a phone in the cell to Itari, who said she had already been in touch with Attorneys George Washington and Sharon McPhail, and they said to let them know what you needed them to do. However, she called them back after speaking with Chokwe in Mississippi. He talked to Jeff, who would be coming to get me out of jail. Unfortunately, Jeff didn't make it there, and I made some mistakes.

The law enforcement agent who initiated the attack from behind me turned out to be the head of Detroit Public School Security. He was also the same officer who was talking to the fellow protester Rose outside the school who encouraged everyone to go into the building. In addition, Chokwe had Attorney Charles Turner, one of the attorneys who handled some of his cases when he was out of town, view all the footage from the board meeting. Charles advised Chokwe and me that after thoroughly going through the footage, he believed the attack upon me by the DPS Security Officer was deliberate. Charles showed me how this officer appears to follow me to the area where the crowd was forming.

It is important to note that I have fibromyalgia. This is a chronic disorder characterized by widespread musculoskeletal pain, fatigue, and tenderness in localized areas. Therefore, it ignited excruciating pain in my body when the security chief and five police officers jumped on me. While I was in jail, I demanded that I go to the hospital for treatment. Of course, I was making demands to people who obviously cared less than a damn for me or any other detainee in that jail. First, they took me back for interrogation. I repeatedly requested that I go to the hospital. When they were finished with my interrogation, my student who had processed me at the front desk came back and told me, "Ms. Hill, you have to be careful what you say. They are considering charging you with aggravated assault on a police officer. You told them you kicked one of them in the groin." What I had told them was "when someone snatched my arm from behind and dug their nails into my hand busting the skin open, I naturally tried to defend myself." I had no idea who that person was or why that person had done that. She left me telling me to be careful.

Shifts changed while I was in jail, and my kind student and her partner left. I then got the disrespectful, rude, and insensitive treatment of the male officers who took their place. It appeared that they were especially annoyed by my supporters in the lobby. My daughters Charlitta, Shushanna, Maisha, and Helen Moore, and a few other people were chanting, "let her go." When I continued to press them to go to the hospital and told them I was a probation/parole officer, one of them said, "Then, you know the drill." In other words, shut up and take it. It wasn't until about 11:00 p.m. that they took me to Receiving Hospital, where the nightmare I was living was heightened. I was escorted in handcuffs through a door where a tall, lanky, mean-looking Black cop received me and ordered me to stand still while he got down on his knees and proceeded to put chains on me. Some people may call them ankle bracelets, prisoner chains.

He then proceeded to escort me with ankle chains and handcuffs on through the emergency room. This was definitely a traumatizing situation for me.

Although Chokwe was in Mississippi, he investigated my case and spoke to Freeman Hendrix at the mayor's office regarding dropping the charges against me. Chokwe and his former law partner, Ernest Jarrett, both discussed with me the possibility of a lawsuit regarding my matter. Ernest Jarrett had won a million-dollar lawsuit for the Malice Green family. Malice Green was killed in Detroit by two pigs, Budzyn and Nevers, where they actually beat a piece of scalp off of his head. Chokwe didn't handle a lot of civil lawsuits. However, he had recently represented a Black woman in Jackson, a nursing supervisor at a hospital who was accused of shoplifting at a store. Both Chokwe and Ernie said I had a fifty-fifty chance of winning a lawsuit in my matter. They also advised me I would have to leave my job. That was a deciding factor for me because I had just completed my master's program and would be receiving a two thousand dollar raise. Also, I loved teaching. Well, I didn't quit my job, and I didn't sue; but I am still traumatized from that experience with the police.

Chokwe was arrested in a Battle Creek case.

Shushanna arrested at a Board of Education meeting.

The Pigs Arrest Chokwe

When I was researching for this book, I came across some video footage of Chokwe being arrested in Battle Creek, Michigan, in a case where he represented members of "Coalition to End Police Brutality and Racism." Chokwe and two of his comrades, Kwame Kalimara, the Minister of Foreign Affairs and Justice on the New Afrikan People's Court in the Provisional Government of the Republic of New Afrika, and Kwame Kenyatta, director of the Malcolm X Center in Detroit and a RNA citizen, were at a city council meeting. The moderator of that meeting deemed Chokwe out of order while he was talking about the many violations of the law and racist acts that had been committed by their police department upon Black residents of Battle Creek. It was painful to see those white racist pigs putting their hands on my brother and arresting him. He did not go peacefully like his hero Dr. King, but they had to take him down like I imagine they would have had to do with his hero Malcolm. It wasn't like he was hitting them, but his body was straight and stiffened, and they had to break it down. Actually, it looked like a couple of those fat pigs were afraid to even approach my brother, with his tall, six-foot four-inch frame. Chokwe's friend Attorney Gerald Evelyn was also involved with helping Chokwe with this case, and he, too, was arrested. This definitely was one of several cases where Chokwe went to jail with his clients.

Eventually, the Detroit Chapter of National Conference of Black Lawyers (NCBL) sent lawyers in to assist with these cases. The NCBL brought the big guns in. They sent the renowned attorney Cornelius Pitts to represent both Attorneys Lumumba and Evelyn. Kwame Kenyatta and Kwame Kalimara were also key leaders in community-organizing with this case and went to jail that infamous day. I wish I could show you how these brave fearless warriors handled themselves against a racist police force and institution.

There were so many situations when Chokwe helped me and many others. However, this next situation is really one I need to mention because he resolved a critical dispute between activists. But the activist that he bailed out of hot water, in my opinion, I found out years later was not worthy of Chokwe's help. Somewhere in the late '90s, Malik Shabazz, a neophyte to many of us in the community, began the New Black Panther Party. Although most of the Detroit grassroots community was not familiar with this brother or had any recollection of work he had done, he wanted to begin the New Black Panther Party in Detroit. How he was able to persuade some of us, including myself, at the time when he was credible to do this, was through his newly founded community work. Malik was organizing his group to march in front of supermarkets (mostly Arabic owned) in the Black community and protest their unsanitary store conditions, selling rotten meat, and price gouging. His efforts were very impressive and many successful, even compelling them to clean up their stores. A few of Malik's store protests resulted in the closing of their stores. At the same time, Malik was marching on what were alleged drug houses in the Black community and insisting they shut down and move out the neighborhood.

Actually, I called for his help with a problem one of my brothers was experiencing with a drug dealer on his block. This particular dealer had disrespected my brother's wife and son. This led to words between the "neighbors," which resulted in my brother's car being shot up. Malik and his group came over and marched on the drug dealer's house. However, the occupant of the property denied having any knowledge of our complaints and claimed the individual who was confrontational with my brother and his family did not live at that house. The police of course did not assist in this situation. However, I did not leave my brother's fate in Malik's hands. Kilindi Iyi, some former RNA security, and a couple of brothers handled the situation.

As time progressed, questions started to arise about Malik's authenticity. One night I was at a program at the Akwaaba Center, a main meeting place for the cultural community. It was there I spoke to two brothers from Cleveland, Ohio, about Malik Shabazz. They shared with me that they believed him to be an informant and they were going to take care of him. The brothers were angry and spoke violently about Malik. The shorter of the two brothers became quite boisterous and told me, "Malik is a traitor, and he cannot be trusted, and he is going to get fucked up." The other taller, thinner brother said, "Malik is going to be taken care of." I didn't know what the brother meant by that statement, and I was scared to find out. This situation reminded me of the altercation Lawrence X, a PGRNA member and a long-time revolutionary activist of the Detroit community, had with Malik Shabazz at the Inner City Sub Center during the time of the DPS protests. Lawrence X, a short-in-stature but muscular and stocky brother, physically confronted big, tall Malik Shabazz and cornered him. It appeared to me that Malik was frightened. I don't recall exactly what the confrontation was about, but I do recall Lawrence X uttering some of the same sentiments that this Ohio brother expressed. He told Malik, "Motherfucker, I'll fuck you up." At that point, I went to retrieve some other brothers to save Malik from Lawrence X. Sometimes I look back and wish that Lawrence X had beat Malik's ass.

The Ohio brothers encouraged me to speak to Malik Zulu Shabazz of the Black Panther Party in D.C., who was operating the true Black Panther Party under the authority of Khalid Abdul Muhammad, an original Black Panther member. Malik Zulu and I spoke for a lengthy time, and he shared a similar viewpoint as the two brothers from Ohio. I also learned from him that the brothers from Ohio were not playing.

Next, I contacted Chokwe and advised him of this situation. It is my understanding that Chokwe boarded a plane that night and came to Detroit and met with Malik Shabazz and other involved parties to resolve the situation. According to Elder Baba Oscar Lucas, a member of Malcolm X Grassroots Movement, the group met at Aknartoons, a vegetarian restaurant on Woodward Avenue in Detroit about 2:00 a.m. to resolve this conflict. Chokwe served as the mediator. Chokwe talked with Kathleen Cleaver and a few other founding members of the Black Panthers and said that Malik Shabazz and any other dedicated activist of our people could form new Black Panther chapters. Thus, Malik was protected.

Years later the grassroots community in Detroit started doubting Malik Shabazz's authenticity, particularly when he publicly supported white Wayne County Prosecutor Mike Duggan, who later became Detroit's mayor. This is the same Prosecutor Mike Duggan who was criticized for attempting to cover up the Malice Green murder by two white cops. Malik was chastised and brought before the community on several occasions for his questionable behavior and activities in our community. The Council of Elders disciplined him for supporting Mike Duggan, a white man. Malik Shabazz supported him for prosecutor and mayor of Detroit. Also, entertainer Arsenio Hall made light of Shabazz on his national TV night show. He mentioned that Detroit has a Black Panther supporting the white candidate for mayor. A couple of Muslim brothers scolded him for not protecting Hakika and me when we were both arrested, and I assaulted, at the DPS meeting. Also, I was at an event where numerous Black leaders gathered and called Malik Shabazz and checked him. Detroit local activist and poet Millard "Owusu" Porter had organized a Youth March Conference subsequent to the Million Youth March in New York. Millard had made arrangements to bring Khalid Abdul Muhammad here to Detroit to speak. However, Malik Shabazz intervened with those plans and rearranged them with Khalid. I recall seeing the following brothers sitting at the table surrounding Malik Shabazz, Amiri Baraka, Kwame Kenyatta, Dawud Muhammad, Brother Owusu, and a few others. I was not privy to their conversation, but I was told afterwards that Malik was checked for his wrongful and inappropriate behavior.

Chokwe demonstrated time and time again his continuing commitment to his Detroit family and community even when he moved to Jackson, Mississippi. When Recorder's Court, Detroit Public Schools, members of his family, and members of the grassroots community experienced injustices and needed his assistance, he was there to assist, even when he had to take a flight out of Jackson, Mississippi, in the wee hours of the morning to resolve a critical dispute. Many people did not know and do not know the sacrifices this revolutionary brother made for our people, and this is why he is an unsung hero whose songs need to be heard and stories need to be told!

Thursday, May 20, 1999 at the Fine Arts.
(From left to right) Hikika, CPA, Greg Frazier,
Helen Moore with microphone, the late Chokwe Lumumba,
Attorney Sharon McPhail and George Washington.

CHAPTER 8

Chokwe Joins Politics

*"Mayors typically don't do the things we're trying to do.
Revolutionaries aren't typically mayors."*
– Chokwe Lumumba

Free The Land: Mayor Chokwe Lumumba (1947-2014)
"one city, one aim, one destiny"

It is rough to love a people
who do not know or love themselves
rougher if
one is a Black intellectual-activist committed to
out working the workers,
out studying the studious, committed to
bright sun tomorrows today and understands
in political & legal language the value of
land, off-centered ideas and honored governance.

rougher still to live among and love
a people who are too often defined by their
athletes, comedians, talk-show hosts, sit-coms,
high-school-pushed-outs-confused rappers, the N-word,
youth prison population, male dress-wearing actors,
incarcerated politicians, and prosperity ministers
whose definitions of their god is how close they
can get to him in their lear jets.

Memories of My Revolutionary Brother, Chokwe Lumumba

it is rough & rougher
to dearly love a people
who believe more in others than themselves
forgetting that the only life-substance that nobody,
nowhere is making anymore of is land, and that
most life-giving & life-saving sources come from land,
not fast food chains, canned broccoli or fried chitterlings.

Chokwe knew this and took the necessary,
often detoured, yet unrestricted 21st century corrective steps
always in league with Garvey, Douglass, DuBois, Nkrumah,
Malcolm, King, Evers, Wells-Barnett, Rodney, Parks, Bishop,
Sibeko, Brooks, Lumumba (his name sake), Obadele, Cabral,
Afrik, Baker, Cortez, Baraka, Mandela and all the unknown
Black faceless fighters stamped into dried earth to become
right melody,
liberated songs & yeses,
a quick study & smile,
a city's head, inspiration and clear possibilities,
whose Afrikan consciousness prepared him
to be us, teach us, lead us and to love us
more than we loved or love our selves.

(for his family, the people of Detroit,
Michigan and Jackson, Mississippi)

Haki R. Madhubuti
3/3/14
Poet, Founder and Publisher of Third World Press,
former University Distinguished Professor and
Founding Director of the MFA Program in Creative Writing
at Chicago State University, and former Ida B. Wells-Barnett
University Professor at DePaul University

Councilman

Chokwe did not find politics; politics found Chokwe. He never aspired to become a politician or run for any elected government office. It is my understanding that some people of Jackson, including members of the Malcolm X Grassroots Movement, went to Chokwe and recruited him to run for a seat on the Jackson City Council and, later, for mayor of Jackson, Mississippi.

When Chokwe called me and announced that he was running for a seat on the Jackson, Mississippi, city council, I was not a bit surprised. To me it was just something else he decided to do for the liberation of our people. I remember Chokwe told me that he needed my help to organize fundraisers in Detroit for his campaign. That, too, did not surprise me because he always called me to organize petition drives and fundraisers for various matters like the one for his reinstatement to the bar, support for his clients in the Brink's expropriation case, the Pontiac Illinois case, and several others. Although I was experiencing some medical issues at that time, Chokwe assured me that Kwame Kenyatta would assist me in procuring the location for the fundraisers and give me the support I needed. And that is how it was done. Chokwe's friend Gerald Evelyn told me when I contacted him for his support, "You are like the Energizer Bunny. You keep going for your brother." Those complimentary words and the support of Chokwe's friends like Gerald and Kwame enabled me to continue providing the support and assistance my brother needed.

Chokwe announced publicly that he was running for a seat on the city council on December 29, 2008. Fundraisers were organized to support Chokwe's candidacy within and outside of Jackson, Mississippi. In Detroit, we held several fundraisers. I recall one fundraiser we had at our beautiful Detroit Charles Wright Museum of African American History. It was scheduled for February, perhaps one of the most troublesome months with the weather. I believe the motivation for this time frame was to do it during Black

Memories of My Revolutionary Brother, Chokwe Lumumba

History month. Unfortunately, on the day it was planned, a blizzard was forming. Congressman John Conyers, a staunch supporter and advocate for Chokwe, was our featured speaker. The congressman was present consistently to support Chokwe with his many legal cases and causes. When members of the Detroit media and political critics demeaned, slandered, and ostracized Chokwe, Congressman John Conyers stood by his side, had his back, and threw his support behind him. In my opinion, there was no one better to give the keynote speech. Conyers's assistant was calling me every couple of hours to see if the event was still on. When I was able to get in touch with Chokwe and discuss the weather situation, he was already en route to Detroit. I advised the congressman's assistant. We held the event, but it ran a little late. Of course we did not have the big crowd we anticipated, due to the inclement weather, but about fifty family members and friends made it there. I found out later that Queen Mother Osun Dara, our community culturalist and a friend of Chokwe, was in a car accident on the way to the event. People who loved Chokwe *really* loved Chokwe.

Congressman John Conyers

Apparently, Congressman John Conyers was one of those people. He arrived at the museum and in the midst of his dynamic speech, a representative from the museum pulled me aside and advised me that we would not be able to stay over our scheduled time. I pled with him to allow us extra time due to late arrivals because of the weather conditions. He told me no. That meant I had to end the congressman's speech and the remainder of the program, including refreshments we had prepared. As I slowly kept working my way to the congressman to give him the note I wrote, he stopped speaking and said to me, "Yes, Shushanna, is there a problem?" I said, "Yes, Congressman, the museum representative said we have to close the program down now and leave the building because we are over our time." "You tell them we aren't closing this program down, and we aren't leaving this damn building, and if he has a problem with it to take the matter up with me after I finish speaking." He proceeded to speak, the program proceeded to go on, and I never did see the museum representative say a word to Congressman Conyers.

In 2009, Chokwe Lumumba was elected to the Jackson Ward 2 council seat with the help of the Malcolm X Grassroots Movement (MXGM), which he had helped found. He also gained support from the Jackson People's Assembly, the Mississippi Disaster Relief Coalition, and other community activists. While serving as a Jackson, Mississippi councilman, Chokwe remained true to his principles and beliefs. He did not sugarcoat his feelings on political positions. Chokwe may have upset the white establishment when he gave a keynote address at the Organization for Black Struggles' 31st anniversary celebration in St. Louis in February 2011. Chokwe spoke about the recent experience of the Scott sisters, whose fame had grown nationwide since their release from prison. But one St. Louis newspaper found Chokwe's comments about Mississippi governor Haley Barbour interesting: "We knew he was a redneck governor from the hills of Mississippi," Lumumba was quoted in the *St. Louis American*. "We knew he couldn't stand that baggage he had in Mississippi—one was the Scott sisters—if he was talking about having a presidential run."[59]

While serving on the city council in Jackson, Chokwe recommended some innovative ideas for the city, including the creation of a "five-person commission composed of a City Council member, a member of JATRAN management, a bus driver, a rider, and a representative

---

[59]"Lumumba Redneck Barbour Earns No Credit," *Clarion-Ledger* (Jackson, MS), February 6, 2011, 16.

Memories of My Revolutionary Brother, Chokwe Lumumba

(Back, L to R): Martez McElwine-Potts, Kamri Hill, Delon Tillman, Treyvon Wells; (Front, L to R): Charlitta Hill, Jay Hill, Jordan Hughes; (Kneeling) Reggie Glaspie

(L to R): Qadir Lumumba-Benjamin, Kofi Miller

(L to R): Sarah Torres, Kofi Miller, Dynasty Hardy, Essence Fields

(L to R): Delisa Glaspie, Kenya Taliaferro, Zipporah Coleman

Millard Owusu Porter, Kwame Kenyatta, Mario Taliaferro, Chokwe Antar Lumumba

Alivia Zuri Ogobonnoya

Chokwe Joins Politics

Rukia

Shushanna & Halima Olufemi

(L to R) Camille Jackson, Zipporah Coleman, Kwasi Akwamu, Nubia Morenike, Verbena

of the mayor's administration." Chokwe wanted "to see a plan to make JATRAN profitable. 'Jackson is supposed to be a growing city,' he said. 'If that's true, and we have a poor transportation system, let's fix it.'"[60] Halima Olufemi, who once served as executive assistant to Chokwe, said that Chokwe also proposed a single home development while he was serving on the city council. Unfortunately, the proposal was not adopted. Olufemi recalls that Chokwe, while serving as councilman, brought the People's Assembly to the city. A People's Assembly member, Akil Bakari, of MXGM explains the history of a People's Assembly: "Assembly" is exactly how it sounds—an assembly or coming together of community members to share ideas about the city and let the city know what matters to us as residents. People's Assemblies (PAs) happen all over the world. Some are very large and take on national issues. Some, like ours in Jackson, are focused on local issues. One of the first PAs took place in Lowndes County, Alabama, in the 1960s and there have been a number of assemblies in Jackson and throughout the South ever since. Initiated by the Malcolm X Grassroots Movement in coalition with Jackson residents and community groups, PAs are where community members make their voices heard.[61]

Another resolution Chokwe sponsored on City Council that was backed by Occupy Jackson was the Jackson City Council endorsement of state and U.S. constitutional amendments that would deny corporations the same rights as individuals. Chokwe said, "'Corporations have taken advantage of this identity,' pointing to large campaign donations made possible by a recent U.S. Supreme Court decision. Two council members abstained their vote and one member, Quentin Whitewell, voted against it."[62]

---

[60]Bill Campbell, "Funding Changes Will Still Take More Work by the City," *Clarion-Ledger* (Jackson, MS), February 6, 2011, 4.
[61]https://jxnpeoplesassembly.org/about.
[62]Brian Eason, "We're the City Council," The Buzz, Clarion-Ledger (Jackson, MS), March 11, 2012, 16.

Mayoral Candidate

When Chokwe decided to run for mayor, our family and his friends were thrilled. However, there were some naysayers outside of the family and his friends. There were rumors that a few people initially thought he was selling out. However, these fears were quickly dispelled when they saw the work he was doing. Despite the hard work that Chokwe and the Malcolm X Grassroots Movement were putting into the campaign, members of Jackson's media and Chokwe's political opponents continued to incite members of the community by publishing false stories. Primarily, there were two stories they would disseminate. The first was that Chokwe was a radical and believed in disunity of the people. They were likely basing this assertion on his years of involvement with the Provisional Government of the Republic of New Afrika (PG-RNA). Chokwe was no longer involved with the PG-RNA, and even when he was, he never preached disunity among the people. The RNA believes that Black people should control their own government and communities. The RNA taught us self-determination, and those who mistake this for disunity must have an issue with Black independence.

(Left to Right) Mario, Robert, Kwame Kenyatta, Itari Greg, Denise, Reggie, and Shushanna

The second false story that Chokwe's media critics and opponents circulated was that he was not a Christian man. To combat these false stories and rumors, Detroit City Council member and friend Kwame Kenyatta encouraged Chokwe to run a commercial. Chokwe and I were able to coordinate with Father Thomas to film the commercial at Sacred Heart Church, Nubia and Chokwe's church home in Detroit. On the day of the commercial shoot, Father Thomas and Chokwe's siblings were all asked to say one thing about Chokwe's character. Our siblings said things like "Chokwe Lumumba has integrity," "Chokwe Lumumba has courage," and "Chokwe Lumumba is our brother, and he is your brother, too." Then Father Thomas said, "Chokwe Lumumba is a Christian family man." The Jackson media and critics that were slandering Chokwe abruptly stopped. Father Thomas is and always has been a revolutionary priest.

Chokwe, Father Norman Thomas, Shushanna

Fundraising

The Malcolm X Grassroots Movement and Chokwe's campaign team organized fundraisers throughout the country for his mayoral campaign. Chokwe's friends Judge Adam Shakoor, Attorney Gerald Evelyn, and Kwame Kenyatta were particularly instrumental in fundraising efforts in Detroit. One event took place at the Seafood

Market Restaurant in Detroit, where friends, activists, and lawyers who had been supporting Chokwe throughout his professional career gathered to donate money. When his team learned that Jonathan Lee, Chokwe's opponent, was outraising Chokwe by a large margin, they sprang into action and began calling everyone they knew in Detroit; and people started sending money. A week prior to the elections, the campaign was suffering a severe shortfall of funds. Kwame and I were in Jackson at that time. Kwame immediately got on the phone and called in numerous donations. I explained the situation to Adam, and he told me to get back on the phone and call a list of people he suggested. I said to him, "Adam, I already called each of the people on this list and they gave." He said, "So what? Call them again. They are his boys, and they will give again. Tell them I said so!" I did just that and they did just that. We were able to help the Jackson campaign procure the much-needed funding. Many people gave twice. Detroiters did not forget about their native son Chokwe Lumumba.

Shushanna and Mario Taliaferro holding campaign signs.

"The People Must Decide"

Chokwe's campaign may have been underfunded, and he may have been considered the underdog by Jackson media, but he had something that his opponent did not have. He had the support of Jackson's treasures like Myrlie Evers, widow of civil rights activist Medgar Evers. When Congressman Bennie Thompson threw his support behind Chokwe, that helped make up for the big financial disparity between the two campaigns. "When Thompson, a powerful African American politician in Mississippi, endorsed Chokwe, he solidified the connection: 'When I see Republicans from Rankin and Madison counties endorsing the other so-called Democrat, I know something is fishy,' Thompson said in a campaign ad, though he never specifically named Lee."[63]

Our siblings, children, friends, and comrades of Chokwe, as well as some friends of the family, all went to work on the campaign. Some flew in, some bussed in on Wright's 54 passenger tour bus, some carpooled, a few took the train, but we all traveled to Jackson, Mississippi, from Detroit, Michigan. My buddy, Malcolm Lewis, whom we referred to as "Malcolmferro" because he was around our family so much, even brought a group of his chess players down to campaign.

---

[63] Ronnie Mott, "Making of a Mayor," *Jackson Free Press*, June 19–25, 2013.

While campaigning on the streets of Jackson, it was exciting but sometimes hot. Most of the people were so friendly, even the people who were leafleting and campaigning for Chokwe's opponents. However, when the race was down to the two Democratic top candidates, Chokwe Lumumba and Jonathan Lee, it got a little more contested. I recall as if it was yesterday, my brother Greg, sister Itari, daughter Nani, nephew Reggie, and my grandsons Jay, Kamri, and Jordan, along with some Jacksonians, were passing out leaflets to occupants in cars and holding up "VOTE FOR CHOKWE LUMUMBA," " ONE CITY, ONE AIM, ONE DESTINY," and "LET THE PEOPLE DECIDE" campaign signs. A brother from Jackson who was passing out Jonathan Lee material said "that guy Lumumba don't need to win. He is too old and he is going to die." That comment incensed me, but I was not going to let him know that. Itari on the other hand was involved in teaching class to Lee's campaigners. I always said Itari should have been a teacher. She loves to teach about our history and culture. By the time she was through, the four Lee people she was talking to said they were going to vote for Chokwe Lumumba.

While I worked in Jackson, Mississippi, on Chokwe's mayoral campaign, I learned about "Jackson Rising," The Struggle for Economic Democracy and Black Self-Determination in Jackson, Mississippi. You see, when we were chanting "One City, One Aim, One Destiny" and "Let the People Decide," Chokwe's campaign was explaining that Chokwe represented the people. And if he became mayor, the people would exercise decision-making power. Chokwe's platform pledged to encompass social solidarity, mutual aid, reciprocity, and generosity, including worker cooperatives to informed, affinity-based neighborhood barter networks. The plan also included housing co-ops, community development, credit unions, local urban farms, and farmers markets working with young people to increase civic engagement and challenging "right to work" laws. Expanding green public transportation and creating a network of solar and wind generators is also among its goals.

Chokwe's campaign was truly the "People's Campaign." Chokwe would represent the people—not the corporations, not the lobbyists, but the people. My brother loved the people, and the people evidently loved my brother.

Victory!

(Left to Right) Chokwe, Khalil Allen, Shushanna, Chokwe Antar, Greg, Kamri Hill

After several months of fundraising, organizing trips to Jackson from Detroit, and three days of canvassing, leafleting, and standing on the hot streets of Jackson, Mississippi, Chokwe's family, Detroiters and other out-of-town comrades, and Jacksonian supporters and campaign workers gathered at a local hall for the results. Because Chokwe won the mayoral election with 55 percent of the vote, that meant there would be no run-off against his Democratic opponent, Jonathan Lee. That also meant he was the next mayor, as the final election would include a contest between Chokwe and the Republican candidate, and in a predominantly Black city like

Jackson, that was no contest. As the headlines of the *Clarion Ledger* and other papers similarly stated, **"Lumumba Wins!"**

Mayor Chokwe Lamumba
(Photo courtesey of Clarion-Ledger (Reis Imagin))

Inauguration

(Photo courtesy of Jay Johnson)

Inauguration day was a beautiful, happy, and unified occasion. Our family and Chokwe's friends flew, bussed, and carpooled to Jackson, Mississippi, to celebrate his victory. Every event planned was beautiful, from the prayer breakfast to the inauguration ceremony to the ball. Jackson treated Chokwe's family like royalty. Everyone wanted to talk to him and congratulate him, and he wanted to share this special day with all of his fellow Jacksonians and everyone who represented a special time in his life and who had contributed to his success at that moment.

Chokwe began his inauguration speech by thanking his family and friends. Ministers surrounded him and prayed over him—a very moving experience. Walking into the convention center where Chokwe would make his inauguration speech was priceless. I was fifth in line behind my older brothers and sisters. Following me and my two younger brothers was a long parade line of nieces, nephews, cousins, and friends from Detroit. It was particularly special to hear Chokwe start his inaugural speech with recognition of my parents and his siblings. It was very moving to see the ministers surround Chokwe and pray over him. Chokwe's speech was great, the audience was in sync, and everyone was having a wonderful time, except my great-nephew Khalil experienced a seizure prior to the start of the ceremony. So his mother DeLisa, who was caring for him, arrived late. When she did arrive, there was not a seat for her. I had already asked two people to leave the reserved seats for the family because those people disrespectfully jumped in line with the family. When my niece DeLisa arrived, I noticed there were two men sitting at the end of my row who were also not related to us. I was told previously by Chokwe's assistant Halima that there would be several rows reserved for the family and our Detroit guests. Thus, I politely went over to the gentlemen and informed them their seats were in the row reserved for family. One gentleman looked at me a bit awkwardly but proceeded to get up. However, the second gentleman spoke irately and rudely to me in an African accent. My brother Jasiri jumped up and moved toward me. As that guy proceeded to walk away, I heard him clearly and plainly say, "Do you know what you did? You unseated the ambassador to Nigeria." *Humph*, I thought, *I did that?* I later learned they mixed the dignitaries in with our family as opposed to reserving seats for them.

Oh my God, I was in trouble now. Later at the hotel, we ran into the two gentlemen, and the one was still rambling on and pointing at me. Thank God for Mahamadou Sumareh, my sister Itari's friend and owner of the African shop Djenne Beads and Gems, Inc., where Itari managed the store. Mahamadou is from Mali, Africa, and he speaks five languages. Itari told Mahamadou what was happening, and he intervened. He had a conversation with the two men in their language, I believed. At least it was foreign to me. After about ten minutes, Mahamadou brought the two men over and said, "I would like to introduce you to the ambassador of Nigeria and his assistant." He understands that a mistake was made. I apologized profusely, and it resulted in laughter and hugs. Mahamadou, with his serene nature, resolved that conflict diplomatically and quickly.

Ministers pray over Mayor Chokwe Lamumba

Memories of My Revolutionary Brother, Chokwe Lumumba

Errin Taliaferro, Maisha Hill, Kenya Taliaferro, Maurice Bowie, Chokwe, Qadir Lumumba-Benjamin, Rukia Lumumba, Kayla Taliaferro, Maya Cain, Nia Bailey Hill, Charlitta Hill (Photo courtesy of Sylvia Davis)

Mario, Shushanna, Chokwe, Reggie, Itari, Greg, Denise, Robert
(Photo courtesy of Gloria Elmore)

Sherman, Shushanna
(Photo courtesy of Jay Johnson)

Jendayi Iyi, Itari, Mahamadou Sumareh, Shushanna, Kilindi Iyi, Ayana Ife Iyi
(Photo courtesy of Jay Johnson)

Chokwe Joins Politics

There were many beautiful moments throughout the events, but there was one that really tugged at my heart. At the Inaugural Ball, everyone—I mean everyone—was going up to Chokwe to congratulate him. After an hour or two had passed, Kilindi Iyi, who had traveled with us from Detroit, came to me with instructions. Kilindi had provided security for Chokwe on numerous occasions in the RNA days. Kilindi said, "Shushanna, you have to get your brother out of here for a while. He is tired, and he needs to sit for an hour and drink water and replenish himself." It made sense to me, so I made my way to Chokwe to tell him what Kilindi had suggested. He said, "Okay Shushanna, this is what I want you to do, tell Watani Tyehimba (who was his comrade in NAPO and his head security that day), Reggie (our eldest brother), Gerald Evelyn (his close friend and colleague from Detroit), Jerry Fuller (his childhood friend), Hondo Lumumba (Chokwe's campaign manager and friend from Jackson), and Kwame Kenyatta (Detroit friend and comrade) to meet me in the room where they will take me. It was difficult to move Chokwe in a room because he kept stopping and talking to people. Watani was trying to get him there. I could see that, so I decided Watani needed some help. Therefore, I bogarted my way through the crowd, telling the people at the front of the line that Mayor Lumumba would return shortly, and Watani escorted him out.

After all the beautiful inaugural events ended, I thought about how Chokwe had requested that I find Johnny Woodle (his high school best friend and teammate), his ex-wife Anasa, and Jerry Fuller to invite them to his inauguration. I knew then that those people were very important to him in his life, and he wanted to share this monumental moment with them. Thinking about the group he asked me to send to the room with him at his Inaugural Ball, all represented special friendships and relationships: his eldest brother, childhood best friend, high school best friend and teammate, colleague and current close friend, longtime Detroit comrade, NAPO/MXGM comrade, and Jackson comrade and friend. I thought to myself, *those were the people he wanted to share that momentous occasion with at that time, and each of them represented a special time in his life that contributed to his success at that moment.* Witnessing these special moments inspired me to respect and love my brother even more. He never forgot where he came from, who he was, and who he loved.

Later, after we arrived back in Detroit, Chokwe and I talked. He wanted to know how everything went for us and if there were any problems. He obviously seemed more relaxed than he had in several months. I think he was happy. I reported to him the wonderful time we all had and told him there was one problem.

Mayoral Photo of Mayor Chokwe Lamumba
(Photo courtesy Jay Johnson)

"Yes, what was it?"

"I unseated the ambassador of Nigeria at your Inauguration."

I just remember him saying, "What?" Then I explained the whole thing and how Mahamadou resolved everything. He didn't respond, I knew he was thinking, but he never mentioned it again, nor did I.

Mayor Chokwe Lumumba

Chokwe spoke often about his political platform and agenda as mayor. On the day he was sworn in, he gave an interview to the *Sun Herald* where it was mentioned, "During a debate leading up to the election, Lumumba closed a strong performance with this message: 'If you vote for Chokwe Lumumba you're voting for not just an individual, you're voting for a movement of change.' In an interview with the *Clarion-Ledger*, Lumumba was asked what it means to elect a movement. 'What we're doing is something which is in my view special, historically,' Lumumba said. 'Usually when people come into the door, even if they've had any credentials in terms of fighting for change movements... a lot of times they leave that at the door when they go into office. They basically become just policy makers. What we're saying is we want to bring some of these principles in to help government work.' Among his goals, Lumumba says [he'd] like to see more city contracts go to minority-owned businesses, providing jobs to a city whose majority black population lags far behind the white community in employment. 'Let's give the people without the money the jobs, that's what's missing. We have some good businesses here in Jackson. We want to bring more. But they can't really prosper, and they can't stay here if the people in the population don't have the money to support them.'"[64]

Mayor Chokwe Lumumba's time in office was cut short due to his untimely and unexpected death. According to one journalist, in just seven months, "Lumumba charted a course of open government, welcoming anyone and everyone to the table to offer ideas and strategies to reduce crime, improve roads and utilities, make the city a more welcoming place. He gently distanced himself from hangers-on, goofballs and loudmouths who had dominated conversation. He

---

[64] Associated Press, "Lumumba Will Be Sworn in as Jackson's Mayor Today," *Sun Herald*, July 1, 2013, https://www.newspapers.com/image/678395863/.

engendered optimism by action, not rhetoric."[65] Perhaps his biggest accomplishment in that time was the passing of the 1 percent sales tax. Mayor Lumumba said he would support a 1 percent sales tax increase to help pay for the city's infrastructure needs, even with a controversial oversight commission in place. The tax has long been looked to as a key element of funding for the city's $400 million consent decree and other infrastructure needs, and previous estimates have projected that the tax will collect $15 million to $20 million annually.

---

[65] Charlie Mitchell, "Firebrand Becomes Effective Mayor," *Enterprise-Journal*, March 11, 2014, A005, https://www.newspapers.com/image/1020758260/.

CHAPTER 9

Chokwe Lumumba's Legacy Continues

"I hope people will remember not only do I support Black people's independence but believe it will occur, and that support does not suggest in any way that I hate anyone, but my beliefs are based upon love for our people."
– Chokwe Lumumba

Mayor Chokwe Antar & Mrs. Ebony Lumumba
(Photo courtesy of Jay Johnson)

Chokwe served many purposes on planet Earth. He was many things to many people. His activities, contributions, and work were spread throughout this country and in some cases throughout the world. I am grateful that his children are his legacy.

Kam

Chokwe's oldest son Kam awakens each day, despite his disability, and spreads joy and encouragement to those surrounding him. He has his father's love and compassion for others and desire for people to live in peace. Chokwe's youngest two children have continued his work and legacy in the community and the fight for justice.

> There is no doubt that my Dad
> was a king of a man
>
> He conquered his goals
> And he made history
>
> My Dad was a very strong
> and good man
>
> There will never be
> another one like him
>
> He loved
> His People,
>
> and he definitely
> laid out a blue print
> for the People
>
> to Free the Land
> by any means necessary
>
> My Dad, Chokwe Lumumba
> did this!
> – Kam

Rukia

Rukia, who is truly her father's daughter, emulates him every day of her life. Rukia walks in his footsteps continuing his work in many facets. Rukia is executive director of the People's Advocacy Institute and co-coordinator of the Electoral Justice Project. She is a founding board member of Black Voters Matter and legal advisor to the Mississippi Poor People's Campaign. Rukia has worked tirelessly and extensively to change the conditions of the prison systems, particularly with women's issues. In addition, she has devoted time and dedication to our youth working with mentoring programs for at-risk youth and Operation Good and Safe Streets Cure Violence Program, a gun violence prevention program. Some of her most phenomenal contributions to the community happened when she was working in Mississippi as lead coordinator of MS Rapid Response Coalition. Rukia along with her co-workers provided infrastructure and crisis relief to 100,000 community members throughout the state during Mississippi's recent water crisis. Rukia's remarkable and significant contributions in the realms of justice, advocacy, and community empowerment is the continuation of her father's, Chokwe Lumumba's, work and principles.

One of the things he taught us was that our struggle is to create a better world: a world where it didn't matter what color you were; a world where we as Black people, yes, had control over our own destinies; a world where we had control over our own governments and had the right to determine how we wanted to be governed and live. That was the core of one of his messages to us, and that was really the core of all of his messages to us. We have the right to govern and to have power and to be in power. We have that right to govern ourselves and to govern our own communities. We have that right to fight for it, and that is not something that is crazy or absurd, but that is real, right? Every human being has the right to govern themselves.

–Rukia Kai Lumumba at Chokwe Lumumba's Celebration of Life, March 8, 2014

Chokwe Antar

Chokwe Antar Lumumba, understanding the necessity to continue his father's important work, unsuccessfully ran for his father's seat after he transitioned on February 25, 2014. Chokwe Antar was newly married, with a baby on the way, and the death of his father all upon his shoulders. He fought the good fight but lost the seat to Councilman Tony Yarber.

Chokwe Antar, determined and driven, returned to the campaign trail after Yarber completed his father's term in office. When Chokwe Antar ran for mayor, Detroiters did not forget about their native son's son. Attorney Gerald Evelyn, Chokwe's good friend and colleague, took up the fundraising mantle with me and Georgia Manzie (Chokwe's former paralegal and friend). With Gerald's extensive connections, the first fundraiser was a huge success. It was hosted by attorneys Gerald Evelyn, Jeffrey Edison, and Todd Perkins and judges Earl Ashford and Adam Shakoor. It was well attended by lawyers, judges, and community activists who all donated. Gerald managed to pick up funds or have funds dropped off to his office of those who were unable to attend the fundraiser. Detroit raised over $30,000 for Chokwe's son to run for mayor. Gerald Evelyn funded a trip for volunteers to go from Detroit to Jackson to campaign, and family friend John Royal assisted in procuring sponsorship for Detroiters to commute to Jackson from the National Lawyers Guild.

Chokwe Antar Lumumba resoundingly won the mayoral election in Jackson, Mississippi, on June 17, 2021, with 93 percent of the vote. At the age of thirty-eight, Chokwe Antar Lumumba began his second term as mayor of Jackson, despite the tremendously challenging times he has experienced as mayor of Jackson through the break-down of the water infrastructure and takeover of some of the city's departments by the right-wing Republican governor and legislature. Mayor Chokwe A. Lumumba remains vigilant in continuing his father's work and legacy while preparing to run for his third term in 2025. The unsung revolutionary hero Chokwe's song and story is told and realized each day more and more through the legacy he built!

 My father once told me, "always put we before I." That is exactly who my father was. He was love and inspiration. He had a special gift for embracing you and imparting wisdom at the very same time. He not only gave us those wise quotes we all love, but more importantly he taught us through his actions. He showed you the type of leader you wanted to be. He showed you the type of father you wanted to be and for many of us, he showed you true friendship. He fashioned himself to struggle without cease, not because of any hatred he had, but because he was filled with love. He would often say, "If you don't love the people, sooner or later, you will betray the people."

 Love freed the Scott sisters. Love led to a basketball program that saw hundreds of young men go to college. Love led to the representation of thousands of clients in over sixteen jurisdictions. Love led to a changed Jackson, Mississippi. Chokwe Lumumba was love.

 My father fought for human rights for human beings at a time when few followed suit, but he said that "we do not measure our movement by the size of the crowd, but by rather the size of our revolutionary hearts." It is the struggle that makes us victorious. Chokwe Lumumba lives in the People's Struggle. He will never die... Chokwe Lumumba lives in me!"

–Chokwe Antar Lumumba at Chokwe Lumumba's Celebration of Life, March 8, 2014

※※

Chokwe the lawyer, councilman, mayor, human rights activist, and freedom fighter positively impacted thousands of people in this country and some outside this country. His remarkable contributions are preserved through the numerous programs and organizations he developed to assist with procuring justice for all. His selfless work changed and, in many cases, saved the lives of others. His death is not in vain, and each of his children will continue the legacy that their father, Chokwe Lumumba, built.

Paul Taylor, JoAnn Watson, Helen Moore, Greg Reed, Ivy Thomas-Riley, Daphne Means-Curtis

John Royal, NLG

Top: Reggie, Shushanna
Bottom: Itari, Greg, Denise

Mutope Alkebulan

Chokwe Lumumba's Legacy Continues

Adam Shakoor, Jeff Edison,
Ebony Lamumba, Chokwe Antar

Gerald Evelyn, Chokwe Antar

Helen Moore, JoAnn Watson,
Chokwe Antar, Adam Shakoor

Michael Sharp,
Gerald Evelyn

Front: Georgia, Itari, Greg, Charlitta, Reggie, Kamri,
Jeaco, Jordan, DeLon; Back: Tez, Hodari, Lee, Kwasi
(Photo courtesy of Kwasi Akwamu)

Millard Owusu Porter, Shushanna,
Ivy-Thomas Riley, Marilyn
Morehead, Malcolm Lewis and
Robert Taliaferro (back)

Memories of My Revolutionary Brother, Chokwe Lumumba

Continue the Legacy: A Poetic Introduction of Panelists for Detroit's Tribute to Revolutionary Mayor Chokwe Lumumba Liberation Film Series, Museum of African American History January 10, 2015

Continue the Legacy

A panel
A panel of Jurists
A panel of Attorneys, Colleagues, Friends,
A panel of Comrades

Distinguished Trailblazers
Established Icons
Warriors of the People
Comrades of Chokwe

A Black Legal Alliance of
Like-minded
Fighters for Freedom

Carl Edwards
From Wayne Law School
To the People's Law School
Free The Land!
Continue the Legacy
Follow the Blueprint
Fighting Discrimination
Fighting for Progress
Fighting Against Poverty
Leading Others to Fight for Justice

Adam Shakoor, The Honorable
Friend from the Cradle
to the Grave
Passing out Justice
on the People's Court
Passing out Knowledge
at WC3D
Free the Land!
Continue the Legacy
Follow the Blueprint

Alice Jennings
Comrade Sister
Fighting for the People
Fighting for Water like
Fighting for Breath
Carl and Alice
Jennings and Edwards
Partners
Continuing the Legacy

Elliott Hall
Mentor, Trailblazer
Paving the Way
Against the Wind
Providing Counsel
Providing jobs for our People
Much Respect to the Elder

Jeffrey Lee Edison
The Backbone
The Support
The Foundation
For NCBL

Memories of My Revolutionary Brother, Chokwe Lumumba

For Chokwe
Being a Partner is
Like being a Spouse
Free the Land!
You Freed Chokwe
to Help the People

Continue the Legacy
Rukia Lumumba
Follow the Blueprint
You can't help it
Being the seed of
Chokwe and Nubia
The niece of Shushanna
The sister of Antar
You can't help it
You have to be that
Warrior Queen
Fighting for Justice in New York
I can't breathe
Keep the Fight Going
Give us Hope
Free The Land!
Continue the Legacy
Follow the Blueprint
Keep it Going
Jackson Rising
Detroit Returning
New York Choking
Free the Land!

– Honorable Ivy Thomas Riley

Chokwe's Legacy

(L to R): Qadir Lumumba-Benjamin, Rukia Lumumba, Kambontope Thurman

(L to R): Chokwe Lumumba, Rukia Lumumba, Chokwe Antar Lumumba

Chokwe Antar and Ebony Lumumba

Nubia Lumumba and Alake' Lumumba

EPILOGUE

When our parents began to age and their health deteriorated, Chokwe and I took on the personas of patriarch and matriarch of the family. We worked collectively to assess family situations and determine what actions should be taken. In critical situations, all eight members of our sibship would weigh in and the majority position would be taken; but most matters, like maintenance of their home and financial and legal concerns, were under the jurisdiction of Chokwe and me. Later on, when my eldest sister, Denise, became our parents' caregiver, she and our brother Greg made most of the decisions related to our parents. When Chokwe and I worked on family matters together, I was in constant contact with him about them. I was his eyes and ears in Detroit.

This relationship worked out well for the most part, but it had its painful times. I kept him abreast of our parents' health concerns and their status when our mother had a heart attack and our father had a stroke back-to-back. When our father and mother both began to exhibit signs of mental deterioration, I kept him updated. Our father, who had been healthy his entire life, began losing his memory first, and although his doctors could never confirm it, he had symptoms of both Parkinson's and Alzheimer's disease. He often found pleasure in speaking to anyone who came along. He liked to reminisce about yesterdays and name-drop. For example, my father shared the story of how he and a boy who later became Judge Damon Keith were in elementary school together. My father protected Judge Keith from bullies. Father explained that Judge Keith was built in a smaller stature than he was, and my father was better built physically to handle the bullies. Actually, my father's assessment of the bully situation

Epilogue

proved to be correct; Father became a boxer as an adult. However, my father's favorite name to drop was his son's, Chokwe Lumumba. Our mother cared for our father until she herself was diagnosed with Alzheimer's. Dr. Rachel Keith (Judge Damon Keith's wife), her primary physician, told our mother and me during one of her routine appointments that she should not have been trying to take care of our father. Another one of her doctors said the same thing—that she was showing signs of dementia and needed to look out for her own health. We were so surprised to hear this; we were so focused on my father's condition that we never saw her condition. Although our mother had numerous physical medical problems, we never saw mental decline at that time.

When our parents were nearing the end of their lives, Chokwe relied on me to let him know when to return to Detroit. He visited our parents many times; however, the other seven of us, along with the grandchildren, were with both of our parents around the clock. When Chokwe came to visit our father about a week before he died, that was perhaps the last day our father was able to speak and was in good spirits. When I called Chokwe a couple of days prior, Chokwe said, "Should I come now?"

"Yes," I told him, "you should come now." I don't know how I knew, but I knew.

Although Chokwe was able to say goodbye to our father, the situation with our mother was a little different. When Chokwe went to see her in the hospital, she was not alert and would not say one word. It was a painful thing to witness. Chokwe bent over our mother's bed and said, almost whispering, "Mama, it's me, Chokwe. I'm here, Mother. It's me, Chokwe." She did not respond; she was too far gone. I often wonder if that meant Chokwe would be the first one of us she would see in the afterlife—that that was why he was the only one who was not able to say goodbye to her. My mother completed her transition on October 1, 2012, and Chokwe made his transition on February 25, 2014, approximately sixteen months later.

Who would have thought that one day I would get a call about Chokwe? I did not think in a million years that Chokwe would be leaving this planet when he did. Kwame Kenyatta, who was working in Jackson, Mississippi, in Chokwe's administration, called me one afternoon and asked me had I heard anything. I began chattering away about the realtor he had referred to assist me in my house hunt in Jackson. Upon my retirement, the year Chokwe was beginning his campaign for mayor of Jackson, my husband Sherman and I decided to move to Jackson. We, who were both suffering from some physical issues ourselves, thought a warmer climate would be beneficial. But the primary reason I wanted to move to Jackson was to help Chokwe with his campaign. He and I had talked about me moving several times previously, but this time it was not talk. We were leaving our home in Detroit, which we had lived in for seventeen years. This was for real, so I told Kwame that I had talked to the realtor and she had been helpful, and that I was making plans to fly down to Jackson.

Kwame responded strangely. "No, Shushanna," he said, "that is not what I'm talking about. Did anyone call you about Chokwe?"

When I responded that I hadn't heard anything, he told me that Chokwe was in the hospital after having chest pains. I hung up the phone and began calling all six of our other brothers and sisters.

By the time I had hung up with the last sibling, my phone rang. It was Kwame Kenyatta. "Shushanna, he is gone. Chokwe is gone." Kwame was distraught; he wasn't able to share much information. I remember robotically hanging up the phone and calling each of my sib-lings back to give them the news. Almost immediately, my phone began to ring off the hook. This was the case for the next three to four days. People were calling from all over the country and around the world: family, friends, and comrades; representatives from the Nation of Islam, the National Action Network, the National Lawyers Guild. It got so bad that, at one point, my husband told me to put my phone away or give it to him. I could not do either. I had

Epilogue

to take care of things, and I did not have time to rest, digest what had happened, or grieve. I just had to utilize every moment taking care of things. That is what I saw my mother do with her family members, and that is what my brother and I had done previously. I was not about to stop now.

Visitors also called at my house and Itari's. My first visitors were "The Girls," Valarie, Lorna, and Dee Dee. They are my childhood friends who I still manage to socialize with every other month. They handed me an envelope containing $100 from each of them to use toward airfare to Jackson. Elaine was out of town and sent me something later. I thanked and kissed them each and enjoyed their visit. The next group of visitors was a total surprise and unexpected: Jeff Edison, Chokwe's former law partner and good friend, who has always been like a brother to me; Chokwe's former law partner Earl and his lovely wife, Daisy; and Chokwe's close friend Gerald Evelyn. We spent a nice time together just talking about the plans for Chokwe's services in Jackson and Detroit. There were no tears, just love extended, and then before they left, they each handed me an envelope containing $1,000. Their generous donations helped with the costs to charter a bus for family members to go to Jackson for Chokwe's homegoing services. Most of the siblings were able to fly, but a couple rode on the bus with our children, Chokwe's nieces, nephews, and cousins. We were going down to Jackson, Mississippi, family strong. Chokwe's partner and good friend Adam Shakoor paid for Rukia to come to Chokwe's Detroit memorial. All I could think of was how loved my brother was and how the support of friends held our family up during those most challenging and difficult times.

There was lots of speculation about the cause of Chokwe's death. Many people believed "they" (white people) who opposed his mayorship in Jackson, Mississippi, killed him. Minister Farrakhan of the Nation of Islam suggested there may have been foul play involved in Chokwe's death. He donated money to assist the children with the costs of an autopsy, for which the National Conference of Black Lawyers had already begun organizing contributions. Rukia announced, after her and Chokwe Antar's investigation of their father's death, that the autopsy concluded he died of an aneurysm in his heart. *How ironic*, I thought, *that my brother had died as a result of an aneurysm in his heart, where his beloved wife, Nubia, had also died from an aneurysm in her brain.* I accepted the findings. However, I do believe my revolutionary brother was murdered, not by a physical being but by an invisible killer—*stress*. Chokwe loved people so much that he worked himself to death. He gave all he could, from defending his people, organizing his people, and representing his people to dying for his people.

Homage to New African Revolutionary Warrior Chokwe Lumumba
Memorial Service at Fellowship Chapel, Detroit, MI
March 15, 2014

The fire was kindled
in the heart of his childhood:
There would be no tolerance for injustice.
His soul announced:
No tolerance
for injustice.

Growing tall and strong, an athlete's energy for the fight to come.
Honing insight and wisdom, a piercing mind for the fight to come.
His spirit, a warrior spirit, like a smoldering fire,
slow burning fire
patient fire,
preparing for the fight to come.

Epilogue

His warrior's calling so fervent, so urgent, it summoned the saints:
Gabriel Prosser, Nat Turner, Harriet Tubman, Sojourner Truth, Marcus Garvey,
magnificent invisible army, hovered around him, and called out further to
that multitude of African spirits
whose bones lie under the Atlantic,
whose moaning haunts the Georgia breeze,
whose blood soaked the Alabama soil,
whose toil, prayers, baptisms, jubilees, and burials
bind us to the Southern earth itself.
This ground he returned to claim as the new African nation.

Settling in the drowning heat of that plantation called Mississippi,
he took up the work young trailblazers had begun:
teaching, guiding, making the way clear,
gathering others for the tedious journey to free the land!
Giving his time, mind, strength, wealth, faithful to the New African creed.*

With all means at his disposal, he affirmed our sovereignty as a people.
In the courts of American injustice,
he was the incarnation of African genius,
his arguments fierce
in defense of fellow fighters;
his blazing intelligence torching the structure of lies and deceit
holding up this racist regime.

In the halls of a hostile government,
his righteous indignation uncovered
the treacherous plots of white supremacy.

Memories of My Revolutionary Brother, Chokwe Lumumba

No devious designs
or illegal calculations could prevail against his purpose:
to secure the people's human rights and unity.

In community and home,
his presence was peace,
sweet reassurance for mother, father, sisters, brothers, children, wife
--
carrying the abiding ache of loss
in a love as deep as the marrow in our bones.
No one's need or desire too small for his notice,
nothing too trivial for his care.
This was a New African revolutionary.

Pushing on
beyond
exhaustion,
pushing on.

So weary at times, each pause, a respite for painful legs, shoulders, back;
each moment of silence, a siege of ideas, strategies, campaigns, plans,
circling without end in his consciousness;
burdened sometimes by the quiet misgivings of even closest comrades,
but reassured by the embrace of Malcolm and Martin,
who had walked this path before him.

Always pushing on,
pushing on,
beyond exhaustion.

Epilogue

What can we do now that our warrior has fallen?
What must we do now that our warrior has fallen?

We advance the mission of self-determination for which he lived!
We advance the mission of self-determination for which he lived.

Get up, rise up, realize the vision that pulled him forward:
The vision of our freedom, our regeneration as a people.
Speak to his spirit. Ask for instructions, a task.
Chokwe, what next, my brother? What now?
Speak we are listening. Pass your fire!
Send us! We will go!

– Aneb Kgositsile (Gloria House)

*New African Creed of the Republic of New Africa

Memories of My Revolutionary Brother, Chokwe Lumumba

(Left to Right) Denise, Greg, Millie, Mario, Shushanna, Reggie, and Robert

(Left to Right) Kenya Taliaferro, Shushanna Hill, Charlitta Hill, Maisha Hill, Mark Taliaferro, DeLisa Glaspie, Asha Akineyele (Back row) Dr. Demetrius Marshall and Oronde Taliaferro

Chokwe Antar, Rukia and Shushanna
(Photo courtesy of Jay Johnson)

Epilogue

Graveside photo
(Photo courtesy of Jay Johnson)

APPENDIX 1

Legal Resume

General Practitioner 1991–2013
Chokwe Lumumba, Esq.
Jackson, Mississippi

Attorney - Criminal Lawyer 1985–2013
Chokwe Lumumba, Esq.
Attorney at Law
Detroit, Michigan

States Licensed to Practice Law
Mississippi April 24, 1991 to 2014
Licensed in all state courts

Michigan May 6, 1976 to 2014
Licensed in all state courts

Federal Jurisdictions Admitted to Practice
Eastern District of Michigan May 6, 1976 to 2014
Southern District of Mississippi April 14, 1991 to 2014
Fifth Circuit Court of Appeals May 1991 to 2014

Other Employment
Legal Services Attorney,
Southwest Mississippi Legal Services March 1, 1991–July 7, 1991

Law Practice, Attorney and Partner
Criminal Lawyer and Firm Management

Appendix 1: Legal Resume

Davis, Edison, Jarrett, Lumumba, Ottison, and Shakoor 1980–1982
formerly Ashford, Edison, Lumumba, and Shakoor 1979–1980
formerly Ashford, Cannon, and Lumumba 1977–1979

Criminal Defense of Indigents
Defender's Office, Detroit, Michigan May 1975–September 1977
Position: Deputy Defender
Attorney for indigent clients in criminal cases

COURTS PRACTICED
As member of State Bar
(or on a pro hac vice basis)

STATE OF MICHIGAN
Supreme Court, Court of Appeals
Circuit and/or District Courts of the following counties: Wayne, Washtenaw, Jackson, Calhoun, Kalamazoo, Van Buren, Berrien, Kent, Clinton, Ionia, Ingram, Livingston, St. Clair, Oakland, and Macomb

STATE OF MISSISSIPPI
Hinds County Circuit Court
Hinds County Court
Hinds County Chancery Court
Pike County Chancery Court
Pike County Court
McComb Municipal Court
Amite County Chancery
Gulfport Municipal Court

STATE OF LOUISIANA
District Court of Lincoln Parish

STATE OF NEW YORK
Brooklyn Supreme Court
Rocklyn County Court
Queens Supreme Court
Rocklyn County Supreme Court

STATE OF OHIO
Canton Municipal Court

STATE OF ILLINOIS
Cook County Criminal Court

STATE OF INDIANA
Indiana Supreme Court

STATE OF GEORGIA
Atlanta Municipal Court
Fulton County Court

STATE OF ALABAMA
County Court in Bessemer, Alabama

FEDERAL COURTS
U.S. Supreme Court
Second Circuit Court of Appeals
Eastern & Western District of Michigan D.C. District
Southern District of New York
Central District of California
Northern District of Louisiana
Southern District of Mississippi

CANADIAN COURT
Ontario Court, Provincial Division

Appendix 1: Legal Resume

PRIOR CLINICAL EXPERIENCE AND LAW STUDENT EMPLOYMENT

July–August 1969, Wayne County Neighborhood Legal Services
Domestic Affairs Division Detroit, Michigan

Position Job: Law Intern: Assisted counsel in divorce suits

January 1971–May 1972: Wayne County Neighborhood Legal Services
Home Purchase and Economic Development
Division Detroit, Michigan

Position Job: Law Intern: Defense counsel for indigents in misdemeanor cases and legal researcher for ACLU-Detroit

May 1975–September 1975
Legal Aid and Defenders Association
Landlord Tenant Clinic, Detroit, Michigan

Position Job: Law Intern: Represented tenants in landlord/tenant actions

September 1975–December 1975
Free Legal Aid Clinic, Inc.
Wayne State University Law School, Detroit, Michigan

Position Job: Law Intern: Represented indigent clients in misdemeanor cases

APPENDIX 2

Words My Brother Left Us

Reparations Conference

Free the Land Brothers and Sisters.[1] Free the land Brothers and Sisters. Free the Land Brothers and Sisters the land is ours. We have gathered over many years of struggles, and we can take that energy and transfer it to the youth. We must always no matter what we do in a revolution and anything in life, keep everything we talk about and everything we do in perspective. It will not do just to talk about the tactics that we must do in order to fight for reparation. Just like if you are going to build a house you have to have a blueprint. Just like if you are going to build a road or a city you have to have a blueprint. The only way you are going to get to where you are going is if you know where you are going and you lay out the plan to get there. We have to lay out the strategy for reparations. The strategy for reparations has to be consistent with all other reasonable strategies to achieve our freedom. This is what we must do; there is no way around it. So we must share with each other our thoughts on these strategies, and all of us in the family must not always agree, but we will listen to each other. And we will open our minds and realize the time is now so we must shorten things. See I know about family conversations. There were ten people in my family and all of them liked to talk. I have four brothers and three sisters and all of us liked to talk. The problem is that none of us could talk until our

---

[1] Chokwe was introduced by Nkechi Taifa, attorney-activist, head of National Conference of Black Lawyers-DC Chapter, National Coalition of Blacks for Reparations in America (N'COBRA).

Appendix 2: Words My Brother Left Us

mother and father got finished talking. So there are always a lot of disagreements, a lot of chatter, a lot of squabbles and sometimes some fights. But that is how it is in a family.

When I say the politics of reparations, you first must understand what politics is. Brother George said it is the authoritative allocation of values in a society or the authoritative allocation of things that are valued between societies. What does that mean? It means the process of whereby you determine. It means who gets what, when, and how. This is politics. Politics is not just going to a ballot box and dropping a vote in. I don't want to disdain voting, because sometimes voting is an important task. But you have to grow up now. You have to understand voting is a very small part of politics. Few decisions are made anywhere in the world especially about people who are trying to change the world through voting. Nobody has ever voted in a revolution anywhere. Nobody has ever voted themselves reparations anywhere. You ought to know about voting. Look at all the decisions that have been made about you. Nobody voted to bring you over here. Nobody voted to have Jim Crow come after you over here. Nobody voted to lynch you. They just went out and lynched you. That's what they did. This is what they did. So you must understand that there are many things that happened in the transition of a society.

Tell them what you did that was wrong. If you screwed somebody up than you owe them something that is going to help them straighten out again. And we must understand not only is there a definition for reparations, but for different kind of reparations. There is what we might call inadequate, sham reparations, make believe reparations. One brother recently called it welfare reparations. And then there is what we might call real reparations, down to earth adequate reparations. And the difference between one and the other is that real reparations will contribute and put you in a position where you can gain self-sufficiency politically, economically, and culturally. That's what the real reparations will do for you. Welfare reparations will just put you in a position where you will need reparations again the next day. So, who has gotten reparations, what have they gotten, and how did they get it? This is how you can analyze the situation and see what you want to do to get your reparations. The Israel so-called Jews got reparations. They got reparations to build a state that they did not have a right to build. At least they did not have the right to build it where they built it. Do you understand that? It seems to me if the Germans were the ones who exterminated them or tried to then they should have gotten some of Germany to set up a state. I mean after all most of them come from Germany or Milwaukee. Right! This is where they come from. So why go over there and invade the Semitic people and then call us anti-Semitic when we expose their hypocrisy in what they are doing. They were on the right side of the war, and they were persecuted by the people on the wrong side of the war. How did they get the reparations? The people that were on their side won the war. As a result of the winning of the war they got real reparations. When did they get them? Anytime they want them. That's when they get them. This is what they did. The allies got reparations from Germany. You know who the allies are. Those jokers France, Britain, United States, and all other people they were using back then. Those folks had to attack Germany because Germany was getting ahead of them in this world conquest thing. The allies they got reparations from Germany. This is what they got. How did they get them? They won the war. They had a war and they won the war, and because they beat Germany, they were able to get real reparations. When did they get them? They get them anytime they want them. They still get them from time to time.

Now we look at the Vietnamese. Even the Vietnamese got real reparations. How did they get them? They kicked Nixon's butt in the war. They kicked the United States' butt and kicked them out. Then when the people came looking for the prisoners of war, the so-called MIAs, the people said where is the payback? Where is the money for these cities that you bombed? Where the lives the money for the lives you disrupted? How did they get it? They got it as a result of a war. This is how they got it.

As we look to wars of national liberation. Most of those nations are still corrupt and the people are still involved in revolutions where they have to get their reparations. But they got partial payment. Yes they did. So when they took over the Gullah what did they do? They snatched every institution that the colonizer had left there. They did the same thing in Nicaragua. They didn't go out and ask them if they could take it, they just took it. That's what they did, because they knew it belonged to them in the first place. So this is how you have gotten real reparations if you look at the world. We look at the Native Americans who certainly deserve reparations as much and more as we deserve reparations. But how have they got their reparations, as we paid for them through the Indian Claims Commission? They got them because the government was trying to disguise the fact they had screwed the Native Americans up in the first place. There was no war that the Native Americans won. They got them because the government was trying to dodge its historical responsibility of giving the Native Americans what they really needed. So they got reparations, so-called reparations yesterday, but they are still in bad shape today. When do they get the reparations they get, when the government decides to give it to them, only then?

The Japanese that we talk about so much, we have to look at it seriously. If we don't want to look at it seriously then it is no use talking about it at all. What have they gotten and how did they get it? They haven't gotten anything yet, number one. They got a vote that says they are supposed to get $20,000 a piece for all the lives that were destroyed in that incarceration situation. This is all they got a vote. They got a promise. When do they get the reparations promised them? Whenever the Congress decides to give it to them and if they decide they want to give it up. I heard a guy on the TV the other day say, "We really don't have the money to pay." So there was no revolutionary war there. At least there was no war in the beginning. So if we look at the circumstances in the world today, and we look at people who have successfully gotten reparations then we must understand that war is at the center of it all. Now a lot of us don't like that. Of course we have been talking about war during this conference. We talk about war when we want to talk about how bad the white man has treated us. Right! Have you ever seen anybody vote themselves out of a war? Have you ever seen anybody pray themselves out of a war? Have you ever seen anybody demonstrate themselves out of a war? Do you know what you are saying? Now if you don't want to use the word, then I'll give you a chance to go back and take it back. But if you really mean war, then you have to understand how we resolve war. First of all you are in bad shape if you are in war, but you are not at war. If you are in war but you are not actively participating in trying to win the war then you have already lost the war. So this is what we have. It is not a question of whether or not you want to be in war. You don't even have a choice in the matter. You were in war from when they took the first African off the African continent.

Detroit Juneteenth Celebration Sponsored by Malcolm X Grassroots Movement in Detroit, 2011

The most significant times in our history are when you get the right people in the right place at the right time, and I think that is where we are now. When you talk about a building that is designated to being built by slaves that's the right place. When you talk about people that have been under this oppression all of their ancestors' lives and all of their lives, those are the right people to make a change and this is the right time.

Recorder's Court is a fundamental part of my development and a fundamental part of life itself. Because it represents an institution

Appendix 2: Words My Brother Left Us

that partakes in the incarceration of more people than any other place in the world. The United States of America incarcerates more people than any other place in the world. More than China, Cuba, and Russia...more than any other place in the world.

It is too disproportionate and it really speaks for this day. It is a great day because it speaks to one of the milestones in our peoples' struggle for freedom. It was a great day I'm sure in 1865 when the general rode in and told our people they were no longer enslaved. They were never slaves. They were just enslaved. They were always human beings. Don't never forget that. So that brightened their spirits to give them a certain qualified freedom. And so it was in 1863 January 1st when Abraham Lincoln was forced to issue the Emancipation Proclamation. He didn't do it because he likes you. He didn't do it because he believed in freedom of all people. In fact in his debate when he was running for office he said I'm like any other white man, believed one race has to be first and the other after that, and I'm of course for the white race. That is what he said. So he lets you know he was a white supremacist. He also realizes in certain degree and practicality that he was a little smarter than some of the southern plantation owners the southern aristocracy.

The problem was never slavery. The problem was the fact that we had lost our self-determination when we were taken from Africa. The problem did not start when we got enslaved. The problem started when they snatched the first African off the coast of Africa, and that is still the problem today. The problem is not that you are being discriminated against.

The problem is you don't make the decisions that control you. The problem is that you don't get paid enough. The problem is that you don't represent. The problem is fundamental.

New Afrikan Liberation NUAFRIKAN History

When we look at the fact that this is a place that was stolen from Native Americans, and then it is a place where they stole us to bring us here to develop this county. If we look at the bombs they dropped over in Iraq bombing people day after day and then cry crocodile tears because a few scudded missiles landed in Israel. If we look at the climate today in America as well as yesterday, we realize that there is no place in the world which deserves a revolution more than the United States of America.

Why do I call the United States an empire and you should think about it? You might not call it an empire but you first of all should call something what it is. What do you call Rome? They call it an empire, because these folks started out in a little bitty city and they stole everybody else's land, that's why they call it an empire. What do you call Britain? You call it an empire because they started off on a little bitty island and they took everybody's stuff. Now the United States didn't start from a little bitty island or a little bitty land, but they jumped off the boat stealing everybody's stuff. So if you took everything away from them that they shouldn't have they would have to go back on the *Mayflower*. So this is why we call it an empire, based on they stole the native American land and they moved across the North American continent on the basis of manifest destiny that means that God gave them the right to do it. Manifest destiny white man takes all. They stole the upper part of Mexico and now they make it illegal for Mexicans to cross borders which are illegal in the first place and then they stole us and brought us over here in order to develop one of the most powerful economic systems that have ever been built. And so this is an empire and this is why we call it that. First of all understand that we are Africans and that we should unite as Africans, fight as Africans and seek our self-respect, self-defense, and self-determination as Africans, but we should also understand that there are people in the world who are similarly situated to us that we need to understand their struggle and not get bulldozed out of the struggle and get all confused and wind up supporting the enemy thinking you are supporting a friend.

Appendix 2: Words My Brother Left Us

Wolverine Bar Association Conference, Detroit

I am really very happy to be here tonight. I love talking to Black people. You have to understand something; I come from a family with eight brothers and sisters. And we all love to talk. All the children loved to talk and my mother and father love to talk too, but we could not talk until my parents were finished talking. So whenever we got an opportunity to articulate what we had to say, there was a whole lot of talking and a whole lot of disagreeing, right! The fact that I love you does not necessarily mean you agree with everything I say. But I think it is important that we share ideas and we set terms for trying to arrive at an agreement so we can work towards the just ends of which we all seek.

The only way to climb is to lift, and the only way to lift is to climb. It is a challenge to understand the politics of power and the economics of reality of survival of advancement and the social forces which possess this planet which knows that no one individual who comes from an oppressed people is ever going to climb but so far by themselves...which understands there are ceilings even if you are not smart enough to know that there is a ceiling there...that understands that anytime you go up against an oppressor the fundamental laws of physics apply to human dynamics but the force of millions is much more powerful than the force of one. So if you must climb then you must lift, for it is a task that you cannot do by yourself. You must understand that only the people can create the type of forces that must be and can create the opportunities to allow you to pass through and allow the people to move up. And most black lawyers I know still depend upon black people. So if the people are poor, then you are poor. Although you can look quite prosperous [*laughter from audience*]. I think coming here tonight is somewhat of a tribute and somewhat of a reinforcement of people's beliefs that most of us have.

I see so many people here today like Professor Littlejohn, Ed Littlejohn. He talked so much about what I had done, and I am very honored to hear that, but the reality is that I have done nothing where a whole lot of people did not help me. I see two brothers sitting in the corner Jeffrey Edison and Gerald Evelyn. You see you hear my name but quite often it is them doing the things that allow me to do the things that I do. Me and Jeff led a people's law firm and didn't make a lot of money for about fifteen years. But as I would go to New York and be on the Brink's case sometimes for nothing and go to Pontiac more so then, because I was doing what I wanted to do, working with the people that I wanted to work with; but he had to keep going to court getting those cases, working those cases and paying those bills. So I salute Jeff and I salute Gerald, who also has been very supportive.

Gerald Evelyn, Jeffrey Edison, Chokwe Lumumba
(Photo courtesy of Earl B. Ashford)

Judge Geraldine Ford is the person who I give the credit for having taken me to school. I was on a roll when I first started practicing. I was winning these cases and winning these cases. And I went to her court room, she probably does not remember, but me and Daphne Means Curtis went into her courtroom and what did they call her [*crowd giggles and shouts back*] "Mean Geraldine" and I was mad at her just because of her reputation. So I went in there and I just knew we were going to win. We were defending two white gentlemen. I really liked these guys, because most people never went to court in Judge Geraldine's courtroom. They said they would go, and I said right on [*more laughs from the audience*]. We get in there and we go through this trial and boy did she take us to school. I tried one tactic, and I said that is not working. So I know when these judges are meaning, a lot of times, they don't know the law. So I am going to exploit that, but she knew the law [*more laughs*]. And she knew the law well enough to apply the law against me, although I thought I knew the law. So we worked with it and worked with it, but still it did not work. So I really was angry about that case for a long time. So I just planned and plotted, and I said the next time I go in there I'm going to....Finally one of the things that happened when I was talking to Judge Ford one day in her courtroom and we were talking about something that had to do about Black history. She came up and said something that had to do with Black history, and she saw how wide my eyes got. She said, "Well I know you didn't think I knew that." And so I got to know her better. Although, I still do not agree with her, but I got to love her because she loves Black people like I love Black people.

Helen Moore, I just want to mention, is one of the most courageous fighters we have in this city. She is struggling for our children. Judge Craig Strong was here. I don't think he remembers, but we use to deliver papers at the same time, and you know how long ago that was, the *Detroit Times*. Greg Reed, I remember going with him over to this little department with meeting Derrick Humphries and this is when I had left school and came back to school, and he was telling me about all these things he had started doing. I just sat there and listened and said Yeah and actually he had done just about all of them. I don't want to say anything about Conrad Mallet, because I might have to come before him one day. There was a brother by the name of Charles, a brother who I defended in an extradition case, who was very happy that a Conrad Mallet was around and actually working for the governor's office. The brother got exactly what he deserved an opportunity not to go back.

I want to thank Donna Batchelor, and I want to remind Edward Littlejohn that it is not exactly true that I never came to the office asking for something for myself. I went to school in 1969 for a year or so. I will get back to this later. There came a time when they unjustly terminated some fourteen out of twenty-two Black law students who were in law school at the time. So what we did we decided to take some direct action. So we took over the school. We chained it up and we basically said if we can't go here, then you can't go here. So everybody ended up getting back in and everybody ended up graduating with the exception of one or two and some of them are judges now. You can take that for what it's worth [*loud laughter from crowd*]. In fact some of them are over in Africa representing some countries over there, and most of them are doing quite well. In fact the real rebel of the group was not me although I got credit for it....It was Derek Humphries. I understand Derek is now a very conservative communications lawyer. But the thing I remember most is after I left and went down south with the Republic of New Afrika for two or three years, and I was told when I came back that I could not get back in. I was told by a certain dean, that they were not quite sure that they really wanted a fella like me around there that was raising all that Cain. So you know how sometimes people likes to shift that responsibility. He had said, you see it's not me. It's this new dean who just doesn't take that stuff, and his name is Ed Littlejohn, so he is the one that you are going to have the problem with. Fortunately, I had already gotten a letter from Ed encouraging me to come back to school. So basically all I did was say, if he is the problem, than there is no problem. Right! [*More laughter from audience.*] So I was able to get back in and once I got back in I was surprised to learn as I stood in line registering where I had completed classes that I had As and Bs in, and while I was registering I was told by the same dean, that I had to repeat everything, no matter what it was, no matter what grade I had in it, because I was coming back too late, and this was a new rule they had passed...for me, right! Now I was very, very upset, and I am saying this for a reason, because I think many of us get into this kind of situation, and I want tell you what kind of language I was using I ran into Jeff Edison in the library, and actually he was using worse language than I was [*lot of laughter from audience*]. He wasn't even there. So I said if he can go there, then I guess I can go there. So I decided to come back and go to Wayne. I think I'm happy that I did, because I really had decided that perhaps with Nixon and this Supreme Court and the other things that were occurring, and actually if I had known what happened after Nixon, I really wouldn't have wanted to go, because it has gotten worse since then. I was thinking the law had limited utility. I'm a revolutionary, and if you don't know it, you will know it before the speech is over. I believe in total and complete change. So I had some questions about this court system and whether or not really helps us that much, then my father, who I love very dearly encouraged me to come back. Then I read that book again Malcolm X, and I read Malcolm in the back of the book in the appendix, he said when he was talking to Alex Haley, author of *Roots*, "I always wanted to be a lawyer. I wish I could have been." Then he told that story as how he expressed that desire to his teacher, his teacher who liked him a lot, said Malcolm that is an unrealistic dream for a Negro. So what I decided is that I would come back and be the kind of lawyer Malcolm would have been.

"Heritage"

I see Ray Jenkins too along with Cindy Owens, who is very active in the Reparations world. I once again want to say that I am very happy to be here today and I am happy to be here with this esteemed panel, and I am particularly happy to be here with you. I commend the Wolverine Student Bar Organization for organizing this event.

Memories of My Revolutionary Brother, Chokwe Lumumba

And placing this topic before us, because it really emphasizes the topic on what I asked to speak about. They asked me to talk about heritage as it relates to the theme of living. Heritage you understand, first of all I think all too often we really don't understand the words that we use, so we have to be careful to say what we are talking about. Heritage you understand is our treasured knowledge and experience from past culture. It is the legacy that we have received from days gone by. Culture you understand is not just a dashiki, it's not just the tiki, it's not just a song, and it's not just a poem. Culture you understand is a people's way of dealing with their environment, their physical and social environment which is around them. There is a medium between them and their environment and there is a way that they handle it, deal with it, transform it in order to meet benefits of advanced life. So when we talk about heritage, we talk about something very important. We talk about something that lives, not just something that you can put up on a wall. So when heritage comes to us in understanding that heritage lives we must understand that a people have culture which must meet the needs of the circumstances that the people find themselves in. So a people who are at war must have war days. They cannot just stay at peace. A people who are oppressed must have a culture which is designed to eliminate that oppression. So when I say that I am proud of the Wolverine Bar Student Association then I am telling you they are keeping up tradition by having forums like this, they are carrying it on. They are bringing to you that tradition of the student movement and of the larger movement which is reflected that comes to us consistently and tells us of some things that you don't want to hear; that we have a price to pay. That we owe a debt. It reminds us of the civil rights movement after long years of the historical figures who Littlejohn could tell you about who worked out every little space they could in this legal system but still couldn't get to the place they deserved to be. It was the civil rights movement, demonstrations and

Appendix 2: Words My Brother Left Us

protests. It was Martin Luther King and it was people right here who walked the streets, thousands more than most places when King came here who cracked the doors for the first time who allowed few more judges to come in and a few more lawyers to come in; perhaps a Littlejohn, perhaps a Sam Gardner, perhaps a Geraldine Bledsoe Ford and perhaps some others; a few more that would have been able to come.

Even beyond that, because I know that I came to school in '69 through a program that was only created a couple of years before that called CLEO. It was only created in the King rebellions. It was blood and sweat...blood and sweat and pure rage in the streets that created programs that got me into school. Elsewise I never would have been here. Actually when I came to the school, they were actually recruiting Black people they were so desperate getting Black folks in [*laughter from audience*]. I know to some of you it sounds strange, but they were looking for us. They found me at Kalamazoo College with a name they actually thought was Hispanic at the time. So they actually had to...I am glad they didn't know who I was. So I came into Wayne, but it was that kind of sacrifice. It was the sacrifice of many who sacrificed once they were in school, and who stood up when it was time to stand up.

They carried on this tradition. And if we look around today my brothers and sisters and we tremble a bit because we see that now they tell us there are more Black young men in prison than there are in college. Now they tell us—and we know it is true—that we only make 57 percent of what white people make. A few years ago, it was even better than that. In a society that says when we are going forward but we are clearly going backwards. Ten times the value of the average Black person is the value of the average white person in this society. Ten times! The United States of America incarcerates more Black People than any other place in the world, including South Africa. Incarceration rates since the time of our movement of the '60s and early '50s have become absolutely astronomical. It is not purely coincidental.

At the same time though, on these very streets that the Panthers walked who sold newspapers to young children and had young children selling newspapers. Now the same government that brought the drugs into the country or allowed them in destroyed the Black Panther Party. So now we have children selling drugs where the Panthers use to walk. Now this is not just wild rhetoric. Read your congressional record sometime, you will find that it is very interesting. This government that you cried crocodile tears for, this government that you were willing to go over to Saudi Arabia for or send somebody else over to Saudi Arabia for. This government that is trying to collect reparations from Saddam Hussein, although they have not paid us reparations.

From the plantation [*long and loud applause from audience*]. This same government according to congressional record waged war against its own people. They killed Fred Hampton in Chicago. I tell you they killed Fred Hampton in Chicago! They admit that they tried to get Martin Luther King to kill himself. So this poor little white man who had nothing gets all the way over to England after Martin Luther King was killed. After the FBI successfully through their counterintelligence program got King to move from one hotel which was considered to be relatively secure to another hotel when he was killed. Malcolm X, he died at the hands of some ex-Muslims. The ex-Muslims were being tampered with and manipulated on string by forces which still have not clearly been exposed. Although we know that the French would not let him come there because someone was trying to kill him in France. Muslims don't have anybody in France [*laughter from the audience*]. We know that he was targeted in Egypt, and we know other things.

So I say all these things, because first of all I say them because you are not going to hear them all of the time. But I'm going to make sure you hear them now. I say these things to tell you we are in a critical period and the reason why some of you don't know it is because of the illusion that has been cast upon you. You had better study your history clearly. You had better read it very carefully and particularly read the reconstruction period. And even more particularly read the post reconstruction period sometimes called "100 Years of Lynching." You see in the reconstruction period there were many more Legislatures and Congressmen representing Black people than ever before. In this country the whole legislative firstly in Mississippi was Black. In South Carolina over 70 percent of the legislature was Black. In the state of Louisiana over 80 percent of the legislature was Black. You ask why, because that was the population of those states. That is how it ought to have been. In Alabama and Georgia, the majority of the legislatures were Black. And this was at a time when voting could have really meant a lot more than it really means today. Because this was an opportunity to exercise some sense of state power; an opportunity to really have some control with your politics over state resources related to economic development: right there at the top of the Caribbean community which was already Black; right across the 30th parallel from Africa, which more sooner than later would be in rebellion, and Africans would be taking over their own territory; right there almost next to and alongside the east coast of Central America where there are Black nations and Black people; right there not too far from Brazil where is 60 million Africans living in Brazil; right there where there was all kind of potential where cotton was king. King Cotton not only built the United States but it built the world.

If anybody ever questions you when you ask them about reparations, you ask them about cotton [*lots of applause from audience*]. But at the end of that period there were prosperous good-looking Negroes back then too. They looked every bit prosperous as you do, and as other people do. I am not trying to isolate you. I mean gentlemen, ladies, high steppers, you know what I'm saying, but they lost perspective. They fell for the Okie doke. They began to believe [*laughter from the audience*]. They really began to believe that because they could sit in the legislature that they could trust the people who patrolled the country just as much as the white people who sat there before them. They didn't understand that they were just a passing circumstance in history. They didn't understand that in fact what was really occurring is that the north was temporarily mad at the south and contrary to what the "Right of Glory" says it has some good things in it but it basically has a bad theme. You need to reread about the civil war. The civil war was not initially about freeing the slaves in the south. Lincoln himself said as the president, that if he could preserve the union and keep slavery he would do it. Lincoln said more than that in his debates with Douglas. Abraham Lincoln this guy you get all folly eyed about [*laughter from audience*]. The one you want to name all of your schools after. He said himself, this is what he said, and in the debates with Douglas before he was elected president, he said, "I enjoy white supremacy as much as any other man." He said it was better that the races be separate if they leave here, but if they can't I like any other person wants the whites to maintain a superior position. And they called him "Honest Abe" and actually he was pretty honest [*lots of applause by the audience*]. It's the people that write about him that you have to be careful about [*more laughter*]. Good old honest Abe said it all along when he mentions the Emancipation Proclamation. Read the book. Read what he said. It doesn't say that I let the slaves go because they should never have been caught as slaves, because they never should have held a slave and because of humanity, and this is the reason and all of these other nonsensical things that about racism. He said, this is basically what he said reading between the lines is that "we are losing this war" and he had said himself several months before he actually issued the Emancipation, that he is convinced that military necessity was required, but he wanted to wait until the north would have enjoy

Appendix 2: Words My Brother Left Us

some semblance of a victory because at the beginning of the war, the South was kicking their butts. I'm telling you Old Stone Wall Jackson and other "crackers." I use that as a word often. I learned that in the South, that's where I learned it from...

(Photo courtesy of Jason Clark)

NATIONAL CONFERENCE OF BLACK LAWYERS

Photos courtesy of Attorney Jeffrey L. Edison

Photo 1.   Chokwe Lumumba
Photo 2.   Chokwe, Wilhelm Joseph, Jr., Lew Myers, Gerald Evelyn
Photo 3.   (Front) Milton Henry, Judge Claudia Morcum, Myzell Sowell, Sr., (Back) Jeffrey Edison, Sarida Scott, Desiree Ferguson, Chokwe, Judge James Roberts, Regina Jemison, Emily Hall, Barbara Wynder, Gerald Evelyn
Photo 4.   Chokwe, Deborah Gaskin, Myzell Sowell, Jr., Brenda Maxwell, Gerald Evelyn
Photo 5.   Gerald Evelyn, Mark Fancher, Maya Cain
Photo 6.   Gerald Evelyn, Earl Ashford
Photo 7.   Chokwe Lamumba
Photo 8.   Jeffrey Edison and Chokwe Lamumba
Photo 9.   Chokwe Lamumba and Milton Henry
Photo 10. Chokwe Lamumba and Myzell Sowell, Sr.
Photo 11. Margaret Burnham, Frank Chapman, Chokwe Lumumba, Lani Guiner,
Photo 12. Roxanna Gordy, Itari Shakur, Judge Craig Strong, Shushanna Shakur, Maya Cain, Asha Akinyele
Photo 13. Congressman George W. Crockett, Jr. Chokw Lamumba, Wilhelm Joseph Jr.

Memories of My Revolutionary Brother, Chokwe Lumumba

National Conference of Black Lawyers

Memories of My Revolutionary Brother, Chokwe Lumumba

About the Author

Shushanna Shakur, also known as Bernadette Taliaferro-Cain and fondly called Mama Shushanna, is an activist and artist who has engaged her community for most of her life. She was born into an activist family in Detroit, Michigan. Her parents, Lucien and Frances Taliaferro, participated locally in the Civil Rights Movement, while her older brother, former attorney and Jackson, Mississippi, mayor Chokwe Lumumba, fought for the freedom of his people throughout the country.

Like her family members, Ms. Shakur's activism is extensive in her own right. As a former member of AFSCME, the Detroit

Federation of Teachers, and Concerned Teachers United, she organized rallies and protests while advocating for improvements to the education system and juvenile justice system. Ms. Shakur has also provided extracurricular and after-school services to more than four thousand young people through her work as a Detroit Public Schools teacher and as the founder and director of the Heritage Youth Program.

In addition, she has organized and coordinated political, cultural, and educational forums through her involvement with the Malcolm X Grassroots Movement–Detroit, the Detroit Jericho Movement, Shakur Squad (Freedom Fighters for Political Prisoners), the Coalition for Detroit Police Transparency and Accountability, and the Sacred Heart Church Education Commission. Ms. Shakur has also advocated on behalf of Detroit homeowners who are overtaxed and facing foreclosure.

Additionally, Ms. Shakur is a contributor to the arts as a poet and as the director of numerous school and community plays.

www.ingramcontent.com/pod-product-compliance
Lightning Source LLC
LaVergne TN
LVHW091619070526
838199LV00044B/863